50 YEARS

lonely planet

OF TR

UTA[illegible] NATIONAL PARKS

Capitol Reef National Park p181

Arches, Canyonlands & Southeast Utah p130

Zion National Park & Southwest Utah p46

Bryce Canyon National Park & Southern Utah p89

Lauren Keith

Double Arch, Arches National Park (p138)

CONTENTS

Zion Canyon National Park (p52)

WILLIAM EUGENE DUMMITT/SHUTTERSTOCK ©

Goblin Valley State Park (p199)

UTAH'S NATIONAL PARKS

THE JOURNEY BEGINS HERE

On trips to the library as a kid, I checked out the same book dozens of times: a small hardback about Utah, wedged in with 49 others about each US state. I can't recall why I picked this one originally, but I remember staring in amazement at the photos inside. Utah hooked me instantly even though I had never been. Was this place even real? How could it be that only one state stood between where I was sitting on the library floor and this alien planet?

Childhood was well behind me when I visited Utah for the first time, but its national parks – these huge, all-natural playgrounds – immediately made me feel like a kid again. Everything in this state feels ready-made for big adventures: dipping into Earth's wrinkles to explore mystical passageways, dizzyingly deep canyons that hark back to the planet's past, soaring pinnacles and arches and rainbow-colored, otherworldly-looking rocks.

Lauren Keith

MY FAVORITE EXPERIENCE

The Narrows, Zion National Park (p54)

STEPHEN MOEHLE/SHUTTERSTOCK ©

My favorite experience is hiking the Narrows in Zion National Park. Wading through the river and wondering what's around the canyon's next corner always brings back that childlike sense of awe.

Lauren Keith

@noplacelike_it

Lauren is a travel writer and an avid hiker whose boots have trekked trails all over the world, including in the US, England, Egypt, Jordan, Iran, Borneo and New Zealand.

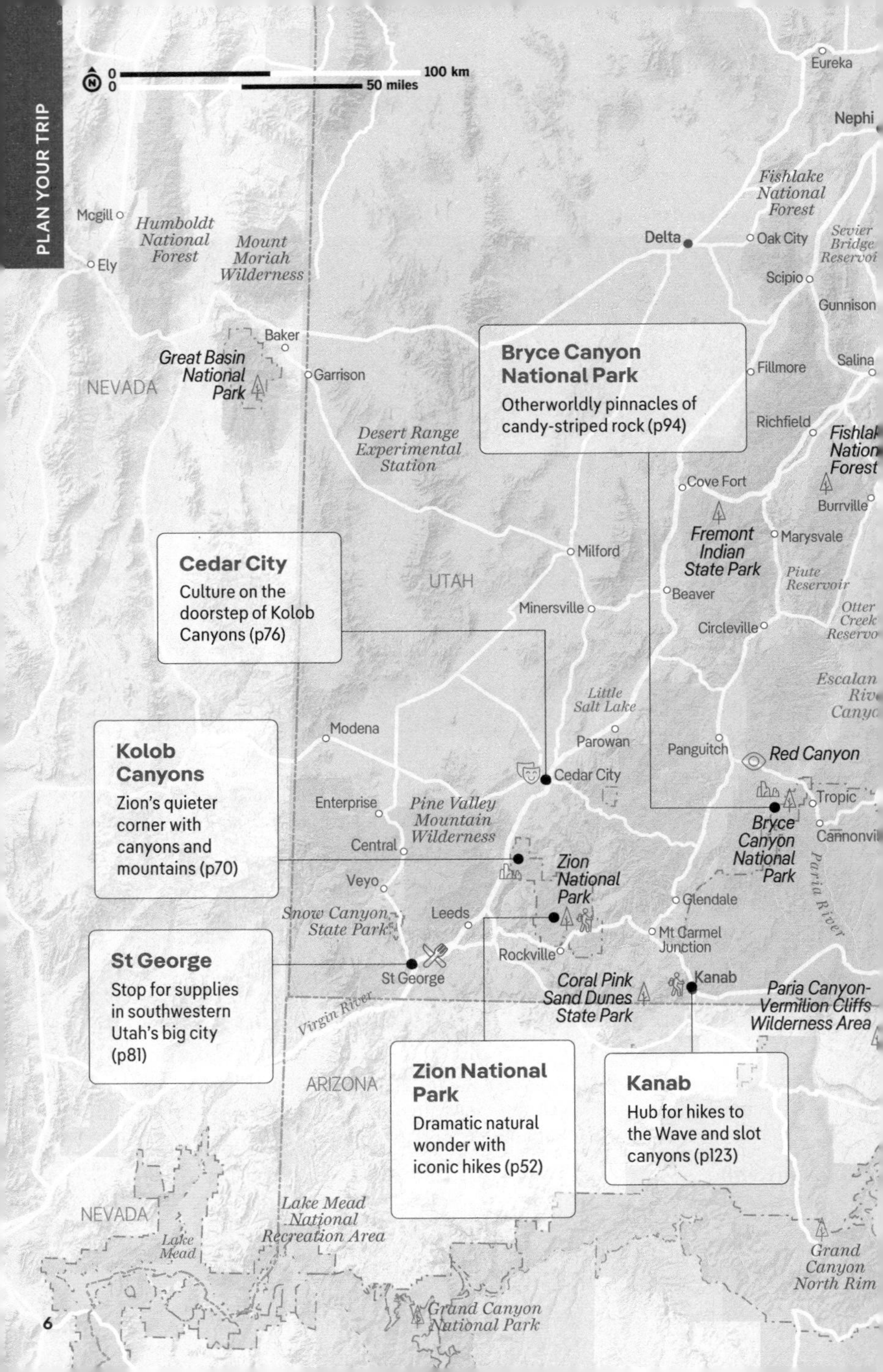

Bryce Canyon National Park

Otherworldly pinnacles of candy-striped rock (p94)

Cedar City

Culture on the doorstep of Kolob Canyons (p76)

Kolob Canyons

Zion's quieter corner with canyons and mountains (p70)

St George

Stop for supplies in southwestern Utah's big city (p81)

Zion National Park

Dramatic natural wonder with iconic hikes (p52)

Kanab

Hub for hikes to the Wave and slot canyons (p123)

0 100 km
0 50 miles

Eureka
Nephi
Fishlake National Forest
Mcgill
Humboldt National Forest
Mount Moriah Wilderness
Ely
Delta
Oak City
Sevier Bridge Reservoi
Scipio
Gunnison
Baker
Great Basin National Park
NEVADA
Garrison
Fillmore
Salina
Desert Range Experimental Station
Richfield
Fishlak Nation Forest
Cove Fort
Burrville
Fremont Indian State Park
Marysvale
Milford
UTAH
Piute Reservoir
Beaver
Minersville
Otter Creek Reservo
Circleville
Escalan Riv Canyo
Little Salt Lake
Modena
Parowan
Panguitch
Red Canyon
Cedar City
Tropic
Enterprise
Pine Valley Mountain Wilderness
Bryce Canyon National Park
Cannonvi
Central
Zion National Park
Paria River
Veyo
Glendale
Snow Canyon State Park
Leeds
Mt Carmel Junction
Rockville
St George
Coral Pink Sand Dunes State Park
Kanab
Paria Canyon-Vermilion Cliffs Wilderness Area
Virgin River
ARIZONA
NEVADA
Lake Mead
Lake Mead National Recreation Area
Grand Canyon North Rim
Grand Canyon National Park

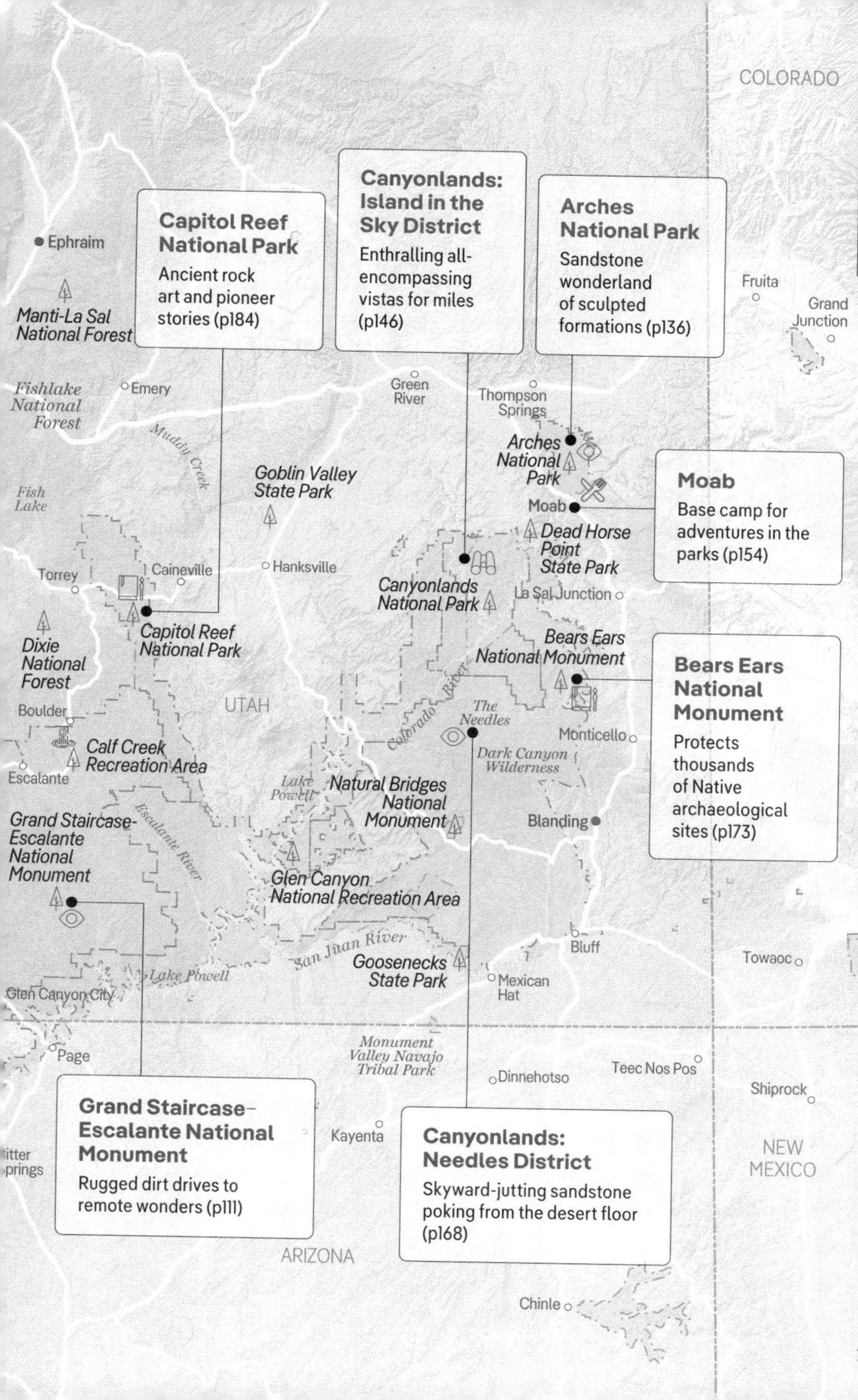

Capitol Reef National Park
Ancient rock art and pioneer stories (p184)

Canyonlands: Island in the Sky District
Enthralling all-encompassing vistas for miles (p146)

Arches National Park
Sandstone wonderland of sculpted formations (p136)

Moab
Base camp for adventures in the parks (p154)

Bears Ears National Monument
Protects thousands of Native archaeological sites (p173)

Grand Staircase–Escalante National Monument
Rugged dirt drives to remote wonders (p111)

Canyonlands: Needles District
Skyward-jutting sandstone poking from the desert floor (p168)

COLORADO
UTAH
ARIZONA
NEW MEXICO
Ephraim
Manti-La Sal National Forest
Fishlake National Forest
Emery
Muddy Creek
Fish Lake
Green River
Thompson Springs
Fruita
Grand Junction
Arches National Park
Moab
Goblin Valley State Park
Dead Horse Point State Park
Torrey
Caineville
Hanksville
Canyonlands National Park
La Sal Junction
Capitol Reef National Park
Dixie National Forest
Bears Ears National Monument
Boulder
Calf Creek Recreation Area
Escalante
Colorado River
The Needles
Monticello
Dark Canyon Wilderness
Lake Powell
Natural Bridges National Monument
Blanding
Grand Staircase-Escalante National Monument
Escalante River
Glen Canyon National Recreation Area
San Juan River
Goosenecks State Park
Bluff
Towaoc
Lake Powell
Mexican Hat
Glen Canyon City
Page
Monument Valley Navajo Tribal Park
Dinnehotso
Teec Nos Pos
Shiprock
Kayenta
Bitter Springs
Chinle

EPIC HIKES

A wonderland of soaring sandstone cliffs and surreal hoodoos, Utah is a paradise for hikers of all levels. Hiking is the main and most accessible activity in the state's national parks and can be done at any time of year as long as you're properly prepared. The wild landscape might be unlike anything you have ever experienced – and designating certain parcels as 'national parks' has not tamed it.

When to Go

Hiking in Utah is best from spring to fall. In winter, snow and ice can cover trails in all the state's national parks.

Slot-canyon Gear

Besides hiking shoes, you might also want to buy or rent neoprene boots, waders or a wet suit, a walking stick and a dry bag.

Permits Required

A few iconic hikes – and not just those in the national parks – require permits (p34). Some are only issued by lottery.

LEFT TO RIGHT: INC/SHUTTERSTOCK ©, JAKUB STANEK/SHUTTERSTOCK ©, ORXY/SHUTTERSTOCK ©

Angels Landing, Zion National Park (p58)

BEST HIKING EXPERIENCES

Wade 16 miles up **The Narrows** ❶, Zion's most impressive canyon, where the water is the trail. (p54)

Make Zion's iconic ascent of **Angels Landing** ❷, with chains and precipitous drop-offs. Permits are required to reach the grand finale. (p58)

Devour Arches' full buffet of red-rock treats at **Devils Garden** ❸, including North America's longest span, space to scramble, and a wayfinding-required return. (p142)

Explore a pastel dream of towering hoodoos and Martian landscapes on **Fairyland Loop** ❹, a quieter and more challenging trail in Bryce. (p96)

Stroll past petroglyphs, carved pioneer names and life-sustaining potholes on the easy slot-canyon saunter of **Capitol Gorge** ❺. (p196)

Rim Trail, Bryce Canyon National Park (p100)

DRAMATIC VIEWS

Southern Utah is an unfurling tableau of sweeping panoramas that will defy your camera's wide-angle lens, from viewpoints in the national parks to scenic road trips. Shutterbugs in particular will enjoy all that these parks have to offer, and it's likely you'll fill your phone's storage with photos by the trip's end.

Early Start

Soft morning light is often best for taking photos in the desert. Later in the day as the sun climbs overhead, it casts much harsher light.

Golden Hour

The last hour before sunset is prime time for photography, as the red rock glows in the sun's waning rays. Leave enough time to linger.

BEST VIEWS

Make the intensely rewarding – and deliciously easy – hike along the top of Zion Canyon's cliffs to **Observation Point ❶** looking out from more than 700ft above Angels Landing. (p65)

Take in the immensity of the Colorado Plateau from **Grand View Point ❷** at the end of the road in Canyonlands' Island in the Sky district. (p151)

Revel in the best views of the Colorado River, like, ever at **Dead Horse Point State Park ❸**. (p153)

Walk the flat and partially paved **Rim Trail ❹** at Bryce Canyon, which gifts views of hoodoos with no climbing required. (p100)

Witness the wildly eroded natural amphitheater of **Cedar Breaks National Monument ❺**, where sculpted cliffs and hoodoos glow like neon tie-dye. (p78)

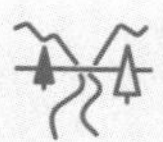

SCENIC DRIVES

As amazing as Utah's national parks are, sometimes it's the drive between them you remember most. Officially designated scenic byways crisscross the state, promising plenty of oohs and aahs as you curve around cliffs, navigate through national forests and ride the roller coaster of desert plateaus. Backroads lead into remote areas where few others dare to tread. All of the national parks also have paved scenic drives that wind through their hearts to trailheads and jaw-dropping viewpoints.

Zion National Park (p52)

Canyonlands National Park (p146)

Get Gas

Gas stations can be few and far between, so fill up. I-70 between Green River and Salina is the longest stretch in the country with no services.

Pack a Picnic

Services are sparse, and most of the national parks have no food options once you're inside. Prepare for a long drive with plenty of snacks and water.

Sun Protection

If you have a choice, opt for a lighter colored rental car, which absorbs less heat. Bring or buy a sun shade for the windshield.

BEST DRIVING EXPERIENCES

Take in the stretch from Capitol Reef to Red Canyon on 124-mile **Highway 12** ❶, which passes desert slickrock, photogenic hoodoos and even drive-through arches. (p114)

Tackle one of America's most iconic 4WD adventures on **White Rim Road** ❷, blazed by uranium prospectors in the 1950s. (p152)

Cruise along **Arches Scenic Drive** ❸ for views of balanced rocks, delicate arches and the La Sal Mountains. (p144)

Climb to 10,000ft on **Highway 14** ❹, the back road between Bryce and Zion that passes Cedar Breaks National Monument. (p83)

Hug the river's serpentine route on the **Colorado River Scenic Byway** ❺, stopping for hikes near Fisher Towers. (p167)

Newspaper Rock, Bears Ears National Monument (p173)

BEST NATIVE EXPERIENCES

Stand in awe of **Newspaper Rock** ❶, a large sandstone rock panel packed with more than 300 petroglyphs attributed to Ute and Ancestral Puebloan groups over a 2000-year period. (p173)

Hike into remote **Horseshoe Canyon** ❷ to witness the 'Louvre of the Southwest,' a collection of huge pictographs painted between 2000 BCE and 500 CE. (p200)

Get up close to the Hollywood-famous red-rock spires of **Monument Valley** ❸ on a Navajo-led tour. (p178)

Walk in the footsteps of the ancients at **Parowan Gap** ❹, where petroglyphs detail celestial knowledge. (p76)

See six sets of unique Ancestral Puebloan settlements at **Hovenweep National Monument** ❺. (p175)

LEFT TO RIGHT: BARBARA ASH/SHUTTERSTOCK ©, LAUREN KEITH/LONELY PLANET ©, LAUREN KEITH/LONELY PLANET ©

NATIVE HISTORY & CULTURE

Home to cliff dwellings and centuries-old rock art, southern Utah has a bounty of fascinating places to get to know the Native people who have lived – and continue to live – here. The state has eight federally recognized tribes, five of which formed a coalition to push for the preservation of sacred lands filled with archaeological sites. Bears Ears National Monument is the first in the country established at the request of Native people.

Fremont Indian State Park (p199)

Fremont Indian State Park & Museum

This park contains one of the largest collections of Fremont rock art in the state – more than 500 panels on 14 interpretative trails.

Native American pottery collection

Edge of the Cedars State Park Museum

This museum (p173) in Blanding has the best Native pottery collection in the Southwest. Climb into a preserved kiva built by the Ancestral Puebloans around 1100 CE.

Respect the Land

The area now called Utah has significant spiritual and historical value and is sacred to many Native Americans. Do not touch sandstone structures or rock art.

ON THE WATER

The Utah desert may be arid, but water plays a critical role in shaping the state's landscape. Powerful rivers, winter's freeze-and-thaw cycle and summer monsoon season sculpt and reconfigure the scenery in microscopic and mighty ways. Contemplate the importance and sheer force of water while riding rapids and hiking through a slot canyon.

Carving Canyonlands

From the top of the plateau, it can be hard to see the Colorado (above) and Green Rivers thousands of feet below, which have sliced near-vertical walls.

Record Rainfall – or Not

The most rain Utah has ever received in a 24-hour period was a little more than 5in in 1963, the lowest amount of all 50 states.

LEFT TO RIGHT: FAYSAL06/SHUTTERSTOCK ©, WESLEY ASTON/SHUTTERSTOCK ©, ANDRE LUIS MICHELON/SHUTTERSTOCK ©

Lower Calf Creek Falls (p119)

BEST WATER EXPERIENCES

Get your feet – and more – wet on a half- or full-day trip on the **Colorado River** ❶ outside of Moab, a great rafting intro for first-timers. (p157)

Rip through class IV and V rapids on **Cataract Canyon** ❷, one of the USA's hallmark stretches of white water. (p158)

Swim in the emerald pool beneath the ribbon-like cascade of **Lower Calf Creek** ❸. (p119)

Take the whole family out for a slot-canyon hike at **Willis Creek** ❹, splashing in the gentle stream. (p110)

Look for scarlet monkey flowers, mosses, golden columbines, maidenhair ferns and violets clinging to the rock face in the lush hanging gardens at **Weeping Rock** ❺, where water seeps from Zion Canyon's walls. (p61)

Rock climbing, Indian Creek (p174)

BEST ADVENTURES

Ride a roller coaster of descents, curves and lung-busting cliffside climbs on the famous **Slickrock Trail** ❶ near Moab. (p156)

Swim and rappel your way through the **Subway** ❷, one of Zion's most impressive geological formations. Apply for a coveted permit in advance. (p74)

Explore the sandstone **Dry Fork Slot Canyon** ❸ for a taste of sculpted landscape in remote Grand Staircase–Escalante National Monument. (p121)

Test your grip on vertical lines in a sea of sandstone at **Indian Creek** ❹, the world's best spot for crack climbing. (p174)

Combine routes for an all-in-one descent to some of Moab's most distinctive mountain biking features on the **Whole Enchilada** ❺. (p156)

LEFT TO RIGHT: ZACHJ6497/SHUTTERSTOCK ©, GALYNA ANDRUSHKO/SHUTTERSTOCK ©, KARA GRUBIS/SHUTTERSTOCK ©

GRIPPING ADVENTURES

What adrenaline-fueled activity isn't possible in Utah? The scenic slickrock playground outside Moab turned the area into a mountain biking hub decades ago, while the slot canyons around Zion are prime canyoneering and rock climbing territory. Squeezing your way through the twists and turns of a dark slot canyon, racing down red rock and ascending a sheer multipitch spire above the desert floor are just some of the adventurous ways to gain a new perspective on this place.

Grand Staircase–Escalante National Monument (p121)

Slot Canyons

Utah has the most slot canyons in the world. These formations can be narrower than your shoe, while the walls shoot hundreds of feet skyward.

Slickrock Trail, Moab (p156)

In the Park

The national parks don't allow some commercial guided activities, such as canyoneering and rock climbing, inside the park boundaries, but similar landscapes are just beyond the borders.

Outfitters

Adventure companies around Utah's parks are great resources. They have everything to set you up for a safe outing, from fully guided courses to DIY rental equipment.

THE PARKS

Find the places that tick all your boxes.

Bryce Canyon National Park & Southern Utah

HIKING AMONG HEAPS OF HOODOOS

A visit to Bryce Canyon is a trip to another dimension. These cliffs were deposited as sediment in a huge prehistoric lake some 60 million years ago, slowly lifted above sea level, and then eroded into wondrous ranks of pinnacles and points, steeples and spires, cliffs and crevices, and oddly shaped hoodoos.

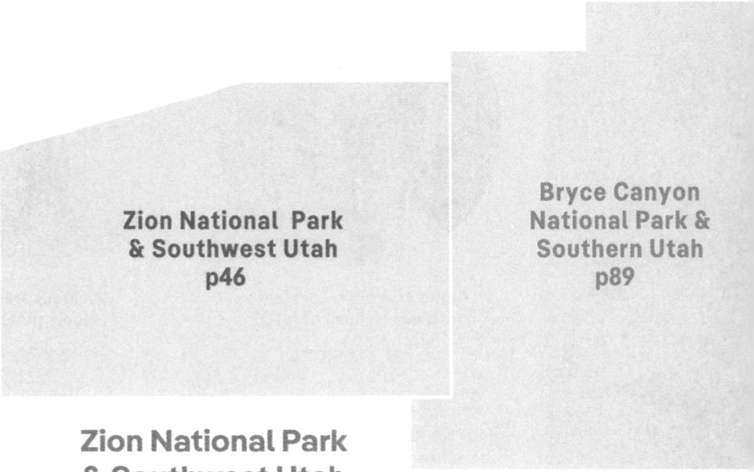

Zion National Park & Southwest Utah p46

Bryce Canyon National Park & Southern Utah p89

Zion National Park & Southwest Utah

UTAH'S CROWN JEWEL

A bold desert beauty, 232-sq-mile Zion National Park is a Utah highlight that's all about the grandeur. The towering sandstone walls of Zion Canyon reach toward the heavens, creating spectacular views and out-of-this-world hiking options that head high into the sky and along deftly carved narrows.

Capitol Reef National Park

A GEM OF GEOLOGY

Called 'the land of the sleeping rainbow' by the Navajo, this colorful desert landscape encompasses buttes and canyons replete with rock art, Mormon history and hiking trails. The remote 4WD roads and mysterious slot canyons of Grand Staircase–Escalante National Monument on Capitol Reef's southern edge are where the real adventure begins.

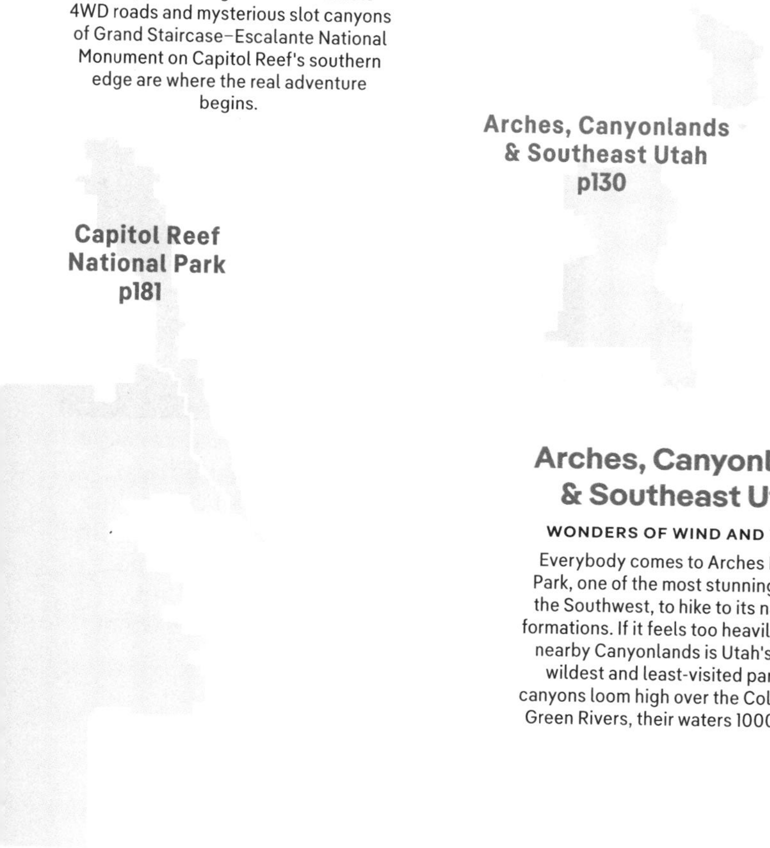

Arches, Canyonlands & Southeast Utah p130

Capitol Reef National Park p181

Arches, Canyonlands & Southeast Utah

WONDERS OF WIND AND WATER

Everybody comes to Arches National Park, one of the most stunning parks in the Southwest, to hike to its namesake formations. If it feels too heavily trodden, nearby Canyonlands is Utah's largest, wildest and least-visited park. Vast canyons loom high over the Colorado and Green Rivers, their waters 1000ft below.

ITINERARIES

Southern Utah Grand Tour

Allow: 10 Days

Distance: 480 Miles

Bryce Canyon National Park (p107)

Each of Utah's national parks has its own unique personality and highlights and you can't pick your favorite unless you visit them all. Taking 10 days gives you enough time to sample each of the 'Mighty Five,' but with more time, you can tack on additional adventures and activities.

1 ZION NATIONAL PARK
3 DAYS

Ride the shuttle into **Zion Canyon** (p52) and exit at the final stop. Follow **Riverside Walk** (p56) and, if you're ready to get wet, plunge into **the Narrows** (above, p54). The next day, hike to the heady heights of **Angels Landing** (p62) or savor the deliciously easy journey to even higher **Observation Point** (p65). Wrap up in the relative solitude of lesser-visited **Kolob Canyons** and **Kolob Terrace Rd** (p70).

2 BRYCE CANYON NATIONAL PARK
1 DAY

Take **Bryce Canyon Scenic Drive** (p104) to Rainbow Point, stopping at as many viewpoints as your eyes can handle. Leave the car behind and head to Sunset Point to glimpse the towering eroded hoodoos of Bryce Amphitheater. Descend into the canyon on the **Navajo Loop** (p98) and return to the **Rim Trail** (p100) around sunset to watch the light play on the hoodoos.

3 CAPITOL REEF NATIONAL PARK
1 DAY

Drive into the heart of Capitol Reef on the **scenic drive** (p194), which ends at **Capitol Gorge** (p196). Park and stroll the flat canyon wash past historic petroglyphs and pioneer carvings. Reward your efforts with a fruit pie from the **Gifford Homestead** (p189) or pick your own sweets from the **orchards** (p189) in season. The nearby trailhead to **Cohab Canyon** (p189) provides bird's-eye views over Fruita.

4 ARCHES NATIONAL PARK
1 DAY

See the major sights from **Arches' Scenic Drive** (p144). Walk among sandstone monoliths on **Park Avenue** (p144) and gawk at **Balanced Rock** (p144) and the **Windows** (p137). Even more arches await in **Devils Garden** (p142), a treat for walkers wanting an easy trail as well as hardcore hikers. As the light and heat fade, visit the famous **Delicate Arch** (p138), a true Utah icon.

Delta
Ephraim
Scipio
Gunnison
Castle Dale
Fillmore
Salina
Emery
Green River
Arches National Park
Richfield
Cove Fort
Monroe
35mins
2hrs 15mins
Canyonlands: Island in the Sky
Moab
Burrville
Marysvale
Milford
Loa
Torrey
Caineville
Hanksville
40mins
Bicknell
Teasdale
Capitol Reef National Park
Minersville
Beaver
2hrs 15mins
La Sal Junction
Canyonlands: Needles District
1hr 30mins
Circleville
END
Parowan
Panguitch
Boulder
Cedar City
Escalante
Hatch
Ticaboo
Blanding
2hrs
Bryce Canyon National Park
Zion National Park
Alton
UTAH
Bullfrog Marina
Glendale
Orderville
Lake Powell
Bluff
Mt Carmel Junction
Mexican Hat
Montezuma Creek
START
Kanab
Oljato
Page
Mexican Water
Paria Canyon–Vermilion Cliffs Wilderness Area
Marble Canyon
ARIZONA
Colorado River
Kayenta
Rock Point
Bitter Springs
Kaibito
Shonto
Grand Canyon National Park
0 60 km
0 30 miles

SEAN XU/SHUTTERSTOCK ©, BOGDAN DENYSYUK/SHUTTERSTOCK ©, ALBERT PEGO/SHUTTERSTOCK ©

5 CANYONLANDS: ISLAND IN THE SKY 1 DAY

Canyonlands has four districts and demands – and deserves – at least a few days. With limited time, head directly to **Island in the Sky** (p146). **Mesa Arch** (p150) is a great hike on the shorter side and it's particularly stunning at sunrise. Stop at **Upheaval Dome** (above, p149) to marvel at the mysterious formation, before driving to Grand View Point for 100-mile views.

6 MOAB 2 DAYS

The adventure multiplies outside the national parks and Moab makes it all possible. Spend a day white-water rafting on the **Colorado River** (p157) or **mountain biking** (p156) before heading downtown for dinner and a drink. The next day, head back to the water along the **Colorado River Scenic Byway** (p167), this time hiking among the rust-colored spires and buttes at **Fisher Towers** (p165).

7 CANYONLANDS: NEEDLES DISTRICT 1 DAY

Though it's only 90 minutes from Moab, the **Needles district** (p168) receives far fewer visitors than Island in the Sky. Before you reach the park entrance, stop to decode the hundreds of petroglyphs at **Newspaper Rock** (p173). Take the three easy hikes that start near the park's main road or get among the namesake sandstone spires on the **Chesler Park trail** (p170).

JASON BUSA/SHUTTERSTOCK ©

Hoodoos, Bryce Canyon National Park (p96)

ITINERARIES

Zion & Bryce Canyon with Kids

Allow: 5 Days **Distance:** 110 Miles

Kids love exploring the wild landscapes of Zion and Bryce Canyon and these two national parks have plenty that appeals to families. Along the way, little ones can become junior rangers, dive into a million years of geological history or just skip from rock to rock in one of Mother Nature's largest jungle gyms.

1 ZION NATIONAL PARK ⏱ 2 DAYS

Pack a picnic to enjoy on the banks of the **Riverside Walk** (above, p56) before getting dripped on in the hanging gardens at **Weeping Rock** (p61) and **Emerald Pools** (p56). Adventurous older kids will love the challenge of **Angels Landing** (p62) or **Observation Point** (p65). Stay at family-friendly **Zion Ponderosa Ranch** (p65) and spend a day rock climbing, horse riding or relaxing in the pool.

2 RED CANYON ⏱ ½ DAY

Exit the park through **Zion–Mt Carmel Tunnel** (p64), keeping an eye out for bighorn sheep (above). Drive through arches on super-scenic **Highway 12** (p114), stopping at **Red Canyon Visitor Center** (p107) to hike among the eerie formations on the multitude of trails. Swap four wheels for two and tackle the paved mountain bike trails at **Thunder Mountain** (p107) or the **Red Canyon Bicycle Trail** (p107).

ROMAN KHOMLYAK/SHUTTERSTOCK ©, MELANIWRIGHT/SHUTTERSTOCK ©

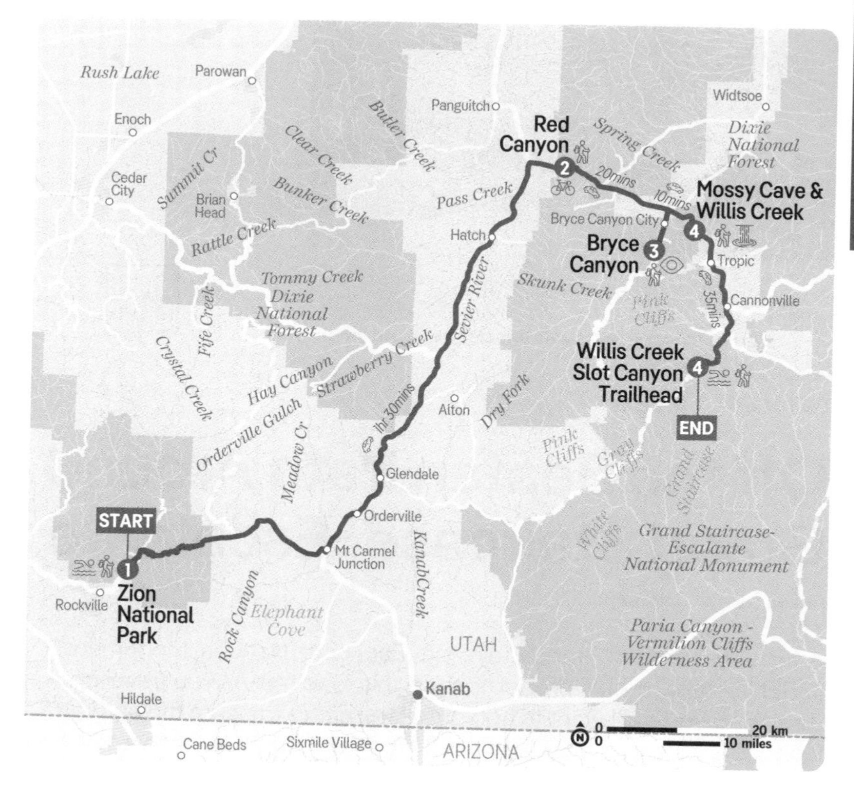

❸

BRYCE CANYON 1½ DAYS

Kids enjoy finding resemblances in the hoodoos and a free park shuttle makes navigation hassle-free. Walk as much of the **Rim Trail** (p100) as you'd like before the temptation to get closer to the hoodoos becomes too strong. The **Queen's Garden Trail** (above, p96), the easiest trail into the canyon, is good for kids. The next day, ride horses around the **Peekaboo Loop** (p99).

❹

MOSSY CAVE & WILLIS CREEK 1 DAY

Seek out water in the desert on these two splash-tastic trails. Outside the main Bryce Canyon boundary (east of the entrance), the easy **Mossy Cave Trail** (p107) leads to a year-round waterfall (above), a summertime treat and a frozen winter spectacle. Further to the south, **Willis Creek** (p110) is a perfect slot canyon for little ones, with a gentle stream and small waterfalls.

FRIEDERIKE KNAUER/SHUTTERSTOCK ©

Grand Staircase–Escalante National Monument (p110)

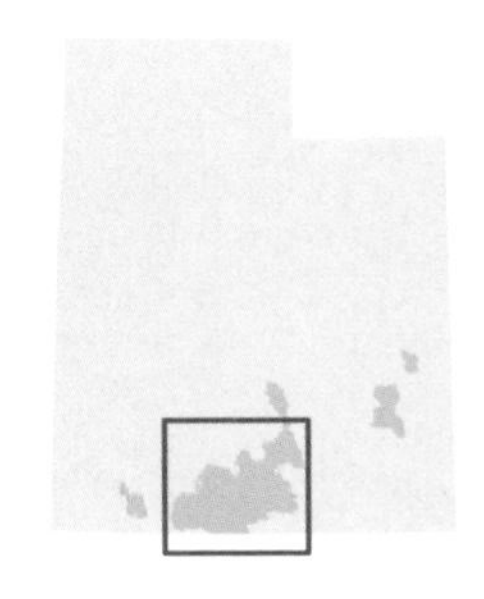

ITINERARIES

Off the Beaten Path Around Grand Staircase–Escalante

Allow: 6 Days **Distance:** 230 Miles

Adventures around Grand Staircase–Escalante National Monument (GSENM) take on epic proportions on this road trip. As you travel up the staircase, you'll want to hop out of the car to treasure the natural wonders in one of the country's last great wildernesses. Take a 4WD vehicle to explore the area to the fullest.

1

KANAB 2 DAYS

Tons of Westerns were filmed around **Kanab** (p123), which still boasts its Hollywood history. If you're ready to do your own stunts, head outside of town to the utterly iconic Southwestern scenes, such as **Wire Pass** and **Buckskin Gulch** (above, p128) and **the Wave** (p126). Day trip to the North Rim of the **Grand Canyon** (p129) for even more splendor.

2

JOHNSON CANYON & SKUTUMPAH ROADS 1 DAY

Stop at the Kanab Visitor Center to get the latest road conditions and then get the heck out of Dodge. Drive **Johnson Canyon and Skutumpah Rds** (p122), GSENM's westernmost route, for cliff views, crumbling movie sets and a hike into the slot canyon at Lick Wash and **Willis Creek** (p110). Watching the sunset colors transform **Kodachrome Basin State Park** (above, p108) is certainly a Kodak moment.

FEEL4NATURE/SHUTTERSTOCK ©, PAUL MAGUIRE/SHUTTERSTOCK ©

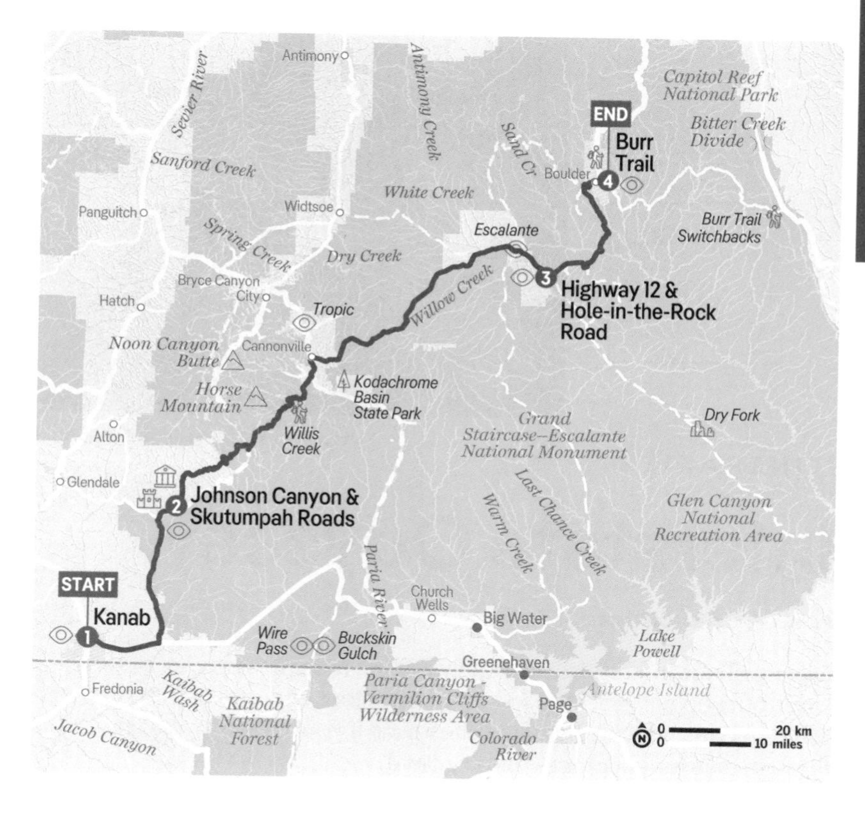

3

HIGHWAY 12 & HOLE-IN-THE-ROCK ROAD ⏱ 2 DAYS

After a night of camping or glamping south of **Tropic** (p108), hit **Highway 12** (p114), arguably the most scenic stretch of road in Utah. Fuel up, get supplies and stay overnight in **Escalante** (p113). In the morning, make your way to historic **Hole-in-the-Rock Rd** (p120), created by 19th-century Mormon pioneers. About 30 miles down the road, feel the squeeze of the scenic slot canyons at **Dry Fork** (above, p121).

4

BURR TRAIL ⏱ 1 DAY

When you've explored far enough, return to Hwy 12 and continue on to **Burr Trail** (p117) near Boulder. This immensely gratifying, dramatic drive is a further lesson in southern Utah geology, with rainbows of rocks in colors from beach-sand white to deep red. On the edge of Capitol Reef National Park, the Burr Trail switchbacks (above) follow an original wagon route through the folded earth.

THE SPEEDY BUTTERFLY/SHUTTERSTOCK ©

Kolob Canyons, Zion National Park (p70)

ITINERARIES

Interstate Odyssey

Allow: 2½ Days **Distance:** 355 Miles

Driving on the interstate is certainly not the most scenic way to see Utah, but you can still stop to stretch your legs at some of the national parks and fascinating historical sites even if you're quickly blazing through on a longer cross-country drive.

1

KOLOB CANYONS ½ DAY

Zion Canyon, the main part of the national park, is almost an hour from I-15, but the lesser-visited **Kolob Canyons** (p70) can give you a taste of Zion's beauty on a whirlwind visit – the visitor center overlooks the interstate. Hike **Taylor Creek** (above, p72) past homesteader cabins to an arched alcove and take the scenic main drive as far as you can.

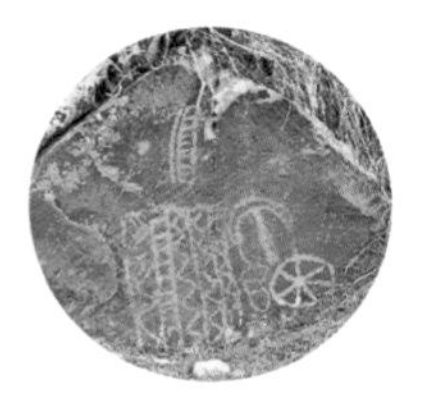

2

PAROWAN GAP ½ DAY

A 15-minute detour from I-15, **Parowan Gap** (p76) has seen passing travelers for millennia, despite how quiet it is now. The road runs through a huge rock split in two, each side covered with thousands of Native petroglyphs (above). Researchers believe the images of entrancing spirals, animal tracks, waves and human figures were carved by the Fremont people, who lived here around 500 CE.

STEVE ESTVANIK/SHUTTERSTOCK ©, KURTIS LEANY/SHUTTERSTOCK ©

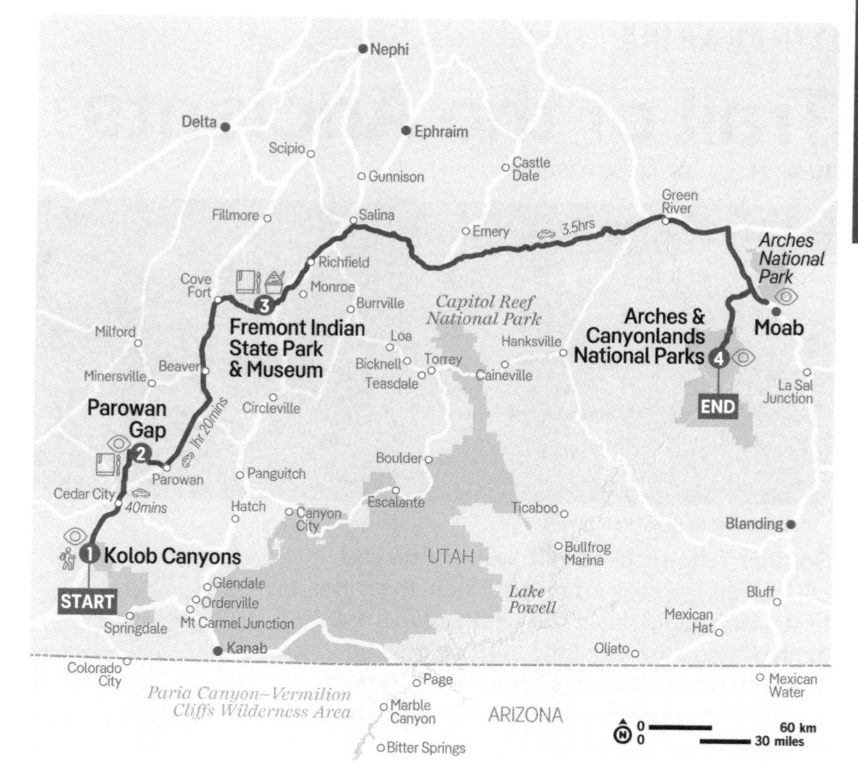

3 FREMONT INDIAN STATE PARK & MUSEUM ½ DAY

After a stop for ice cream and cheese curds at **The Creamery** (p77) in Beaver, turn right to head east on I-70. The interstate plows right over an ancient Fremont village, discovered during highway construction. Thankfully, some artifacts have been preserved in the **Fremont Indian State Park & Museum** (p199). Use the dozen-plus trails to access hundreds of petroglyphs.

4 ARCHES & CANYONLANDS NATIONAL PARKS 1 DAY

Get a peek at two more parks a short distance south of I-70. Start at **Arches** (p136), winding along the **Scenic Dr** (p144) and stopping at as many formations as you can squeeze in. On the other side of Hwy 191, **Canyonlands** (p146) soars above the landscape. Follow the road to its conclusion at **Grand View Point** (p151) for an epic end to your Utah detours.

ITINERARIES

Trail of the Ancients

Allow: 7 Days **Distance:** 425 Miles

SNEHIT PHOTO/SHUTTERSTOCK ©

Capitol Reef National Park (p184)

Southern Utah is filled with well-preserved cliff dwellings, rock art and artifacts that offer tantalizing glimpses of the past, but this area's Native history isn't just the stuff of museums. Tribal culture still thrives in the Four Corners region and travelers can to get know the area's Indigenous people past and present.

RED HERRING/SHUTTERSTOCK ©, LAUREN KEITH/LONELY PLANET ©, COLIN D. YOUNG/SHUTTERSTOCK ©

1 CAPITOL REEF NATIONAL PARK 1 DAY

This national park has some of the most easily accessible petroglyphs of any in Utah. Right off Hwy 24, two **wooden boardwalks** (p191) meander past human figures and bighorn sheep carved by the Fremont people. Head into the heart of the park for an easy stroll down **Capitol Gorge** (p196) to see even more etchings, as well as more recent additions from 19th-century Mormon pioneers.

2 HORSESHOE CANYON 1 DAY

The drive to get here is rough and remote, but it's absolutely worth it for the 'Louvre of the Southwest.' Part of Canyonlands National Park, **Horseshoe Canyon** (above, p200) shelters one of the most impressive collections of rock art on the continent. About 80 haunting human figures spread like paper dolls across the 200ft-long Great Gallery, likely painted between 2000 BCE and 500 CE.

3 AZTEC BUTTE TRAIL 1 DAY

Island in the Sky's **Aztec Butte Trail** (p148) weaves over steep slickrock to an Ancient Puebolan granary (above) tucked safely below the overhang, once used to store food and medicine safely away from the elements. As you leave the park on Hwy 313, stop to see 'Intestine Man,' a human figure with a curled-up snake in his stomach, one of several pictographs on the mesa wall.

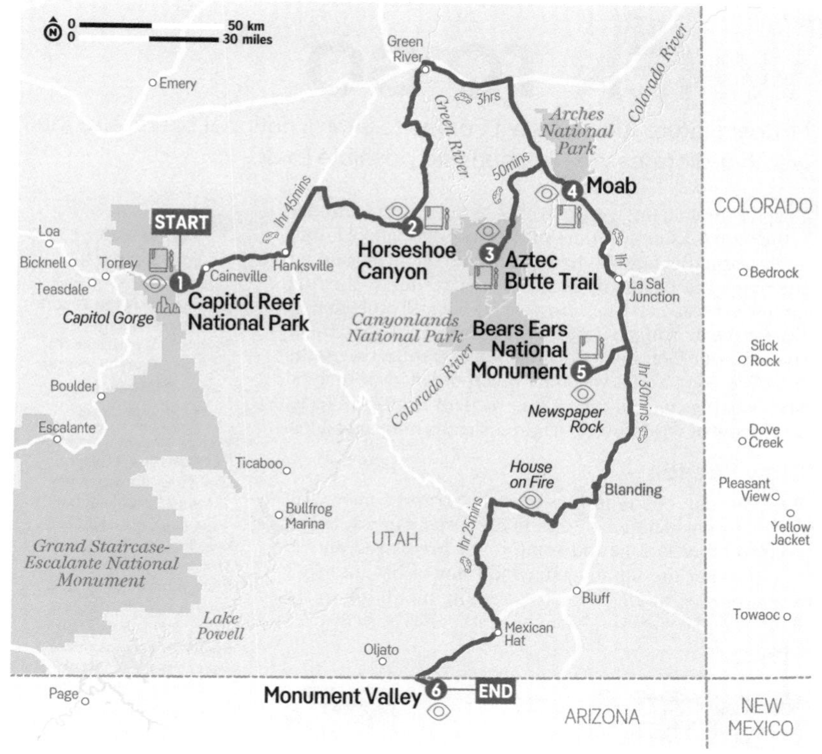

4 MOAB 1 DAY

The area around Moab is tattooed with **petroglyph sites** (above, p160) that are easily accessible from town. Potash Rd on the west side of the Colorado River is particularly rich. Don't miss the roadside site near the Wall Street rock-climbing area, where some scenes were etched as far back as 6000 BCE. More sites await at the Poison Spider trailhead, which also has dinosaur tracks.

5 BEARS EARS NATIONAL MONUMENT 2 DAYS

The first national monument created with Native American tribes, **Bears Ears** (p173) preserves thousands of archaeological and sacred sites. Highlights include thousands of petroglyph inscriptions on **Newspaper Rock** (p173); the granaries known as **House on Fire** (above, p175), due to their unusual gold-orange sandstone overhang; and Moon House, which has 49 rooms across three well-preserved dwellings.

6 MONUMENT VALLEY 1 DAY

Just across the state line in Arizona, **Monument Valley** (p178) has dozens of Hollywood-famous formations. This land is part of the Navajo Reservation and to best get acquainted with it, you can join a Navajo-led tour on foot, horseback or by truck. Guides shower you with details about the curiously named rocks, life on the reservation and trivia on locally shot movies.

WHEN TO GO

Mother Nature rules when it comes to Utah's national parks, and the weather dictates what's open and possible to do.

Despite the soaring temperatures in the desert, summer is the high season for Utah's national parks. School is out, and vacationing families have packed up their cars and hit the road. The blistering heat index is gradually inching up toward seasonal highs, so save hiking and other activities for the morning or late evening. From mid-September to early October, colorful fall foliage paints the parks in new colors, and a welcome touch of warmth lingers. Mild weather makes spring an excellent time to hike, as a rainbow of wildflowers brightens trails and roadsides.

Slow Season

Bargains can be found in winter, but travel comes with different considerations. Some of the parks' gateway towns go into hibernation, and some roads are closed entirely, either because of adverse conditions or because they aren't plowed at all. If you're planning on hiking in the winter, make sure you have (or rent) snowshoes or traction devices.

WINTRY WONDERS

Lance Syrett is the Resort General Manager at Ruby's Inn, which hosts the Bryce Canyon Winter Festival.

@rubysinn.com

"With an elevation of nearly 8000ft, Bryce Canyon National Park is a winter wonderland of natural beauty. Even if you've seen Bryce in summer, you haven't witnessed it at its best until you've seen its world-famous hoodoos with a cap of snow. Think of Bryce Canyon like a cake – everybody likes cake, right? But everyone loves it a little more with some frosting on top."

Wall Street, Bryce Canyon National Park (p98)

FREEZE & THAW

The cycle of freezing and thawing has sculpted many of Utah's iconic formations. When water seeps into the rocks and freezes, it expands, causing the rock to break apart. Bryce Canyon's otherworldly hoodoos are formed this way and were once part of a whole plateau.

Weather through the year

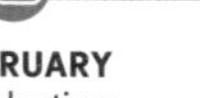
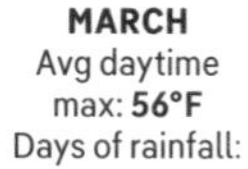

JANUARY	FEBRUARY	MARCH	APRIL	MAY	JUNE
Avg daytime max: **50°F**	Avg daytime max: **49°F**	Avg daytime max: **56°F**	Avg daytime max: **59°F**	Avg daytime max: **69°F**	Avg daytime max: **82°F**
Days of rainfall: **6½**	Days of rainfall: **7**	Days of rainfall: **8**	Days of rainfall: **6**	Days of rainfall: **4**	Days of rainfall: **3**

LIKE THE DESERTS MISS THE RAIN

Utah doesn't have four seasons but five. The southwestern USA's summer monsoon season runs from mid-June to September. Ominous clouds gather on warm afternoons, unleashing deadly bolts of lightning and flash floods, but they sweeten the scene with rainbows and bursts of green in the desert.

Festivals & Events in Southern Utah

Discover high-elevation wintry charm and try cold-weather activities during the **Bryce Canyon Winter Festival** (p92). Participate in guided snowshoe hikes, cross-country skiing, photography workshops and storytelling presentations.
February

Bryce Canyon National Park has some of the darkest skies in the entire country, and even more stars are on display during the **Bryce Canyon Astronomy Festival** (p92) when the Salt Lake Astronomical Society brings out its telescopes.
June

Soak up the sounds among the red rocks at the **Moab Music Festival** (p135). Some shows take place in surreal surroundings, including a secret rock grotto and floating concerts on the Colorado River.
August and September

Run like a bandit at the **Butch Cassidy 10K/5K** (p51), which ends in Grafton ghost town, and don your best outlaw outfit for the look-alike competition.
November

STARRY SUMMER SKIES

Bettymaya Foott is an astrophotographer and dark-sky advocate who grew up in Moab.

@bettymaya.foott

"I take lots of photos of the night sky, and in summer the Milky Way is up as soon as it gets dark. You can pull over at any viewpoint in Canyonlands or Arches National Parks, watch it get dark and take amazing photos of the red-rock canyons as the stars shine above. Summer is also a great time to swim in the Colorado River."

Delicate Arch, Arches National Park (p138)

CLIMATE CHANGE

A 2019 study by a scientist at the University of California, Berkeley, found that climate change affects US national parks more than the rest of the country. Compared to the US as a whole, which has warmed by about 0.7°F since 1895, the temperatures in the national parks have increased by more than double - 1.8°F on average.

Of Utah's five national parks, Zion has seen the highest temperature jump, by nearly 2°F. Zion has also been included on a list of the country's 25 most endangered national parks by the National Resources Defense Council and the Rocky Mountain Climate Organization. Climate change might also be responsible for the recent growth of toxic cyanobacteria (also known as blue-green algae) in the Virgin River and its tributaries.

RECORD TEMPERATURES

Utah is a state of extremes. The highest temperature recorded was 117°F in St George. Meanwhile, Peter Sinks, a natural sinkhole in northern Utah, is one of the coldest places in the country. It has reached -69.3°F, the second-lowest temperature documented in the contiguous United States.

JULY
Avg daytime max: **87°F**
Days of rainfall: **5**

AUGUST
Avg daytime max: **85°F**
Days of rainfall: **6**

SEPTEMBER
Avg daytime max: **78°F**
Days of rainfall: **4**

OCTOBER
Avg daytime max: **66°F**
Days of rainfall: **4**

NOVEMBER
Avg daytime max: **56°F**
Days of rainfall: **5**

DECEMBER
Avg daytime max: **48°F**
Days of rainfall: **6**

LEFT: BLAZG/SHUTTERSTOCK © RIGHT: ALLSTAR PICTURE LIBRARY LTD/ALAMY STOCK PHOTO ©

Angels Landing, Zion National Park (p62)

GET PREPARED
FOR UTAH'S NATIONAL PARKS

Useful things to load in your bag, your ears and your brain

Clothes

Moisture-wicking outdoor wear: Fabrics that are breathable and actively wick moisture away from your skin are better than cotton or wool.

Walking shoes or hiking boots: Trail-running shoes with grippy soles are probably the best all-around footwear for Utah. Hiking boots provide the best ankle support, but you may find them too cumbersome in the desert heat.

Water shoes or closed-toe sandals (not flip-flops): Useful for splashing your way through a slot canyon.

Hat and sunglasses: Utah is one of the sunniest states in the country, so protect your skin while you're outdoors.

Warm and waterproof jackets: In winter you'll need enough clothes to keep warm in a snowstorm. Summer means monsoons. Temperature swings are huge from day to night, and high elevations remain cooler throughout the year.

Manners

Hikers going uphill have the right of way.
If you're going downhill, step to the side while they pass.

Greet others on the trail.
A simple 'hello' or head nod will do. If you approach other hikers from behind, call out and make yourself known.

Don't stack rocks.
In some national parks, hikers rely on these piles of rocks, called cairns, for navigation.

READ

Desert Solitaire
(Edward Abbey; 1968)
Provocative and hilariously cranky chronicle of the author's experience as a ranger at Arches.

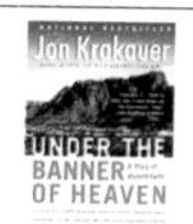

Under the Banner of Heaven
(Jon Krakauer; 2003)
A compelling look into extremist polygamist groups and Utah state history.

The Secret Knowledge of Water
(Craig Childs; 2000)
Includes a heart-thumping account of flash floods raging through a slot canyon.

Beneath These Red Cliffs
(Ronald L Holt; 2006)
Unflinching tale of Indigenous survival, with a foreword by tribal chairwoman Lora Tom.

Words

Slot canyon A narrow passageway with towering rock walls. Slots are formed by water cutting through sedimentary rock, such as sandstone. Utah has the densest concentration of slot canyons in the world.

Flash flood A sudden rush of water that can rise within a few hours – or minutes – of a heavy rainstorm. Flash floods most commonly occur during the summer monsoon season and are particularly dangerous in slot canyons, where they sweep away everything in their path.

CFS Cubic feet per second, ie how much water a river is carrying. One cubic foot is roughly equivalent to 7½ gallons of water. Popular hikes such as the Narrows in Zion National Park are closed when the flow rate of the Virgin River is higher than 150 CFS.

Mormon A member of the Church of Jesus Christ of Latter-day Saints (sometimes abbreviated to LDS). More than 60% of Utah residents identify as Mormon, the most of any state.

Wash A dry stream bed that fills with water seasonally; called an arroyo in some neighboring states.

Hoodoo A column of rock sculpted by erosion; also called a fairy chimney. Bryce Canyon National Park has more hoodoos than anywhere else in the world.

Petroglyph Carving created by chiseling or pecking straight onto a rock surface, often one with desert varnish (a thin and dark mineral coating), which allows the petroglyph to appear more vividly.

Pictograph Painting on a rock surface.

WATCH

Paul Newman, Butch Cassidy and the Sundance Kid

Butch Cassidy and the Sundance Kid (George Roy Hill; 1969) The adventures of two real-life outlaws hiding in Utah.

Thelma & Louise (Ridley Scott; 1991) Two gal pals run from the law and into stunning Southwest scenery.

127 Hours (Danny Boyle; 2010) Aron Ralston's harrowing survival drama after a canyoneering adventure gone wrong in Utah's red-rock country.

Forrest Gump (Robert Zemeckis; 1994) Forrest stopped his cross-country run in Monument Valley, which straddles the Utah–Arizona line.

Big Love (2006–11) Starring Bill Paxton, this HBO drama examines the true romance and intimate humanity of Utah's polygamists.

LISTEN

100 Years: Celebrating a Century of Recording Excellence (Mormon Tabernacle Choir; 2010) 'America's Choir' has performed at six presidential inaugurations.

Native Lands (various artists; 1996) Native American and Southwestern music recorded in Utah's national parks.

Night Visions (Imagine Dragons; 2012) Imagine Dragons was started by former students of Brigham Young University; 'Radioactive' won a Grammy for Best Rock Performance.

TRIP PLANNER

HOW TO GET PERMITS FOR UTAH'S NATIONAL PARKS

Increasingly, Utah's national parks are for the planners. The parks have drawn record numbers of people – a whopping five million visitors came through Zion's entrances in 2021 – which has led the National Park Service to introduce permits and restrictions on popular trails.

FOTOS593/SHUTTERSTOCK ©

Court of the Patriarchs, Zion National Park (p60)

Busiest month June
Quietest month January
Number of visitors (2022) 4,692,417
Increase (since 2012) 58%
Most-visited national parks ranking 3 of 63

Zion National Park

Angels Landing is one of the park's most popular and iconic hikes. Permits (recreation.gov; introduced in 2022) are issued through two lottery systems: two months in advance or the day before.

Permits are required for most activities (besides day hiking) in Zion, including canyoneering, overnight backpacking and rock climbing, and trips on the Virgin River. You also need a permit to hike the Subway and the Narrows from the top down, even if you're not camping overnight.

Busiest month September
Quietest month January
Number of visitors (2022) 2,354,660
Increase (since 2012) 70%
Most-visited national parks ranking 15 of 63

Bryce Canyon National Park

Bryce Canyon requires permits for backpackers wanting to camp in the backcountry. Permits for trips from March through November can be booked on recreation.gov up to three months ahead.

Walk-in permits are available year-round, but before you set off on your hike, you must check in at the visitor center to go through the rules and rent a bear canister (or have yours inspected).

The Wave

For tips on how to get highly saught-after permits for the Wave, see p127

ONLINE MAPS & APPS

AllTrails
Save lists of trails and read reviews and current conditions from recent hikers. The app is free, but it's worth paying for AllTrails+ to download maps offline and get wrong-turn alerts.

Recreation.gov
An indispensable app: reserve permits, campgrounds and day-use passes for national parks and other federal areas.

ReserveAmerica
Book campsites at Utah's state parks.

STAYING IN THE NATIONAL PARKS

Zion and Bryce Canyon are the only two of Utah's five national parks with in-park, non-campground accommodations.

Reservations for **Zion Lodge** (zionlodge.com) and **Bryce Canyon Lodge** (visitbrycecanyon.com) open 13 months in advance.

The main lodge, suites, Sunrise Motel and Sunset Motel at Bryce Canyon Lodge are closed from November to the end of March. The cabins open later, at the end of April.

Opening dates for reservations for the national parks' campgrounds vary. Some are bookable up to six months ahead, while others are available only two weeks in advance. Sites in the backcountry are often by permit or on a first-come, first-served basis.

Arches National Park

In 2022, Arches implemented a timed entry system. If you want to visit from April through October between 7am and 4pm, you must have a timed ticket on top of the park fee. One-hour entry slots are released three months ahead on recreation.gov, and a limited number of tickets are available the day before at 6pm.

Permits are required for backpacking and canyoneering and advised for rock climbing. To visit Fiery Furnace, you must get one of the few coveted slots a week in advance for a ranger-led tour or a self-guided visit.

Busiest month May
Quietest month January
Number of visitors (2022) 1,460,652
Increase (since 2012) 36%
Most-visited national parks ranking 20 of 63

Canyonlands National Park

Canyonlands requires backcountry permits for overnight trips, which become available four months in advance and are highly sought after. You need a day-use permit for 4WD, motorcycle and mountain bike travel on White Rim, Elephant Hill, Lavender Canyon and Peekaboo/Horse Canyon Rds, which you can obtain online the day before your trip. Any remaining permits are available at the visitor centers for day-of trips.

Permits are needed to get on the rivers for both day and overnight trips. If you organize your trip through an outfitter, the company will take care of this for you.

Busiest month May
Quietest month January
Number of visitors (2022) 779,147
Increase (since 2012) 72%
Most-visited national parks ranking 29 of 63

what3words

This company has given every 3m square of the world a unique three-word address. For example, the address for Zion's south entrance is *firms.landing.wrong.* Emergency services are increasingly using what3words so response crews know exactly where to send help.

Scan to download the what3words app

Capitol Reef National Park

Capitol Reef requires permits for backpacking, canyoneering, rock climbing and bouldering, but the permits are free and don't need to be obtained in advance (though some types of permit can be applied for in advance by emailing a form).

Busiest month May
Quietest month January
Number of visitors (2022) 1,227,608
Increase (since 2012) 82%
Most-visited national parks ranking 22 of 63

TRIP PLANNER

TRAVELING WITH PETS IN UTAH'S NATIONAL PARKS

It's only natural to want to explore the great outdoors with your pet, but the national parks have a lot of rules that make bringing your doggo a challenge. While some parts of the national parks are open to pets, state parks are a better bet if you want to spend the day on the trail together.

The National Parks

Pets are allowed in Utah's national parks but under a lot of restrictions (exceptions are made for service animals; emotional-support animals are not considered service animals). These rules are in place to protect the parks' flora and fauna. In areas where they are permitted, dogs must remain on a leash no longer than 6ft and be accompanied by a person at all times.

The national parks' gateway towns have daycare and overnight boarding options. Be aware that most pet-friendly hotels do not allow pets to stay in the room unaccompanied.

DOGGY DAYCARE & OVERNIGHT BOARDING

Near Zion
Canyon Paws (canyonpaws.com) in Rockville has daycare and overnight boarding 4 miles from Zion's South Entrance.

Near Bryce Canyon
Pawz Dogz (pawzdogz.net) offers boarding and grooming and will pick up and drop off your pet; in Panguitch 30 miles from the park entrance.

Near Arches & Canyonlands
Leave your pet at Moab National Bark (moabnationalbark.com), started by a vet tech and her husband. **Moab Vet Clinic** (moabvetclinic.com/boarding) also offers boarding.

Near Capitol Reef
Drop off cats and dogs for daycare or an overnight stay at **Color Country Animal Welfare** (colorcountryanimalwelfare.org/boarding) in Torrey.

LAYNE V. NAYLOR/SHUTTERSTOCK ©

ZION NATIONAL PARK

Dogs are allowed on only one trail in Zion, Pa'rus. You can also take pets on public roads and into parking areas, developed campgrounds, picnic reas and the grounds of Zion Lodge. Pets are not permitted on any other trails or in wilderness areas, shuttle buses or public buildings.

BRYCE CANYON NATIONAL PARK

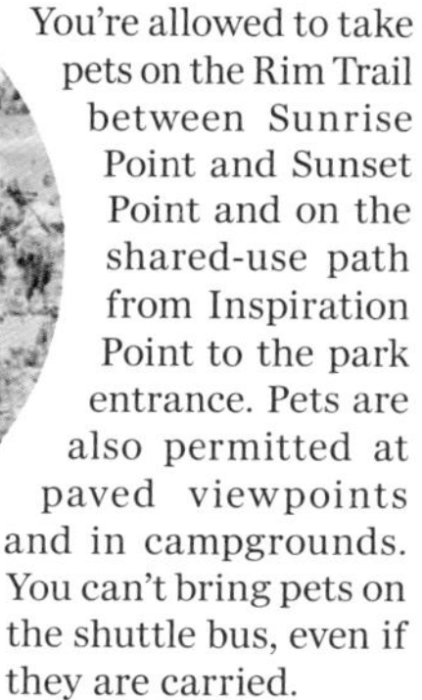

Bryce Canyon

You're allowed to take pets on the Rim Trail between Sunrise Point and Sunset Point and on the shared-use path from Inspiration Point to the park entrance. Pets are also permitted at paved viewpoints and in campgrounds. You can't bring pets on the shuttle bus, even if they are carried.

Sign your pup up for the BARK Ranger Program to get a treat from the visitor center.

ARCHES NATIONAL PARK

Moab

Pets are not permitted on any trails at Arches, but you can walk dogs along established roads and bring them to parking lots, campgrounds and picnic areas.

CANYONLANDS NATIONAL PARK

Pets are allowed on front-country roads, and in parking and picnic areas and campgrounds, but not on any hiking trails or overlooks. You can't take pets anywhere in the backcountry, including on river trips or in your own vehicle, except for the Shafer Trail in the Island in the Sky district.

CAPITOL REEF NATIONAL PARK

Pets are allowed on the Fremont River Trail, the trail between the visitor center and Fruita Campground, in the campground, in unfenced orchards, on roads and in picnic and parking areas.

PET-FRIENDLY PARK ALTERNATIVES

State parks and areas administered by the Bureau of Land Management and the US Forest Service are more pet-friendly than national parks. Some national monuments also allow pets.

Dead Horse Point State Park
Leashed pets are allowed on all hiking trails and at the campground at this state park near the entrance to Canyonlands' Island in the Sky district.

Manti–La Sal National Forest
You can take pets out on any trails in this 1.4-million-acre area that stretches through central Utah and into Colorado. Be aware that black bears and livestock might be present.

Fishlake National Forest
This US Forest Service land covers nearly 1.5 million acres between Capitol Reef National Park and I-15. Leashed pets are permitted on all trails.

Best Friends Animal Sanctuary
The southern Utah town of Kanab is home to Best Friends Animal Sanctuary, a no-kill rescue center that became famous for rehabilitating Michael Vick's pit bulls. You can volunteer, take a tour of the facility or hike the trails with your own pet or one of theirs.

Grand Staircase–Escalante National Monument
One of the largest national monuments in the country, GSENM encompasses a huge swath of south-central Utah and allows pets on its trails.

Red Canyon
Let your hound explore the hoodoos in this gorgeous US Forest Service area west of Bryce Canyon.

ANDREW REPP/SHUTTERSTOCK ©

Double Arch, Arches National Park (p138)

TRIP PLANNER

HIKING THE DESERT SAFELY

Going out in the hot desert means taking extra precautions to make sure you return safely. This is true whether you plan to be gone an hour or a week. The desert has a way of compounding simple errors in judgment very quickly, and consequences range from unpleasant to grave.

DRINK PLENTY OF WATER

Dehydration is the biggest danger of desert hiking. It sounds obvious, but we've seen too many people with a single small water bottle on a half-day hike. Bring lots of water (a gallon per person per day in summer) and protect yourself from the sun.

Because your body can only absorb about a quart of water per hour, it's beneficial to prehydrate before embarking on a long hike. To get a head start on hydration, drink plenty of water the day before your hike and avoid diuretics such as caffeine and alcohol.

FINDING YOUR WAY

Download maps for offline use while you have a strong wi-fi connection – don't wait until you're at the trailhead, many of which have a poor or nonexistent cell signal. Be aware that things go wrong with electronics – batteries and chargers fail or are forgotten – so always bring a paper map and a compass.

WATCH THE WEATHER

Flash floods are an ever-present danger in the desert, and hikers have drowned from them in Zion, including several people in recent years. Check weather warnings at visitor centers or with the National Weather Service, especially if you're planning on hiking through slot canyons.

Lightning strikes are another common danger in the desert. If a thunderstorm is brewing, avoid exposed ridges or summits. Never seek shelter under objects that are isolated or higher than their surroundings, such as a lone tree. In open areas where there's no safe shelter, find a dry depression in the ground and take up a crouched-squatting position with your feet together. Do not lie on the ground.

DANGEROUS PLANTS & ANIMALS

Southern Utah is awash in critters that, if bothered, can inflict pain, including rattlesnakes, scorpions, tarantulas, black widow spiders, wasps and centipedes. Spiders rarely bite unless harassed, which is also true of rattlesnakes, which like to warm themselves on trails or rock ledges. Don't put your hand beneath logs and rocks or into piles of wood and never reach blindly over ledges or beneath boulders.

Tarantula

Learn to identify poison ivy, which has bright-green, serrated leaves that grow in clusters of three. This toxic plant grows in thickets, preferring moisture-laden canyons.

DAY-PACK ESSENTIALS

Hydration Bladder
Makes it easier to carry – and drink – enough water while you're hiking.

Maps & Compass
Carry paper copies of maps and a compass, and know how to use them.

Phone Cable & Spare Battery
Keep your phone charged for maps and in case of emergency.

Sun Protection
Wear a hat and apply sunscreen and lip balm with at least SPF 15. On day hikes, long sleeves and pants might provide more protection.

Salty Snacks
Eat high-energy bars or trail mix to help retain water.

First-Aid Kit
Build your own or buy one premade.

DESERT-HIKING GUIDELINES

Stay on the trail
Whether hiking, biking or driving, stay on the trail. Cryptobiotic crust is present in many areas and can take a century or more to regrow if it's stepped on. If it's muddy, either be willing to get dirty or don't go – it's better than creating wider, braided trails.

If there is no trail
Stay on slickrock, gravel or sand; never step on plants or cryptobiotic soil.

Pack it in, pack it out
Bring resealable plastic bags for trash and toilet paper.

Protect all water sources and riparian areas
Camp 200ft from any water, never wash yourself or dishes in creeks or springs and use minimal or no soap.

Backcountry fire
Usually prohibited.

Never touch artifacts or rock art
Don't move or take any cultural or archaeological artifacts.

Say something
Always tell somebody in advance where you are going and when you expect to be back.

If problems arise
If you do run into trouble, don't panic – sit down (if possible) and regain your cool before making any important decisions.

Know your limits
One little-talked-about risk facing hikers is their own enthusiasm. Remember that even in the middle of a national park, you're in a remote, wild place. Don't tackle a trail that's above your skill level.

Canyonlands National Park (p159)

THE OUTDOORS

The great outdoors is exactly why you've come to Utah, and Mother Nature provides a playground of labyrinthine canyons, red-rock spires, moonlit desert arches and slickrock landscapes.

Outdoor adventures are available for all skill levels, and outfitters are there to get you set up. Challenge yourself by rappelling into the narrow canyons around Zion National Park or mountain biking on the steep and sinister Slickrock Trail in Moab. Or take it easy on your body (though not your vehicle) by going off-pavement along one of the state's many 4WD roads. Whether you're rafting on the Colorado River or skiing fresh powder in the mountains, you'll see the state in a whole new way.

HIKING

Hiking is the main and most accessible activity in the national parks and can be as short or long as you'd like. You can hike at any time of year, but you need to be prepared. Though southern Utah is a year-round destination, variations by location and season are extreme. As the majority of parks, monuments and other hiking destinations are in the desert, spring and fall are often the best times to hike. Summer – the height of tourist season – can be the worst, and temperatures routinely top 100°F.

RAFTING
Enjoy a day of white-water adventure on the Colorado River near Moab or a longer trip through **Cataract Canyon** (p158).

STARGAZING
All of Utah's national parks are certified dark-sky parks. **Bryce Canyon** (p96) has the most astro events and activities.

FOUR-WHEEL DRIVING
Leave the pavement behind on the backroads of **Canyonlands** (p152) and **Grand Staircase–Escalante National Monument** (p192).

FAMILY ADVENTURES

You don't have to wade all the way into Zion's Narrows to splash in the Virgin River – bring a picnic to the 'beach' on the **Riverside Walk** (p56).

Stare in wonder at **Goblin Valley State Park** (p199) as the rock formations turn into otherworldly beings before your eyes. Some of the valleys are free to roam with no trails, perfect for DIY adventures.

Climb ladders and pass an abandoned cowboy camp on the **Cave Spring Trail** (p169) in Canyonlands' Needles district.

Most of the classic hikes in **Arches National Park** (p136) are family friendly, including Landscape Arch, Delicate Arch and the Windows.

Cycle along the **shared-use trail** (p107) that runs from the heart of Bryce Canyon National Park to Red Canyon.

The majority of hikes in the region are day hikes, taking anywhere from 20 minutes to eight hours. On steep trails that lead from canyon floors to rims, or vice versa, a general guide is that it takes twice as long to ascend as to descend.

Rock Climbing & Canyoneering

If Dr Seuss designed a rock-climbing playground, it would look a lot like Utah: a surreal landscape filled with enormous blobs, spires, soaring cliffs and canyon walls in kaleidoscopic colors. Some of the country's best rock climbing lies in southern Utah, though many routes are for intermediate to expert climbers. Zion is famous for big-wall climbs, and you'll find great climbing in Arches, Canyonlands and Capitol Reef, but the National Park Service does not maintain anchors.

If you'd rather rappel down than climb up, Utah is tailor-made for canyoneering. The thrill of squeezing yourself into a dark, narrow slot, rappelling over the lip of a 70ft chute or swimming across a cold subterranean pool is obvious enough. Outfitters run guided canyoneering trips across southern Utah.

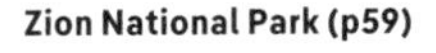

Zion National Park (p59)

Mountain Biking & Cycling

The fat-tire crowd already knows about Moab, a mountain biking mecca for decades. The original Slickrock Trail is for experienced riders only, so if you're a novice, try the Bar M Loop. Even though mountain biking is prohibited on national-park trails, it's permitted on dirt roads. In Canyonlands, Island in the Sky's White Rim Rd and the labyrinth of 4WD roads in the Maze are awesome experiences, as is Cathedral Valley Loop in Capitol Reef and backcountry roads in Grand Staircase–Escalante.

Road cycling the paved scenic drives in Zion, Bryce Canyon and Capitol Reef is an excellent way to take in the parks' sights. The steeper, longer and more challenging paved roads in Arches and Canyonlands are best left for experienced cyclists in good shape. Shorter paths are Zion's Pa'rus Trail and the shared-use Red Canyon Bicycle Trail, on USFS land outside Bryce Canyon that leads into the national park.

SKIING

Yes, you really can ski above the desert. Hit the powder at **Brian Head** (p78) and **Bryce Canyon** (p98).

WILDLIFE WATCHING

Look out for iconic and endangered species, such as California condors soaring above **Zion Canyon** (p56).

HORSEBACK RIDING

See the hoodoos from the saddle on a horseback ride on **Peekaboo Loop** (p99) in Bryce Canyon National Park.

BACKPACKING

Tackle the less-trafficked routes of Zion, such as **West Rim Trail** (p58) or **La Verkin Creek** (p73), on an overnight trip.

ACTION AREAS

Where to find Utah's National Parks' best outdoor activities.

National Parks

1. Zion National Park (p52)
2. Bryce Canyon National Park (p94)
3. Arches National Park (p136)
4. Canyonlands National Park (p146)
5. Capitol Reef National Park (p184)

Hiking

1. The Narrows (p54)
2. Angels Landing (p62)
3. Fairyland Loop (p96)
4. Devils Garden (p142)
5. Hickman Bridge (p186)
6. Chesler Park (p170)

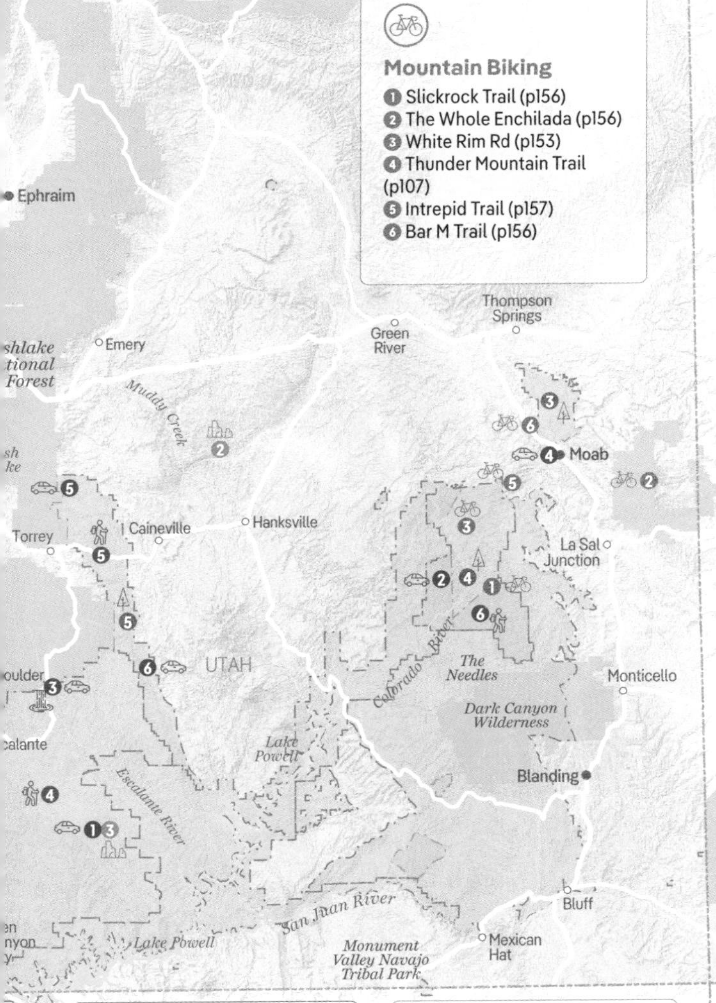

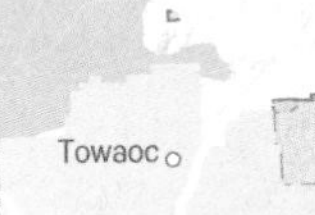

Mountain Biking

1. Slickrock Trail (p156)
2. The Whole Enchilada (p156)
3. White Rim Rd (p153)
4. Thunder Mountain Trail (p107)
5. Intrepid Trail (p157)
6. Bar M Trail (p156)

4WD Roads

1. Hole-in-the-Rock Rd (p120)
2. The Maze (p201)
3. Burr Trail (p117)
4. Potash Rd (p153)
5. Cathedral Valley Loop (p192)
6. Notom-Bullfrog Rd (p192)

Slot Canyons

1. The Subway (p74)
2. Little Wild Horse & Bell Canyons (p201)
3. Dry Fork (p121)
4. Wire Pass & Buckskin Gulch (p128)
5. Willis Creek (p110)

UTAH'S NATIONAL PARKS

THE GUIDE

Chapters in this section are organized by hubs and their surrounding areas. We see the hub as your base in the destination, where you'll find unique experiences, local insights, insider tips and expert recommendations. It's also your gateway to the surrounding area, where you'll see what and how much you can do from there.

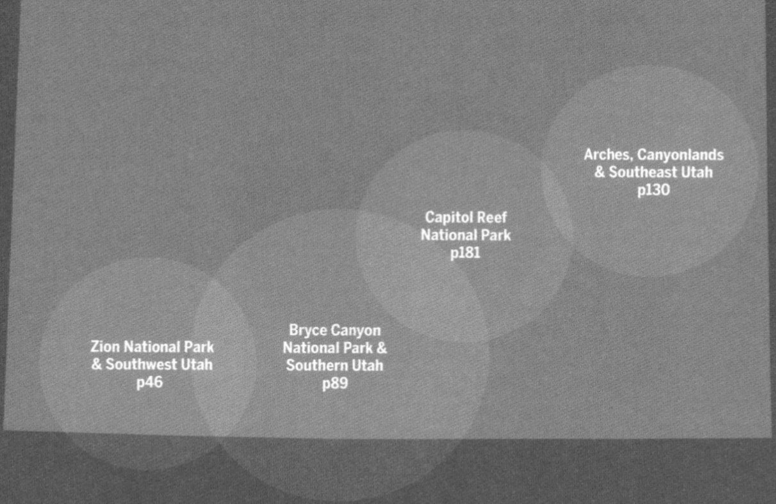

Mule deer fawn, Virgin River, Zion National Park (p56)

ZION NATIONAL PARK & SOUTHWEST UTAH

UTAH'S CROWN JEWEL

Visiting heavenly Zion National Park can feel like a religious experience. Get ready for an overdose of awesome.

The soaring red-and-white cliffs of Zion Canyon, one of Utah's most dramatic natural wonders, rise high over the Virgin River. Hiking through the Virgin River in the Narrows or peering beyond Angels Landing after a 1500ft ascent is indeed amazing, but for all its majesty, the park also holds more delicate beauties: weeping rocks, tiny grottoes, hanging gardens and meadows of mesa-top wildflowers. Zion's treasures turn up in the most unexpected places. That's not to say that the soaring 2000ft sandstone cliffs won't leave you awestruck, but it's the finer details that really make Zion stand apart.

The beauty of Zion (locally pronounced *zy*-in, rhyming with lion) has hardly gone unnoticed. Nearly five million people pass through its entrances, making it the third-most-visited national park in the country. Summers can sometimes feel claustrophobic, and more mandatory permits have been introduced to control the crowds. Quieter corners can still be found. Much of Zion's 232 sq miles are little-visited backcountry, while the surrounding small towns, national monuments and state parks wait to show slow travelers their secrets.

Whether you're capturing the play of shadows on the rocks, admiring the echoes of water in the curves of a slot canyon or wading knee-deep in the adventure-fueled fun of the Narrows, Zion and southwestern Utah will leave you in reverie every step of the way.

Inset: Valley of Fire State Park (p86) Opposite: The Narrows (p55)

THE MAIN AREAS

Find Your Way

Tucked in the southwesternmost corner of the state, Zion National Park is closer to Las Vegas than Salt Lake City. Vast distances mean that a car is essential for exploring the region to the fullest.

Kolob Canyons & Kolob Terrace Road, p70

The national park's quieter corners, with dramatic finger canyons, the world's second-largest freestanding arch, and lesser-visited viewpoints and trailheads.

St George, p81

Southwestern Utah's big city has affordable accommodations, a decent selection of restaurants and plenty of places to stock up before heading into the wild.

SHUTTLE

A seasonal shuttle bus runs along Zion Canyon from March to the end of November. Private vehicles are not allowed on this road when these buses are operating. The shuttle is free to ride.

CAR

Unless you're staying in Springdale, which has a shuttle bus to the park's south entrance, you need a car to get to Zion. A high-clearance 4WD vehicle is necessary for reaching some trailheads and backcountry areas.

BICYCLE

The national-park roads are open to cyclists, and traveling by bike is a beautifully slow way to enjoy the scenery. Zion Canyon Scenic Dr gains only 450ft in elevation.

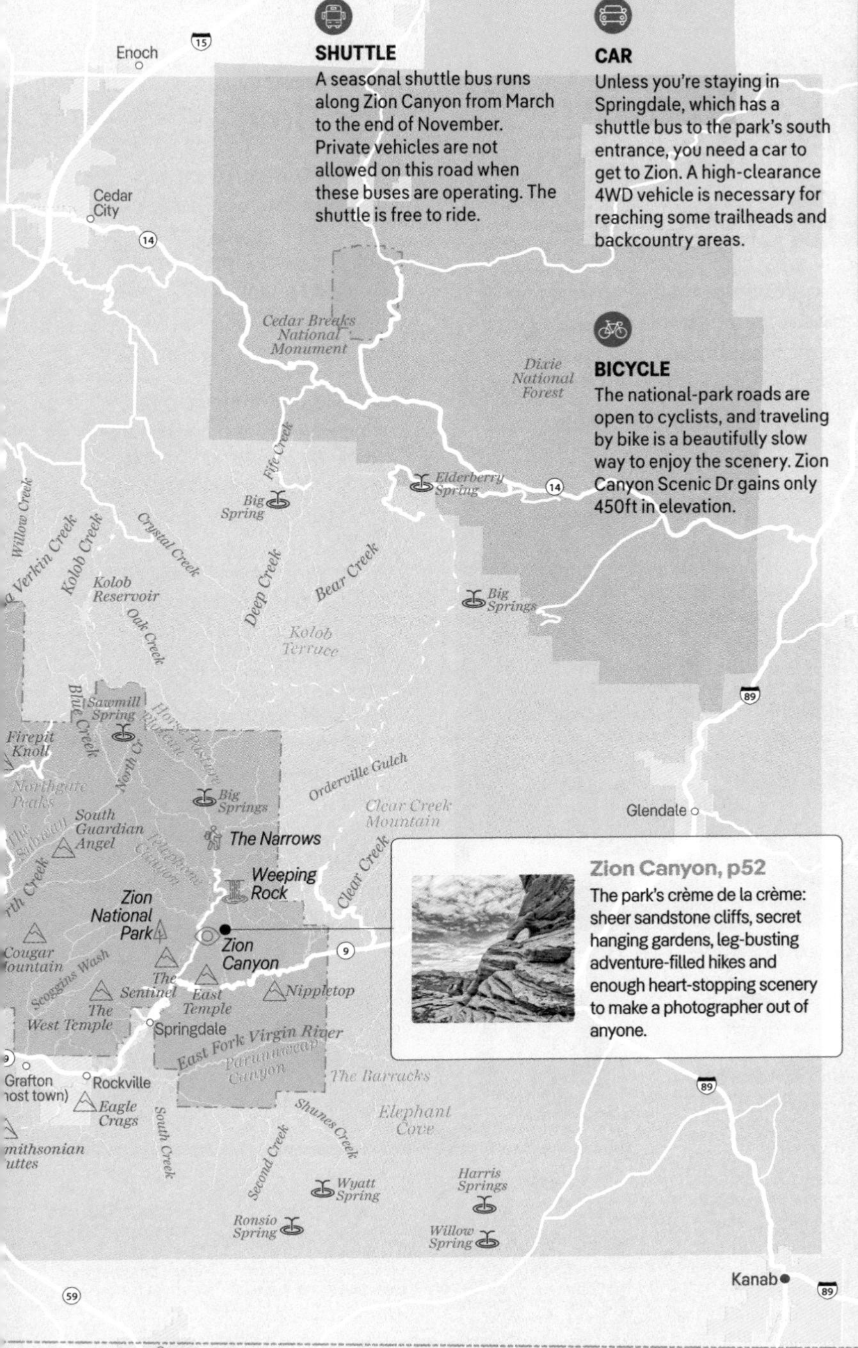

Zion Canyon, p52

The park's crème de la crème: sheer sandstone cliffs, secret hanging gardens, leg-busting adventure-filled hikes and enough heart-stopping scenery to make a photographer out of anyone.

Plan Your Days

Zion Canyon is the star of the show and has the national park's major trailheads, but extra time is easily spent in nearby towns, slot canyons and state parks.

KAN_KHAMPANYA/SHUTTERSTOCK ©

Kanarra Falls (p76)

Pressed for Time

- **Zion Canyon** (p52) is the park's showstopping centerpiece. Hop on the free shuttle that trundles along **Zion Canyon Scenic Dr** (p60) and get off at the Temple of Sinawava, the final stop.

- Plunge into the landscape-carving Virgin River and continue up the **Narrows** (p55) or follow the dry **Riverside Walk** (p56) until your stomach begins to rumble.

- Picnic on the riverbank or catch the shuttle to the restaurants at **Zion Lodge** (p54).

- Hike to the **Emerald Pools** (p56) to see the park's unique hanging gardens.

- Toast to your adventure at the **Zion Canyon Brew Pub** (p69) just outside the park's south entrance.

SEASONAL HIGHLIGHTS

Summer is peak season for both visitor numbers and temperatures around Zion National Park. July and August afternoon thunderstorms bring relief – but also flash floods.

MARCH

St Patrick's Day in Springdale means a parade, live bagpipers and a green Jell-O sculpture competition.

APRIL

Enjoy live music, outdoor food and drink, and impressive chalk-art designs during **Zion Chalk and Earth Fest**.

JUNE

The Bard's plays and contemporary dramas are on stage for the **Utah Shakespeare Festival** in Cedar City.

STUART MONK/SHUTTERSTOCK ©, JULI SCALZI/SHUTTERSTOCK ©, DAVE G. HOUSER/ALAMY STOCK PHOTO ©

A Long Weekend in Zion

- With permit in hand, pull yourself to the top of **Angels Landing** (p58) or take the easy way up to the even loftier panorama at **Observation Point** (p65).

- Adventurous types can tack on the trail to **Cable Mountain** (p67), but if your legs need a break, hop in the car and take the scenic route along the **Zion–Mt Carmel Hwy** (p66).

- Leave the crowds behind and venture to the lesser-visited side of Zion, **Kolob Canyons** (p70).

- Hike **Taylor Creek** (p72) past old homesteader cabins to an arched alcove.

- Wrap up your weekend with a rappel or three on a **canyoneering trip** (p74).

Southwestern Utah Session

- With more time, explore the quirky towns and sights beyond the national-park boundaries.

- Visit the past in **Grafton ghost town** (p69) and hike the smaller slots around **Kanarraville** (p76).

- Staying in **Cedar City** (p76) puts you within easy day-tripping distance of **Cedar Breaks National Monument** (p78), reachable via super-scenic **Hwy 14** (p80).

- Explore the stalactite-studded caves and glaciers of **Great Basin National Park** (p79) in Nevada, pausing on the way to decode the petroglyphs at **Parowan Gap** (p76).

- If you're flying home from Vegas, get one last dose of the desert at **Valley of Fire State Park** (p86).

JULY

Parade through the streets of Springdale and eat your weight in pancakes during the **4th of July** celebrations.

SEPTEMBER

The **Zion Canyon Music Festival** fills Springdale with two days of folk, blues and other music.

NOVEMBER

The **Butch Cassidy 10K/5K run** ends in Grafton ghost town and also puts on an outlaw look-alike competition.

DECEMBER

Christmas in the Canyon brings out live nativity shows and seasonal train rides through red-rock Tuacahn Amphitheater near St George.

ZION CANYON

Zion's unique landscape has to be seen to be believed. It might be smaller than the Grand Canyon, but in a way, this makes it easier to handle, with perspectives that are both monumental and yet still manageable. Bisecting the canyon, the Virgin River has sliced massive 15-mile-long cliffs that expose thousands of feet of Navajo sandstone, and it's still hard at work, cutting downward about 1000ft every million years.

From the canyon floor to Zion's highest peak there is nearly 5000ft of elevation change, resulting in a range of ecozones and experiences for travelers. The park's most famous hikes – the white-knuckle climb up to Angels Landing and wading through the water in the Narrows – set off from here, but not all of them are strenuous. Check out the oasis-like hanging gardens at Emerald Pools or Weeping Rock, where plants cling to dripping seeps on the canyon walls.

Zion Canyon

TOP TIP

To avoid the park's crowds, get a sunrise start (the first shuttle leaves at 6am from mid-May to mid-September) or go in late afternoon.

FOTOS593/SHUTTERSTOCK ©

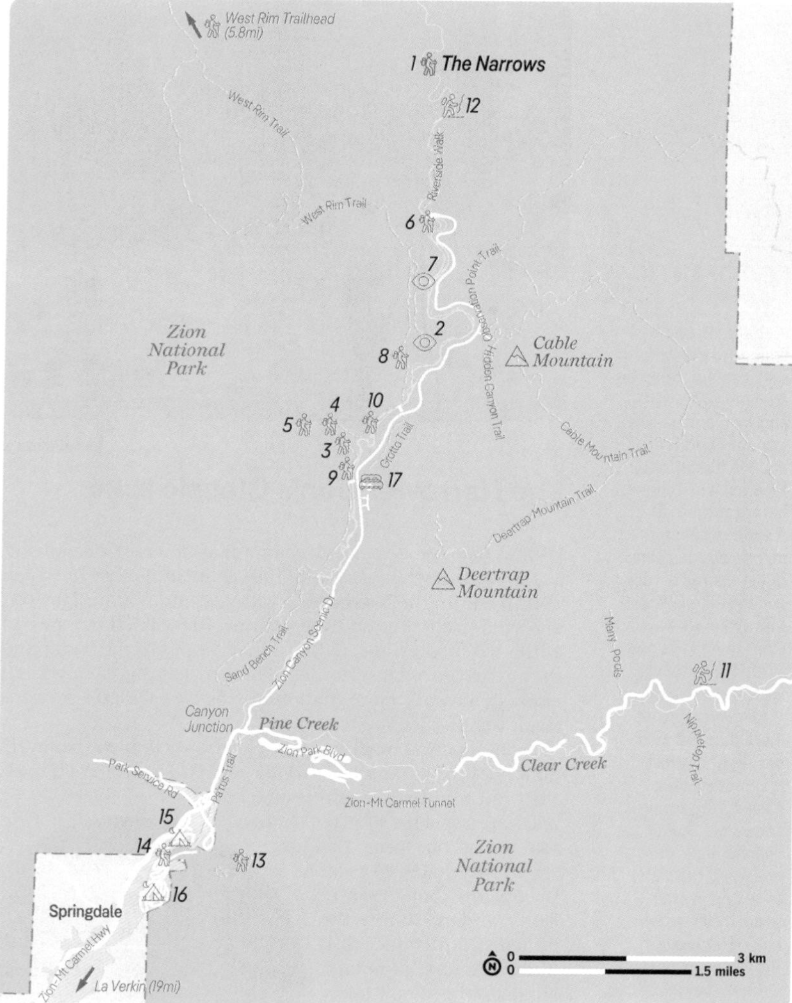

HIGHLIGHTS

1 The Narrows
2 Angels Landing
3 Emerald Pool - lower
4 Emerald Pool - middle
5 Emerald Pool - upper

ACTIVITIES

6 Riverside Walk
7 Scout Outlook
8 Trans-Zion Trek
9 Grotto Trail
10 Kayenta Trail
11 Keyhole Canyon
12 Mystery Canyon
13 Pa'rus Trail
14 Watchman Trail

SLEEPING

15 South Campground
16 Watchman Campground
17 Zion Lodge

Pa'rus Trail (p58)

CAUTIONS & CLOSURES

Preparation and timing are the keys to a successful Narrows adventure. Always – and we mean *always* – check conditions and the flash-flood forecast with rangers before setting off. A sudden rainstorm miles away can send down a surge of rock- and log-filled water that sweeps away everything in its path.

The Narrows hike is closed when the Virgin River runs at more than 150 cu ft per second, which is sometimes the case during spring snowmelt. Some years there is little change in the water level, but in other years the Narrows could be closed in April, May or June. Getting the right gear is imperative for a safe and fun trek.

BROCREATIVE/SHUTTERSTOCK ©

The Narrows

The Narrows: Zion's Classic Hike

WADING THROUGH THE WATER

Hiking through a rocky river in ankle- to chest-deep water as the canyon walls rise up to 1000ft tall and press in to just 20ft in width: the **Narrows** is quintessential Zion. This wet and wild 'trail' is actually the Virgin River itself. At the end of the Riverside Walk (p56), stairs descend to the water and the adventure begins. Hordes of hikers visit the Narrows, but many don't walk more than a mile or two. Quieter sections await the further you trek.

The best part about hiking the Narrows is that you can walk for as little or as long as you'd like and still have a great time. This out-and-back route is not about reaching a specific spot, but simply soaking up the scene. Day hikers are allowed to go as far as Big Spring, though few do. Don't underestimate the difficulty or distance (9.4 miles round-trip, about eight hours): it's a long way to hike against the current.

Around the first river bend, you might catch canyoneers on their final rappel

SLOT IN

Utah has the densest concentration of slot canyons in the world. Explore more from **Hole-in-the-Rock Rd** (p120) in Grand Staircase–Escalante National Monument and the famous formations around **Kanab** (p123).

WHERE TO STAY IN ZION CANYON

Zion Lodge
It's more motel than magnificent, but having Zion's domes on your doorstep is sublime. **$$$**

Watchman Campground
Some 175 sites in a prime location south of the visitor center. Reservations required year-round. No showers. **$**

South Campground
Sites sandwiched between the visitor center and the Zion Human History Museum along the Pa'rus Trail. **$**

at **Mystery Canyon**. About 2 miles in, the **Orderville Canyon** tributary flows from the east. You can explore it for a quarter-mile, but to go further, you have to do the top-down hike (p55). The bottom-up route continues north through **Wall Street**, where the sheerness, nearness and height of the cliffs shatter whatever remains of your perspective.

After this section, the canyon opens slightly and the water gets deeper, usually requiring swimming.

Tackling the Narrows Top-Down

GOING THE DISTANCE

One of Zion's most famous backcountry routes takes on the unforgettable **Narrows**, starting from the Chamberlain's Ranch trailhead in East Zion and ending at the Riverside Walk in Zion Canyon. This strenuous 16-mile one-way journey meanders through the towering slot canyon along the North Fork of the Virgin River. Plan on getting wet: most of the hike is in the river, and full swims are sometimes required. The soaring walls, scalloped alcoves and wading through chest-deep pools with your backpack lifted over your head make it truly memorable.

Some hikers complete this trek as a one-day thru-hike, which can take 12 hours or longer. In shuttle season, you must make it to the Temple of Sinawava stop before the last bus out of the canyon, lest you add another 9 miles to the visitor center to your hike. The better experience is an overnight backpacking trip.

No matter which way you tackle the top-down Narrows hike, permits are always required and are some of the most sought-after in the park. Only 40 permits per day are issued. At 10am on the 5th of each month, reservations for the next month become available online (zionpermits.nps.gov). Reservations cost $5 (nonrefundable) and are often booked out within minutes. An additional fee of $15 to $25, depending on the size of your hiking group, is paid when picking up your permit in person. Last-minute and walk-in reservations are also possible – check online for details.

Backpackers can stay in one of 12 campsites in the canyon. Six campsites are bookable online, and the other six are reserved for day-before walk-ins at the Wilderness Desk at the Zion Canyon Visitor Center.

Permits are not issued when the Virgin River flow rate is higher than 120 cu ft per second, so this hike may be closed at times between March and June. The optimum time to hike is late June through September.

GETTING THE GEAR

As an almost entirely water-based hike, the Narrows isn't your standard walk in the park. Outfitters in Springdale, the gateway town near Zion's south entrance, rent canyoneering shoes, neoprene socks, wooden walking sticks, and dry suits or bibs. You might balk at the price tag ($30 to $75 depending on the season), but what you wear will greatly influence your enjoyment.

The Narrows is cooler than elsewhere in Zion because of the tall canyon walls, and hypothermia can be a risk in colder months. A walking stick helps you navigate the fast-moving currents on slippery rocks, and you'll want to put your phone, camera and anything else you don't want to get wet in a dry bag.

ENDEMIC PLANTS IN ZION NATIONAL PARK

Zion Daisy
White or light pink flower with a yellow center that grows in small bunches.

Crimson Monkeyflower
Four eye-catching lipstick-red petals give riparian habitats a burst of color.

Zion Milkvetch
These delicate purple flowers are some of the first to bloom in spring.

Staying Dry on the Riverside Walk

WATERSIDE WANDER

ROMAN KHOMLYAK/SHUTTERSTOCK ©

Riverside Walk

If you don't want to take the plunge into the Narrows, the easy **Riverside Walk** is the dry and paved part of the journey. Shadowed from the slanting sun by lofty canyon walls, this fun path parallels the slippery cobblestones of the Virgin River and rambles by seeps, hanging gardens and wading spots. Interpretive signs explain the local geology and ecology, and points along the way give access to the riverbank and water, making it a family favorite. The water is a great place to play, though it can be chilly.

The canyon walls around the Temple of Sinawava are popular rock climbing sites, so look up as you set off. From the start, the pavement undulates up and down close to the canyon wall and past water-carved alcoves. Park maps describe the walk as 'wheelchair accessible with assistance.' We think someone fairly strong would have to be doing the pushing, but strollers work fine. The paved trail ends where the Narrows begin, at a raised cul-de-sac with benches. Steps lead down to a rocky fan at the river's edge. Wear shoes you don't mind getting wet; you may not be able to resist the river, which beckons even those not hiking further up-canyon.

The trail is a 2-mile round-trip and starts at the Temple of Sinawava shuttle stop at the end of Zion Canyon Scenic Dr.

BEST PARK MUSEUMS & RANGER TALKS

Zion Human History Museum
Modest exhibit of the geological and human history of Zion. Ranger talks at 10:30am and 2:30pm daily.

Ride with a Ranger
Two-hour bus ride through Zion Canyon with ranger commentary. Free and accessible but limited seats.

Zion Canyon Visitor Center
Talks at 1pm daily on a range of subjects.

Zion Lodge
The 4pm talk here is a good option after a morning hike.

Watchman Evening Program
A 9pm talk at the campground from May to October.

Path to the Emerald Pools

ZION'S HANGING GARDENS

KIT LEONG/SHUTTERSTOCK ©

Lower Emerald Pool

Short and sweet, the Emerald Pools Trails are a superb introduction to Zion's unique ecology and microhabitats. These popular paths lead to a series of bucolic ponds, stunning desert-varnished rocks and a beautiful example of Zion's hanging gardens. The pools fill with water that seeps from the sandstone, augmented by seasonal rains, creating these oa-

WILDLIFE TO LOOK OUT FOR

California Condor
Crane your neck near Big Bend to spot the largest wingspan in North America.

Mule Deer
Large-eared deer frequently spotted near Zion Canyon Visitor Center and the lawn of Zion Lodge.

Bighorn Sheep
Reintroduced in the 1970s; keep an eye out near the east entrance and the Zion–Mt Carmel Tunnel.

ERIC URQUHART/SHUTTERSTOCK ©

Upper Emerald Pool

ses in the desert ringed by algae and ferns. The water is ecologically sensitive, so getting into the pools is not allowed.

The paved **Lower Emerald Pool Trail**, the easiest of the three, gradually rises and falls for 0.6 miles before reaching the first pool. Waterfalls cascade down a multicolored, mineral-stained overhang in a long arc, misting the trail (and you) as you pass beneath. If that was enough walking for you, this is a good spot to turn around. Otherwise, follow the dirt trail as it ascends 150ft to the less dramatic **Middle Emerald Pool** that feeds the waterfalls below.

From here, a steep, rocky half-mile spur leads to the **Upper Emerald Pool**. It's the loveliest grotto of all, surrounded by the sheer-walled skirts of Lady Mountain.

The round-trip hike to all three pools is roughly 2 miles. You could return to Zion Lodge the way you came, but we recommend continuing in the opposite direction, on the **Kayenta Trail**. This path affords spectacular views down the valley. Expect to be picking your way among rocks along the mile-long trail before you descend to the Grotto picnic grounds and shuttle stop.

Backpacking & Multiday Trails in Zion

OVERNIGHTING IN NATURE

Hikers up for a longer adventure are in for a treat in Zion National Park, which has dozens of backpacking sites and more than 90 miles of trails. Some trails start outside the

RANGER RECOMMENDATIONS

Susan McPartland, Park Ranger at Zion, shares her tips for enjoying the national park.

Take it all in
Some of the best experiences are counted in the number of birds you hear or plants you see rather than the number of miles you travel.

Ask a ranger
You may be visiting for a day or a week, but park rangers have lifetimes of knowledge about Zion. No matter when you visit, take advantage of park rangers' collective experience by attending a free talk.

Explore
Whether you experience a frontcountry trail in Zion Canyon or get a Wilderness permit to explore remote parts of the park, take the opportunity to get away from roads.

Ringtails
These nocturnal relatives of the raccoon are agile rock climbers with foot-long fluffy striped tails.

Mountain Lion
Solitary creatures rarely seen; they typically avoid the main canyon. Report sightings to rangers.

Desert Tortoise
One of the park's most endangered residents, these slow movers can live up to 80 years..

HOW TO GET A PERMIT FOR ANGELS LANDING

In 2022 the National Park Service (NPS) started requiring hikers to obtain permits to climb up Angels Landing, one of the most popular spots in Zion. Permits are awarded through seasonal and day-before lotteries. In the seasonal lottery, you pick seven days and times in the next three-month season (eg if you want to hike from June to August, the lottery takes place in April). Apply for day-before permits from midnight to 3pm.

It costs $6 to apply for a permit. If you're successful in the lottery, you'll be charged an additional $3 for each person you registered. Same-day permits are not available. Without a permit, you can still hike as far as Scout Lookout.

park boundaries or in East Zion, Kolob Terrace Rd or Kolob Canyons and end in Zion Canyon.

Backpacking in Zion demands preplanning. All overnight backpacking trips require permits, which include a campsite reservation. Half of the permits are available online (zionpermits.nps.gov) about a month in advance, and the other half are allocated on a first-come, first-served basis the day before or the day of your trip. Many of these hikes are one-way routes, so you'll need to organize a shuttle to the trailhead. Try **Red Rock Shuttle** (redrockshuttle.com) or **Zion Guru** (zionguru.com).

In addition to the Narrows top-down overnight hike (p55), the 14.5-mile **West Rim Trail** is one of Zion's most popular backcountry routes. It starts on a high plateau at Lava Point off Kolob Terrace Rd before descending steeply toward Scout Lookout and Angels Landing. The spectacular views, especially at sunset, are bound to leave you breathless. The **Trans-Zion Trek** (also called the Zion Traverse) is a four-day, 36-mile marathon beginning in the separate Kolob Canyons section of the park. It links up several other trails, including the final descent of the West Rim, taking in Zion's diverse range of landscapes. The Kolob Canyons section also has some long-distance trails perfect for backpacking that stay in that area and don't enter Zion Canyon.

West Rim Trail

EASY HIKES IN ZION CANYON

Pa'rus Trail
The only path in the park open to bicycles and pets on a leash; paved and wheelchair accessible.

Watchman Trail
Ascend 368ft to a short loop that provides fine views of the park's formations, best seen at sunset.

Grotto Trail
This half-mile trail connects the Zion Lodge with the Grotto picnic area on the canyon floor.

Climbing & Clambering on the Canyon Walls

SUCH GREAT HEIGHTS

If there's one activity that makes Zion special, it's canyoneering. Rappelling over the lip of a sandstone bowl, swimming in frigid pools and tracing a slot canyon's curves – canyoneering is daring, gravity-defying and sublime all at once. Zion's slot canyons are the park's most sought-after backcountry experience, and you must get a permit online in advance for all routes (zionpermits.nps.gov).

Commercially guided trips are prohibited in the park. If you aren't confident going on your own or want to try rock climbing or canyoneering for the first time, outfitters in Springdale (p68) put on courses outside the park boundaries, usually on Bureau of Land Management (BLM) land.

Mystery Canyon lets you be a rock star. The last rappel drops into the Virgin River in front of an admiring audience of crowds hiking the Narrows. With multiple rappels of up to 120ft, Mystery Canyon is one of Zion's best, but it's not for beginners. Off Hwy 9 east of the Zion–Mt Carmel Tunnel, **Keyhole Canyon** is a gem of a narrow slot that drops down a few short rappels (the longest is 30ft), interspersed with several cold, dark swims.

Zion Canyon also has some of the USA's most famous big-wall rock climbing spots. However, rock climbing inside the park isn't recommended for beginners because of the difficulty levels, and outfitters run excursions outside the park. The best times for climbing are spring and fall, but some routes are closed from March to late summer to protect nesting peregrine falcons.

Climbers don't need permits for day trips, but they're required for overnight stays. Bolted routes aren't common in the park, and the NPS doesn't inspect, maintain or repair climbing equipment.

IS ZION SUFFERING FROM OVERTOURISM?

US national parks are busier than ever. Visitor numbers to Zion have doubled in the last two decades, and the park had its most-visited year in 2021, reeling in five million travelers – only the fourth national park ever to reach that figure.

New permits have limited numbers on some trails, and with flexible plans, you can more easily find a quieter corner. May, June and July are the busiest months, while winter sees just 25% of peak visitor numbers. Zion Canyon is the park at its finest, but hikes in Kolob Canyons are still stunning and less trodden.

Afternoons see fewer visits, and in summer, sunset is still hours away, allowing enough time for a trail or two.

GETTING AROUND

From March through November, private vehicles are not allowed on Zion Canyon Scenic Dr while shuttle buses are in operation. The Zion Park Shuttle makes nine stops along the canyon, from the visitor center to the Temple of Sinawava. The Springdale Shuttle stops along Hwy 9 between the park's south entrance and the Majestic View Lodge in the gateway town of Springdale. You can ride the Springdale Shuttle to Zion Canyon Brew Pub and walk across a footbridge into the park. The visitor center and the first Zion shuttle stop lie on the other side of the kiosk. Both shuttles are free to ride.

Limited free parking is available inside the park; arrive as early as possible. Otherwise, it costs $20 to park in Springdale.

ROAD TRIP

Zion Canyon Scenic Drive

Discover the heart of Zion National Park on a journey along Zion Canyon Scenic Dr, which threads along the Virgin River between towering sandstone cliffs. If you have time for only one activity in Zion, this route is it. North of Canyon Junction Bridge, the road is closed to private vehicles from March through November, so use the excellent park shuttle instead or go by pedal power on a bicycle or e-bike.

1 Zion Canyon Visitor Center

Get your bearings with a quick intro at the Zion Canyon Visitor Center near the park's south entrance. Outdoor exhibit panels provide a quick lay of the land.

The Drive: Jump on the shuttle from the visitor center (Stop 1) to the Court of the Patriarchs (Stop 4). Cyclists can pedal the river-hugging Pa'rus Trail – the only path in the park open to bikes – before heading north on Zion Canyon Scenic Dr.

2 Court of the Patriarchs

A steep 150ft path leads to a view of magnificent peaks named after men in the Old Testament. Christened by a Methodist minister in 1916, from left to right are Abraham (6890ft), Isaac (6825ft) and Jacob (6831ft), while crouching in front of Jacob is Mt Moroni (5690ft), named for a Mormon angel.

The Drive: Take the shuttle one stop to Zion Lodge (Stop 5).

DENIS UM/SHUTTERSTOCK ©

Court of the Patriarchs

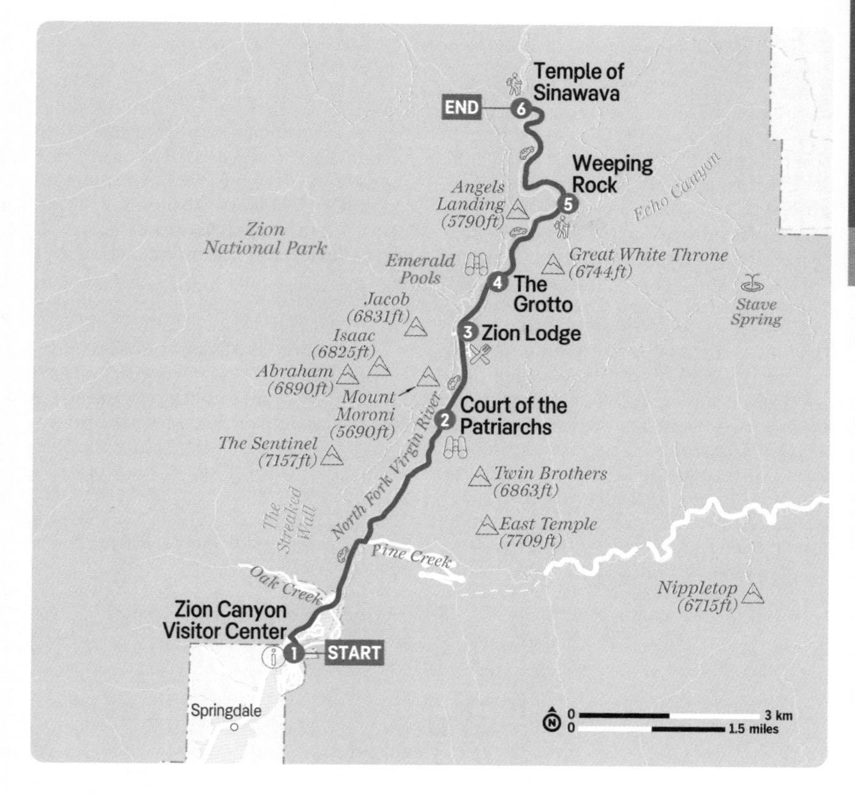

3 Zion Lodge

Zion Lodge houses the park's only hotel and restaurants. The wide, grassy front lawn, shaded by a giant cottonwood tree, is a favorite place for a post-hike ice cream and nap. Stretch your legs on the Emerald Pool Trails (p56) and investigate Zion's incredible hanging gardens, where plant life clings to the cliff walls.

The Drive: Ride the shuttle one stop to The Grotto (Stop 6). If you hike the Emerald Pool trails, take the Kayenta Trail to the Grotto instead of returning to Zion Lodge.

4 The Grotto

The hike to Angels Landing (p62) starts from this large, cottonwood-shaded picnic area. To admire Angels Landing rather than climb it, stroll the flat first quarter-mile of the West Rim Trail for a perfect vantage point.

The Drive: Take the shuttle one stop to Weeping Rock (Stop 7).

5 Weeping Rock

The steep 0.4-mile Weeping Rock Trail ends at a large dripping rock alcove. As water percolates through the Navajo sandstone, it's pushed out by the less permeable layer of Kayenta sandstone underneath, causing the water to seep out, feeding a large hanging garden – and dripping on your head.

The Drive: Ride the shuttle to the end of the line (Stop 9).

6 Temple of Sinawava

Zion Canyon's dramatic conclusion (by way of concrete at least) is a natural amphitheater known as the Temple of Sinawava. From here, you can take the popular Riverside Walk to the ultimate Zion experience, the Narrows (p54).

HIKING TO THE HEAVENS AT ANGELS LANDING

A must-do in Zion Canyon, Angels Landing offers an exhilarating half-day hike with a jaw-dropping payoff. The 5-mile round-trip hike hugs the face of a towering cliff, snakes through a cool canyon and climbs up a series of sharp switchbacks before finally ascending a narrow, exposed ridge where steel chains and the encouraging words of strangers are your only friends. Your reward after the final scramble to the 5790ft summit? A lofty view of Zion Canyon and some unreal photos of your vertigo-defying adventure. A permit (p34) is required for the full hike, but you can go as far as Scout Lookout without one. The **1 trailhead** is on the western side of Zion Canyon Scenic Dr from The Grotto shuttle stop. At the **2 intersection** (p57) with the Kayenta Trail, turn right to follow the West Rim Trail. At first, this trail meanders along the desert floor, before ascending gradually but relentlessly, becoming steeper as you begin climbing long, paved switchbacks up the canyon wall. Beyond a rock overhang, the trail levels out, running deep into the narrow, slightly cooler **3 Refrigerator Canyon**. You'll ascend a few more switchbacks before reaching **4 Walter's Wiggles**, an engineering marvel. Built in 1926, this set of 21 steep stonework zigzags is named after the first superintendent of Zion. Huffing and puffing, you emerge at **5 Scout Lookout** (p58), a sandy area with stellar views. If you have a permit, carry on to **6 Angels Landing**, the razor's-edge traverse where the ridge is just 5ft wide and the sheer cliffs plummet 1000ft. Pull yourself along the chains for the final 488ft elevation gain. At the hike's dramatic conclusion, take in the stunning 360-degree view of Zion Canyon. You've earned it.

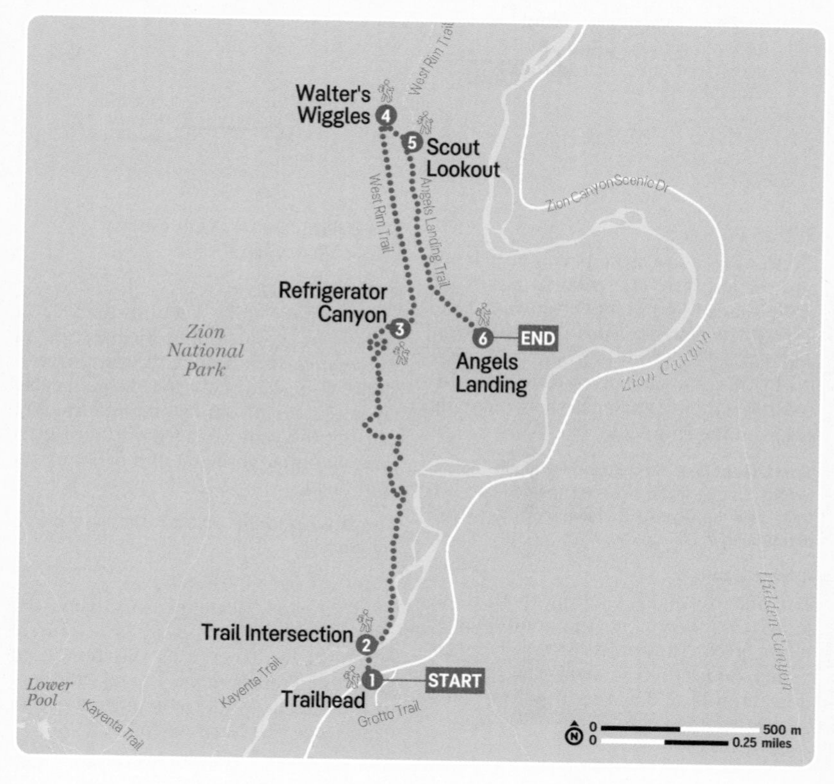

Observation Point
Cable Mountain
Zion Canyon
Canyon Overlook Trail
Springdale
Grafton Ghost Town

Beyond Zion Canyon

Most travelers blaze through Zion's south and east entrances en route to the canyon, but these areas are worth a closer look.

East Zion has several little-traveled, up-country hikes that provide an entirely different perspective on the park. Find the trailheads off the road leading to Zion Ponderosa Ranch Resort. For families, East Zion makes an ideal base camp, with ranch activities and room to roam without the park crowds. Staying on this side of Zion also puts you closer to the hoodoos of Bryce Canyon National Park.

Springdale is Zion's gateway town, bumping right up to the south entrance with loads of accommodations and dining options, and it's where you'll find the vast majority of adventure outfitters that rent gear for the Narrows and can take you out on canyoneering and rock climbing trips.

TOP TIP

Recreational vehicles (RVs) and other oversized vehicles traveling through the Zion–Mt Carmel Tunnel must pay a fee and drive through during specific hours.

Springdale (p68)

MOVING MOUNTAINS: THE ZION–MT CARMEL TUNNEL

Completed in 1930, the 1.1-mile-long **Zion–Mt Carmel Tunnel** was once the longest tunnel in the United States.

Four crews of workers packed the sandstone cliffs above Pine Creek Canyon with dynamite, blasting the tunnel from the inside out. Gallery 'windows' were carved to give motorists views of the canyon (though drivers are no longer allowed to stop).

The 22ft-wide, 16ft-high tunnel has changed little since its opening, which has presented challenges for modern automobiles. If your vehicle is wider than 7ft 10in or taller than 11ft 4in, you must pay $15 for a tunnel permit and drive through during specified hours when rangers are present so that the tunnel can be converted to one-way traffic.

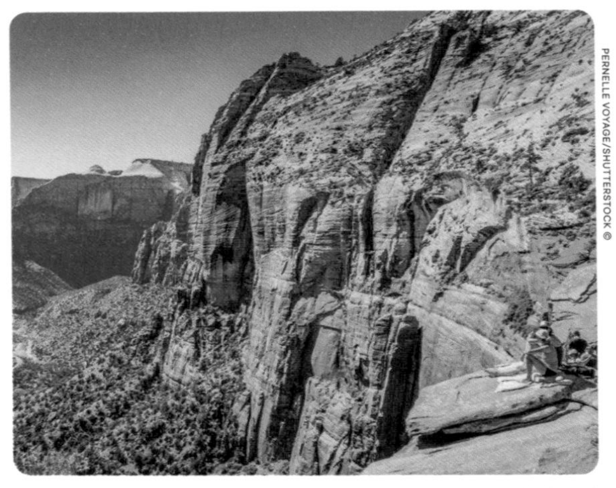

PERNELLE VOYAGE/SHUTTERSTOCK ©

Canyon Overlook Trail

Peeking at Zion from Canyon Overlook

CATCHING SIGHT OF THE CANYONS

A convenient stop off Hwy 9, the 1-mile out-and-back **Canyon Overlook Trail** is a relatively quick hike that rewards walkers with fun desert scrambling and ends in a much-photographed panoramic vista. Although it's not a particularly strenuous hike, the slickrock terrain is somewhat rugged, with exposed ledges and a pretty rocky trail. It's a great hike if you're headed to Zion Canyon from the east, giving you a taste of the wonder to come.

After an initial staircase ascent, the trail clings to the cliff walls, passes beneath overhangs sheltering hanging gardens and traverses bridges over sheer drops. Peer into the dark, narrow recesses below as you cross Pine Creek Canyon, a favorite technical canyoneering route. After crossing the slickrock, you'll arrive at the final sweeping Canyon Overlook, with views of lower Zion Canyon and the West Temple, Altar of Sacrifice and the Sentinel.

DANITA DELIMONT/ALAMY STOCK PHOTO ©

Canyoneer, Pine Creek Canyon

WHERE TO STAY IN EAST ZION

Zion Ponderosa Ranch Resort
Families love this activity-rich ranch on 6.25 sq miles with swimming pools, climbing walls and mini golf. **$$**

Zion Mountain Ranch
Luxury ranch with six different types of cabins, larger lodges and its own herd of roaming buffalo. **$$$**

Dispersed Camping
Free dispersed camping is permitted on BLM lands, but amenities are few; no bathrooms or water. **$**

The Great Arch, visible from the west side of the tunnel, is directly below you, though you won't be able to see it.

The most challenging part of the hike is finding somewhere to park. If the small lot near the trailhead is full or if you're coming from Mt Carmel, park in the overflow lots 300ft east of the tunnel.

Surveying the Scene from Observation Point

THE BEST VIEW IN THE PARK

Zion Canyon from Observation Point

LUCKY-PHOTOGRAPHER/SHUTTERSTOCK ©

It feels deliciously like cheating to wander along a mostly flat woodland path and then descend to **Observation Point**, which towers more than 700ft above Angels Landing – you get all of the rewards with hardly any of the work.

The trailhead, also called East Mesa, is at the end of a small parking lot off a 4WD road in East Zion. The parking lot fills early, and the road is often too rough for standard sedans. Instead, book a spot on a shuttle (round-trip $8.50 per person) run by **East Zion Adventures** (eastzionadventures.com), which leaves from nearby Zion Ponderosa Ranch Resort.

The first 2 miles of the hike meander through open stands of tall ponderosa pines, which may show signs of the periodic park-prescribed burns. In May and June, keep an eye out for showy up-country wildflowers. To the right, canyon views open up in the distance. From here, the main trail turns southwest and starts gradually descending, with glimpses of Echo Canyon on your left and Zion Canyon on your right. A further descent down slickrock and loose stones shaded by juniper and piñon leads past some sandy sites and to the Observation Point spur at 3 miles. Sit and soak up the panoramic vistas and see if you can spot the intrepid and much more tired hikers on Angels Landing.

For a longer and more challenging hike, you can tack on Cable Mountain (p67), descending the spectacular East Rim Trail through Echo Canyon on the backside of Mt Baldy before climbing up to the flatter trail out to the viewpoint. This full route is a little more than 15 miles, and you'll need to use a shuttle service to get back to your vehicle.

PARTIAL CLOSURE OF THE EAST RIM TRAIL

Observation Point was previously accessible from Zion Canyon via the East Rim Trail, but this route has been closed since 2019 because of a landslide.

Hidden Canyon Trail, which branches off from the East Rim Trail closer to the Zion Canyon floor, suffered the same fate earlier that year from a smaller landslide.

Neither trail appears to be reopening anytime soon, so the only way to access the mountaintop viewpoint for the time being is from East Zion.

WHERE TO EAT AROUND EAST ZION

Cordwood
This rustic farm-to-table restaurant offers the only gourmet dining in East Zion, plus beer and wine. **$$$**

Archie's Food to Die For
Burgers and loaded fries are the carb boost (and kid pleaser) you need after a day of hiking. **$**

Blue Mule Cafe & Bakery
Weekday-only spot serving breakfast, sandwiches and salads on a farm with cute pettable goats. **$**

SIGHTS & SWITCHBACKS ON THE ZION–MT CARMEL HIGHWAY

The scenic drive along Hwy 9 certainly rivals the drive in the main canyon of Zion National Park, with a series of magnificent overlooks followed by a landscape of multicolored slickrock, culminating at Checkerboard Mesa. You can start this drive at either the south entrance or, if you're coming from Bryce Canyon on Hwy 89, the east entrance near Mt Carmel. From the **1 south entrance**, follow the main road as it winds north through the park. Pass the turnoff at Canyon Junction, where Zion Canyon Scenic Dr splits off from the highway (closed to private vehicles when the shuttle buses are in operation). Follow the highway east, climbing up a series of six tight **2 switchbacks**. This picturesque stretch offers superb views back to the main canyon and ahead to the Great Arch. Make sure to stop at one of the turnouts on the side of the road before you get to the engineering marvel that is the **3 Zion–Mt Carmel Tunnel** (p64). At the tunnel's east entrance is a small parking lot (often full) and the **4 trailhead for Canyon Overlook** (p64), which leads to the top of the canyon wall you were just admiring. Bighorn sheep are sometimes spotted around this area. After a second smaller tunnel, stop off at the numerous scenic viewpoints. After about 3.5 miles, you'll get your first glimpse of **5 Checkerboard Mesa**, a huge sloping face of crosshatched beige slickrock, etched with both horizontal bedding layers and vertical stress fractures caused by countless freeze-thaw cycles. It's another mile to the official **6 Checkerboard Mesa viewpoint**, your last must-see stop. About a quarter-mile further on is the **7 east entrance**, marking the park boundary.

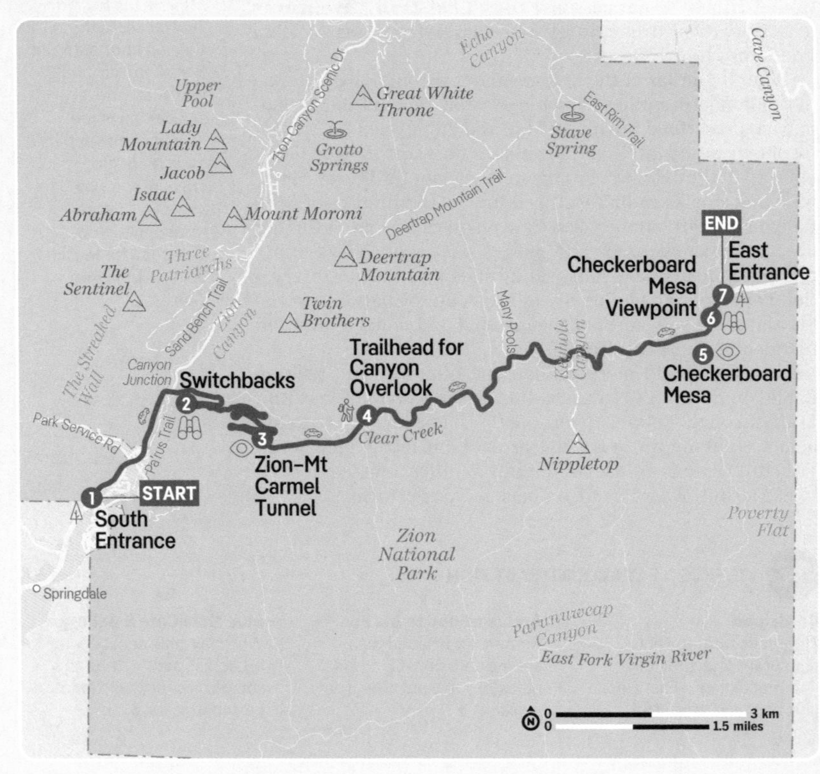

AGEFOTOSTOCK/ALAMY STOCK PHOTO ©

View from the east rim, Cable mountain

View on the Past from Cable Mountain

HIKING TO HISTORY

Seeking solitude in Zion? The route to **Cable Mountain** is an easy way to escape the crowds, and for those who want to make a long day of it, it can be combined with a hike to Deertrap Mountain. Even in season, you'll rarely see another soul. Both are mainly plateau hikes that end at staggering viewpoints over Zion Canyon. The trails are long but have little elevation change.

Like Observation Point and the East Mesa trailhead, the route is best left for high-clearance 4WD vehicles. The small trailhead parking lot fits just a handful of cars and can have huge tire-swallowing ruts. East Zion Adventures (p65) runs shuttles from nearby Zion Ponderosa Ranch Resort.

The well-trodden dirt trail starts by threading through ponderosa pine forest and after a quarter-mile passes a signed junction with a trail to Echo Canyon. After ascending for a steady half-mile through scrub forest, you'll reach a signed junction with the East Rim Trail. A mile further, bear northward at the signed turnoff for Cable Mountain. Deertrap Mountain is another 2 miles straight on from this point.

CABLE MOUNTAIN DRAW WORKS: BOOM & BUST

The Cable Mountain Draw Works, a historic wooden structure that sits on the canyon lip at the end of the trail, was used to lower lumber 2000ft from the East Rim mesa to the floor of Zion Canyon, reducing the timber's transport time from weeklong trips by wagon to just two minutes. Hundreds of thousands of board feet were sent into the valley, including the lumber used to build the original Zion Lodge.

Lightning struck the draw works in 1911 and it burned down, just a decade after its construction. A fire in the 1920s reduced it to ashes once again. It was rebuilt but finally abandoned in 1927 because of decreasing timber supplies.

WHERE TO STAY ALONG HIGHWAY 89

Historic Smith Hotel
Lovely 1929 historic home with big breakfasts and hosts who help plan your day. **$$**

Arrowhead Country Inn & Cabins
Seven cabins on a working ranch, with the East Fork of the Virgin River meandering behind. **$$**

East Zion Resort
Live out your glamping dreams in one of the tiny homes, tree houses, yurts or rustic tents. **$$**

The trail soon tops out and descends a final mile to the historic cable works, the mountain's namesake, once used to haul down lumber. The wooden structure is rickety, so don't climb on it. Instead, enjoy the bird's-eye view overlooking the Virgin River and Angels Landing.

CAR PARKING IN SPRINGDALE

Parking in Zion fills up fast, and if you're not staying in Springdale you'll have to figure out where to stash the car while you're on the trail. Springdale's streets are divided into three zones. It costs $20 for the day to park in Zone A (Zion's south entrance to Springdale Shuttle Stop 4). Zone B costs $15 for all-day parking and Zone C costs $12.

Private lots at Springdale businesses charge $20 or more to park for the day, but you might be able to get a deal. Some outfitters allow free parking for customers. Hoodoos Market, a 15-minute walk from the south entrance, offers free parking with a $25 purchase at its deli and general store.

Springdale: Zion's Southern Gateway

ONE-STOP SHOP

Just outside Zion's south entrance, the town of **Springdale**, population 514, sees many thousands of visitors pass through daily on their way to the park, and it makes an excellent base if you prefer the walls of a hotel to the inside of a tent (or if you couldn't get an in-park campground reservation). The main (and only) drag is packed with adventure outfitters, coffee shops, art galleries and restaurants, and if you're signing up for any activities or need to grab supplies, it's likely you'll be in town at some point.

Outfitters lead hiking, bicycling, climbing and multisport trips on the every-bit-as-beautiful BLM lands near the park. Trips and courses tend to be run as private groups, which

OLOS/SHUTTERSTOCK ©

Desert Pearl Inn, Springdale

WHERE TO STAY IN SPRINGDALE

Under the Eaves Inn
Quaint 1930s bungalow with character-filled rooms; hang out on Adirondack chairs and swings in the gardens. $$

Red Rock Inn
Eight romantic country-contemporary cottages spill down the desert hillside backed by incredible red rock. $$

Desert Pearl Inn
Stylish rooms with molded metal headboards overlooking water: either the pool or the Virgin River. $$$

can be costly for solo travelers. These shops also sell ropes and maps, provide advice and suit you up with rental gear, including harnesses, helmets, canyoneering shoes, wet and dry suits and waterproof bags.

Ideally located at the park's southern entrance, **Zion Outfitter** is particularly handy for renting bicycles (including e-bikes) and gear for the Narrows. **Zion Guru** is a holistic outfitter offering yoga and wellness programs as well as canyoneering, climbing and guided hikes. **Zion Adventures** also has a good selection of climbing and canyoneering trips, including one with a *via ferrata* route.

Ghosts of Grafton Town

PIONEER PAST

Grafton ghost town achieved its 15 minutes of fame in 1969 as the setting for the bicycle scene in the film *Butch Cassidy and the Sundance Kid.* Originally settled by Mormons in 1859, the town was frequently wiped out by the flooding Virgin River. By the 1890s only a few families were left, and the last residents moved out in 1944.

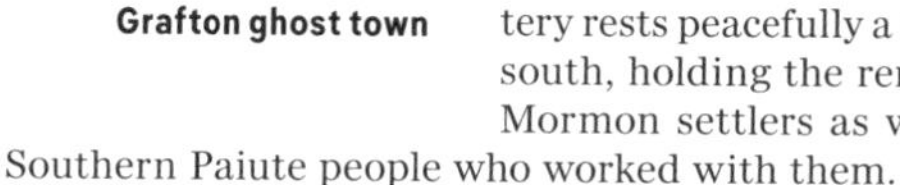

Grafton ghost town

EDDIE J. RODRIQUEZ/SHUTTERSTOCK ©

The Grafton Heritage Partnership Project (graftonheritage.org) has restored a handful of buildings, including an 1886 school and three pioneer cabins built between 1862 and 1879. A well-maintained cemetery rests peacefully a quarter-mile south, holding the remains of the Mormon settlers as well as some Southern Paiute people who worked with them.

You can freely look around the cabins and cemetery from dawn to dusk. Even though it's less than 10 miles from Zion's south entrance, you might not see another soul here.

WHERE TO EAT & DRINK IN SPRINGDALE

King's Landing
This dinner-only hotel-restaurant entices with fried quail, charred octopus and fettuccine with black truffle oil. $$$

Oscar's Cafe
From heaping huevos rancheros to pork verde burritos, Oscar's delivers big servings of Southwestern spice. $$

Deep Creek Coffee Company
Springdale's best coffee, plus smoothies, bagels and sandwiches. $

Zion Canyon Brew Pub
Southern Utah's first microbrewery is mere feet from the park entrance, and a pint of Zion Pale Ale is just the reward for all that hiking. $$

GETTING AROUND

The free Springdale Shuttle runs through town from March through early November every 10 to 15 minutes and makes navigating the town a breeze. It runs from the Majestic View Lodge to Zion's south entrance, with nine stops in total. At the south entrance you can walk across a footbridge to the visitor center and Zion shuttle. Leave your car at your hotel as parking is often a headache.

KOLOB CANYONS & KOLOB TERRACE ROAD

Zion Canyon might hog the spotlight, but the national park doesn't end there. Escape the crowds and seek out two of the park's entirely separate access points: Kolob Terrace Rd, which climbs more than 4000ft from the town of Virgin, and Kolob Canyons, 40 miles northwest of Zion Canyon on I-15.

Kolob Terrace Rd takes off north from Hwy 9, weaving in and out of Zion's highlands, a gorgeous panorama of cinder cones, sandstone peaks and windswept mesas. Even in season, you'll see relatively few other cars on this subtly scenic high-plateau road, where striking rock-formation views alternate with pastoral rangeland. Don't miss Lava Point, one of Zion's highest and best vantage points.

In Kolob Canyons, sheer cliffs jut abruptly from the Hurricane Fault as if they rose out of the ground just yesterday. Sweeping vistas of cliffs, mountains and finger canyons dominate the stunning, 5-mile Kolob Canyons Scenic Dr, rich with overlooks.

TOP TIP

If you're visiting Kolob Canyons, Cedar City is your best bet for accommodations. This part of the park doesn't have any campgrounds, except those in the backcountry, which are for backpackers and require permits. The towns of Virgin, La Verkin and Rockville are closest to Kolob Terrace Rd.

ANDREW HAGEN/SHUTTERSTOCK ©

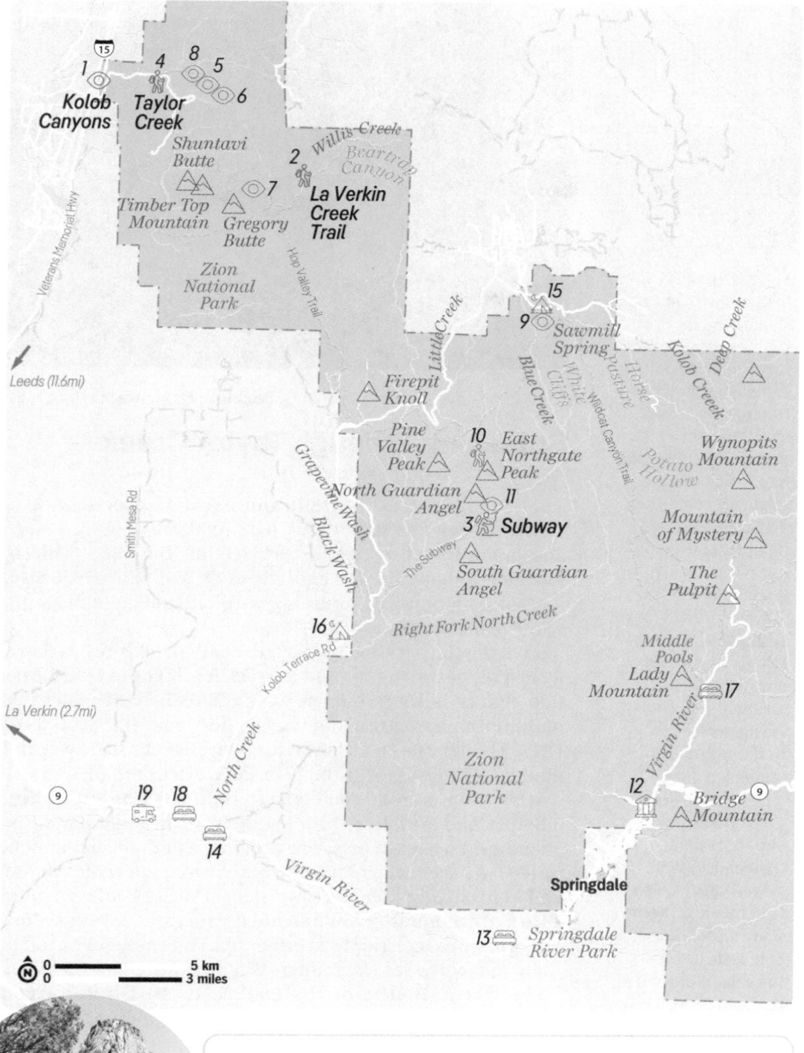

Larson Cabin

HIGHLIGHTS
1 Kolob Canyons
2 La Verkin Creek Trail
3 Subway
4 Taylor Creek

ACTIVITIES
5 Double Arch Alcove
6 Fife Cabin
7 Kolob Arch
8 Larson Cabin
9 Lava Point
10 Northgate Peaks Trail
11 Waterfall Room
12 Zion Human History Museum

SLEEPING
13 2 Cranes Inn
14 AutoCamp Zion
15 Lava Point Campground
16 Under Canvas Zion
17 Zion Lodge
18 Zion River Resort
19 Zion White Bison Glamping & RV Resort

Double Arch Alcove, Taylor Creek

KOLOB CANYONS ROAD CLOSURE

The seasonal freeze-thaw cycle has shaped the rocks of Utah's national parks for millennia, and sometimes Mother Nature's sculpting interferes with human-created works. Small rockfalls are relatively common in Zion National Park, but larger incidents can put areas off-limits indefinitely.

In March 2023 rocks cratered a section of Kolob Canyons Rd, and at the time of research, it remained closed to vehicle traffic with no set reopening date.

For now, Taylor Creek is the only car-accessible trailhead, though visitors are allowed to continue on Kolob Canyons Rd on foot or bicycle beyond the vehicle closure at the South Fork picnic area.

Splashing Through Taylor Creek

HOMESTEADER HISTORY AND AN ARCHED ALCOVE

This 5-mile refreshing out-and-back hike crisscrosses **Taylor Creek** dozens of times, passing through juniper, sage and piñon to get to two historic cabins. But keep walking for the real payoff at the end: views of Double Arch Alcove, a natural amphitheater ringing with birdsong and dripping with spring water.

From the the parking-lot start, the path quickly drops down from a set of stairs and sand to creek level. The overall elevation change is 450ft, but the walk is mostly flat beyond this point. From here, trail and water interweave like strands of DNA. Though the creek is small, expect to get a little wet and muddy, and harassed by bugs in the warmer months.

After about a mile, you come to the 1930 **Larson Cabin**, a homestead established by a state historian that had to be abandoned when the area was declared a national monument in 1937. As the trail enters a finger canyon, the walls narrow and your steady ascent grows steeper still. A mile further, **Fife Cabin**, another homesteader structure, appears. Both buildings are too fragile to enter, but you can peek through the windows to see the remnants of furniture and the floor.

The last half-mile of the trail leads to **Double Arch Alcove**, where the seep-stained red rock glows and echoes with dripping water and swirling wind. It's a cooling break before your walk back.

WHERE TO STAY AROUND KOLOB TERRACE RD

Lava Point Campground
Six summer-only sites situated at 7900ft; reserve online two weeks in advance. Pit toilets, no water. **$**

Under Canvas Zion
Uber-luxe secluded safari-style tents ringed by red mesas and distant sandstone peaks. **$$$**

AutoCamp Zion
Airstream suites, canvas tents and accessible suites in blond wood and modern minimalist monochrome. **$$$**

Go the Distance on La Verkin Creek Trail

BACKPACKING OR PACKING IT INTO A DAY

Doable as a 14-mile day hike to Kolob Arch or as a two- or three-day backpacking trip past the arch and up the creeks, **La Verkin Creek Trail** is Kolob Canyons' most off-the-beaten-path adventure and a wonderful place to camp. The trailhead is just south of the Lee Pass parking area on Kolob Canyons Rd.

Hiking along Timber, La Verkin and Willis Creeks is lovely in spring (late April to May) and fall (September and October). In early summer, biting flies can hound hikers and high-season temperatures are discouraging. It's a strenuous day hike because of its length, sand and elevation changes (1037ft overall). Camping overnight is easier and allows time to explore the remote Willis Creek area. Permits are issued with campsite reservations. Six are available online in advance (zionpermits.nps.gov), while the remaining seven are available for walk-ins. Day hikers do not need a permit.

For the first 2 miles or so, you descend an open ridge with fine views of the finger canyons. Eventually, you'll skirt the spire of Shuntavi Butte and descend more steeply through piñon and juniper forest along Timber Creek. The trail then turns east to the north bank of La Verkin Creek, a permanent, vigorous stream lined with the most convenient campsites (numbers 4 through 10 are closest). The trail is sandy and slow going here.

After about 6.25 miles, follow the signed Kolob Arch Trail turnoff. The half-mile Kolob Arch Spur is as far as day hikers should travel. When you reach a sign advising against further travel up-canyon, look high on the west wall for **Kolob Arch**. Though its opening is the second-longest in the world (287ft), the distant arch is so dwarfed by massive walls that at first it seems strangely anticlimactic. Spend some time watching the sun cloak the rock in ever-shifting shadows, however, and it soon makes a satisfying destination after all.

STARGAZING IN ZION NATIONAL PARK

In 2021 Zion became an International Dark Sky Park, commended for its efforts to preserve natural darkness.

You can't access Zion Canyon by private vehicle from March through November when the shuttle is running, so nighttime visits here are limited to the guests of Zion Lodge or travelers who walk or cycle in. (Shuttle service ends before sunset, but the road does not open to traffic.)

The patio of the Zion Human History Museum is the park's official night-sky viewing area, but instead, astro observers should head to Kolob Canyons or Kolob Terrace Rd for an absolutely epic session with the stars in a quieter part of the park. Look east for the darkest skies.

Through Pines to Northgate Peaks

CHILL AWAY FROM THE CROWDS

On this overlooked canyon-top gem, hikers traipse through meadows and pine forest to reach a lava outcrop with a view of 7000ft-plus peaks. Looking for a cool retreat on a hot summer day? Starting at 6500ft makes a big temperature difference. As the area sees so little traffic, the pleasant **Northgate Peaks Trail** remains largely uncrowded, though it

2 Cranes Inn
Quiet home in Rockville with four rooms, a communal kitchen and an extensive garden. **$$**

Zion White Bison Glamping & RV Resort
A Wild West fantasy of Conestoga wagons, luxury tipis and 'cliff dwellings' designed like Native kivas. **$$**

Zion River Resort
Massive RV resort catering to upscale big rigs; also has a handful of tent sites and cabins. **$**

PERMITS FOR THE SUBWAY

Wilderness permits are always required for the Subway, no matter which way you tackle it. The permitting process is the same for both trailheads, and 80 permits are issued per day (60 of the 80 permits are distributed by lottery). The **advance lottery** takes place two months ahead. If spaces are left after the advance lottery, you can make online **calendar reservations** one month in advance up until the day before your trip. Applications cost $5.

The remaining permits are distributed through a **last-minute drawing**. You can apply a week to two days in advance. Any spaces still available after this are issued as **walk-in permits**. Permits cost $15 to $25 depending on your group size.

doesn't have the wow factor of Zion Canyon or the East Zion trailheads.

For about a mile, you wander through an open meadow of sage and scrub. The ponderosa pines, manzanita and wildflowers (blooming in early summer) are a welcome rest for rock-weary eyes. After you crest a rise to a Y junction, the aptly named White Cliffs tower to the east as you gently ascend and descend to a lava-rock outcrop at the trail's end – a good perch to admire the stunning terrain. On either side, seemingly close enough to touch, are the pale, crosshatched Northgate Peaks. Front and center is North Guardian Angel, with an arch so deep it's more of a cave. Framed amid these in the distance is the heart of Zion Canyon, including the East and West Temples and Deertrap Mountain on the East Rim.

Although the Northgate Peaks Trail officially ends at the outcrop, summiting East Northgate Peak (on the left) provides fantastic 360-degree views and is a fun way to extend the hike.

Up & Down the Subway

MIND THE GAP

The unique tunnel-like rock formations of the **Subway** make it the park's most photographed backcountry feature. This incredibly popular canyoneering route (9.5 miles, 1850ft elevation change) has two or three short rappels, numerous cold swims and a series of stunning rock formations – even by Zion's standards.

The whole sculpted canyon is full of surprises, beauty and camera-worthy moments, including the curving walls that form the tunnel-like subway formations and hard-to-find dinosaur tracks. Along the way, the creek – the only trail – tumbles scenically over waterfalls, collects in deep pools, gives way to boulders and meanders in and out of the stream bed. You'll be swimming, scrambling, rappelling, sliding on your butt and whatever else you have to do to continue on.

Start at the Wildcat Canyon trailhead off Kolob Terrace Rd and finish at the Left Fork trailhead. A hiker shuttle, 60ft of rope, a backcountry permit and a wetsuit are required.

If you don't have the necessary gear, it's possible to start at the Left Fork trailhead and hike up about halfway to the Subway formation and the Waterfall Room (7 miles round-trip). It's not a technical route, but you still need a permit. The approach is long, and the trail is not quite as spectacular, but there's no arguing that the Subway is an awesome destination – anywhere else and this hike would be a highlight.

You'll be hiking in ankle- to knee-deep water most of the time, so dress appropriately. Check with park rangers and outfitters in Springdale for the latest conditions.

GETTING AROUND

You'll need a car to get around these parts of Zion National Park. The trailheads don't see as many hikers, but the parking areas are often small and fill quickly.

Beyond Kolob Canyons & Kolob Terrace Road

Wheeler Peak
Great Basin National Park
Parowan Gap
Dinosaur Tracks
Kanarra Falls
Cedar Breaks National Monument
ring Creek Canyon
Kolob Canyons

Adventure doesn't end at the national-park boundaries, and places outside of Zion's lesser-visited northwestern section are worth tacking on to your trip.

I-15 provides a lightning-quick route for exploring the area around Kolob Canyons, but the real journey begins when you get off the interstate. Secret slot canyons that hug the Zion border shelter waterfalls and provide welcome shade for hiking in creeks. Enigmatic petroglyphs shed light on the area's human histories and mysteries, while just across the state line in Nevada, yet another national park beckons with magical caves and an oft-snow-capped peak rising above the desert.

Cedar City, a sleepy college town that comes to life every summer when the Shakespeare festival takes over, makes the best base. Dining options are decent given the town's size, with more trendy and stylish choices starting to emerge.

TOP TIP

Cooler temperatures prevail in Cedar City, at roughly 6000ft in elevation, than in Springdale (60 miles away) or St George (55 miles).

Utah Shakespeare Festival, Cedar City (p77)

Kanarra Falls

JEREMY CHRISTENSEN/SHUTTERSTOCK ©

Wading Through Kanarra Falls & Spring Creek Canyon

SLOT-CANYON HIKES OUTSIDE THE PARK

The photogenic **Kanarra Falls** offers a fun 4-mile round-trip hike to two waterfalls, with makeshift log ladders adding to the thrill for first-time canyoneers and families. As with the Narrows, this hike plunges into a stream and gets your feet good and wet, so make sure you are dressed appropriately. The average water temperature is 30°F (-1°C) in winter and only 50°F (10°C) in summer, and it might be worth renting neoprene boots and other equipment from outfitters in Springdale (p68).

Beyond the initial slot canyon section is the first waterfall (about 1.75 miles in), an iconic sight that's been captured in thousands of photographs. Many hikers turn around at this point, but if you want to carry on, you need to scale a 20ft aluminum ladder and, later on, several large boulders. The hike continues upstream to a second waterfall, which marks the end of the route.

Kanarra Falls is extremely popular and requires a permit to visit ($12 per person). Only 150 permits are issued per day, so it's best to snag one online in advance (see kanarrafalls.com), though not too far ahead of time – permits are nonrefundable, and the slot canyon can be closed during times of high water.

Slightly south of Kanarraville on BLM land, **Spring Creek Canyon** is longer and covers similar terrain, winding through beautiful slots and riparian habitats, but this hike does not require a permit. The canyon continues on for many miles, but the first 3 miles provide all the necessary wonder. As the trail dives in deeper, it can get overgrown, and huge boulders might block your way.

BEST PLACES TO STAY & EAT IN CEDAR CITY

Big Yellow Inn
This 12-room knickknack-filled B&B is elegantly ornate, with a library, den and chair-filled front porch. $$

Centro Woodfired Pizzeria
Wood-fired Neapolitan pizza with gourmet toppings and heaping bowls of fresh salad in a sleek space. $$

Chef Alfredo's Ristorante Italiano
Impeccable servers dish up lip-smacking authentic Italian pasta and perfectly cooked steaks. $$

Petroglyphs of Parowan Gap

DECODING ANCIENT STORIES

Though the area feels off the beaten track and quiet these days, the **Parowan Gap** has seen people passing by for millennia. At the edge of the flat valley floor, jagged rocks reach toward the heavens and are etched with thousands of petroglyphs, many of which are unique to this place. Parowan Gap is a sacred site for the Paiute and Hopi.

Researchers believe the intriguing images of entrancing spirals, animal tracks, waves and human figures were carved

WHERE TO DRINK IN CEDAR CITY

Policy Kings Brewery
Black-owned craft-beer bar with plenty of pours, games, trivia and open-mic nights.

I/G Winery
Sip Utah-blended wines from West Coast grapes in the sleek wood-and-brick tasting room.

The Grind Coffeehouse
Get into a chilled college-student state of mind over coffee, breakfast or lunch.

Parowan Gap

STEVE CUKROV/SHUTTERSTOCK ©

by the Native Fremont people (Nungwu in Paiute), who lived in the area in the period around 500 CE. One section of petroglyphs is thought to be a seasonal celestial calendar, detailing Native astronomical knowledge of the equinox and phases of the moon, though the meanings aren't fully understood. Native people say that petroglyphs are based on a sign language that was universally understood among all tribes throughout North America, which is why so many similar symbols are seen across the Southwest. The Hopi and Paiute are considered to be the modern descendants of the Fremont people.

But humans aren't the only creatures to have roamed here. Two miles southeast of the Parowan Gap you can hop out of the car to check out **dinosaur tracks**, left in the mud around 65 million years ago by hadrosaurs, slow duck-billed herbivores that foraged for plants and shrubs.

MATTHEW THOMAS ALLEN/SHUTTERSTOCK ©

Petroglyphs, Parowan Gap

ALL OF UTAH'S A STAGE

If you're seeking a post-hike dose of culture, Cedar City puts on one of the biggest and longest-running Shakespearean festivals in the country from June to October: the **Utah Shakespeare Festival**.

Southern Utah University puts on an eight-show season, with half of the plays by the Bard or his contemporaries, plus more modern dramas. Productions are well regarded, but don't miss the extras, all free: 'greenshows' with Elizabethan minstrels, literary seminars discussing the plays, and costume and prop classes. Backstage tours cost extra.

The venues are the modern 769-seat Randall L Jones Theatre, the 200-seat indoor Eileen and Allen Anes Studio Theatre and the outdoor Engelstad Shakespeare Theatre, a replica of Shakespeare's Globe Theatre.

OFF-BEAT SPOTS AROUND PAROWAN

Frisco Ghost Town
Cabin frames and charcoal kilns are all that remain of one of the wildest towns in the West.

The Creamery
Upgrade your road trip snacks with ice cream and signature cheese curds made from local milk.

Mountain Meadows Massacre Memorial
Remote monument to one of the darkest incidents in the Mormon settlement of Utah.

MOUNTAIN BIKING & SKIING IN SOUTHERN UTAH

The highest town in Utah, **Brian Head** towers over Cedar City, 35 miles southwest. 'Town' is a bit of an overstatement: it's basically a big resort. From Thanksgiving through April, snow bunnies come to test the closest slopes to Las Vegas (200 miles away).

Advanced skiers might grow impatient with the short trails (except on a powder day), but it's great for beginners, intermediates and freeriders. Lines move quickly, and it's the only Utah resort within sight of the red-rock desert.

In July and August, the elevation keeps temperatures deliciously cool for hikers and mountain bikers. Ride the summer chairlift up to 11,000ft for an alpine adventure or pack a picnic to enjoy with a panoramic view.

In the Heavens at Cedar Breaks National Monument

HIGH-ELEVATION HOODOOS

Sculpted cliffs and towering hoodoos glow like neon tie-dye in a wildly eroded natural amphitheater encompassed by **Cedar Breaks National Monument**. The majestic kaleidoscope of magenta, salmon, plum, rust and ocher rises to 10,450ft atop the Markagunt Plateau, and time seems to stand still. Despite its name, the park has no cedar trees. Early pioneers mistook the evergreen junipers for cedars.

This altitude gets more than a little snow, and the one road into the national monument, Hwy 148, is not plowed in winter, closing the park from November

CB & BC

The hoodoo formations, rock colorations and plant life at Cedar Breaks are much the same as those found at **Bryce Canyon National Park** (p94), but this national monument sees a fraction of the visitors (600,000 annually vs 1.5 million at Bryce Canyon).

JASON PATRICK ROSS/SHUTTERSTOCK ©

Cedar Breaks National Monument

WHERE TO STAY & EAT IN BRIAN HEAD

Brian Head Lodge
Cozy, log-cabin feel in the lobby and forest-green carpets and accents in the rooms. **$$**

Cedar Breaks Lodge
Post-activity relaxation hub with pool, sauna and spa. All rooms have jetted bathtubs. **$$**

Last Chair Grill & Brews
Winter-only pub with local beer on tap, burgers and fried-food favorites. **$$**

until May – and sometimes far into June. Summer temperatures range from only 40°F (4.4°C) to 70°F (21.1°C), and brief storms drop rain, hail and even powdery white stuff far later than you might expect.

Trails edge along the rim of the amphitheater to gorgeous viewpoints. The 2-mile **Sunset Trail** is paved and accessible and allows pets, while the more challenging **Alpine Pond** and **Southern Rim** Trails dip down to lower viewpoints, requiring steep ascents and descents.

You can stay overnight in the monument at the 25-site **Point Supreme Campground**, which has showers and flush toilets.

Caves & Peaks at Great Basin National Park

UNDER THE GROUND AND IN THE SKY

Just across the Utah–Nevada border, the uncrowded **Great Basin National Park** encompasses the 13,063ft ice-sculpted horn of **Wheeler Peak**, which shelters a tenacious glacier, and the dripping **Lehman Caves**. The colossal marble cavern is home to a colony of Townsend's big-eared bats and features a staggering collection of formations, including stalactites, stalagmites, helictites, flowstone, popcorn and more than 500 rare shields.

To visit the caves, you must join a guided tour. It's best to book in advance through recreation.gov (the website or the phone app), lest you drive all this way and miss one of the park's main attractions. The NPS offers two tour options. The longer **Grand Palace Tour** (90 minutes) takes in all accessible areas of the cave, while the hour-long **Lodge Tour** follows a similar route but doesn't go as far. The temperature inside the caves is a constant 50°F (10°C), so bring a jacket.

Wheeler's slopes are home to a compact but diverse range of landscapes and life zones, which can be explored along the paved 12-mile **Wheeler Peak Scenic Dr**, which rises more than 10,000ft. This road is open only during a short summer window, usually from July through October.

Hiking trails off the Scenic Dr take in superb country of glacial lakes and ancient bristlecone pines. On clear nights, a panoply of stars dances overhead. The tiny gateway town of Baker sits at the entrance to the park and has a visitor center with exhibits and information.

BEST PLACES TO STAY & EAT NEAR GREAT BASIN NP

Great Basin National Park Campgrounds
The park has five developed campgrounds with vault toilets, grills, picnic tables and tent pads. $

Stargazer Inn
Spruced-up motel rooms with wood floors, comfortable beds and a warm welcome; pet friendly. $$

Sugar, Salt & Malt Restaurant
This Baker eatery's menu of lamb burgers, Asian tacos and pizza punches above its weight for such a small town. $$

GETTING AROUND

You'll need a car to get around this southwestern section of Utah and eastern Nevada.

CRUISING AT 10,000FT ON HIGHWAY 14

This paved scenic route, a back road between Bryce Canyon and Zion, leads 40 miles over the Markagunt Plateau, ending at Hwy 89. The road rises to 10,000ft, with splendid views of Zion National Park. Though Hwy 14 remains open all year, check weather conditions before you travel and use snow tires or chains in the winter months. Heading east out of **1 Cedar City**, Hwy 14 mimics the bends of Coal Creek and climbs steadily. After about 5 miles is a turnoff for the **2 Kolob Reservoir Scenic Backway**, which winds through Zion backcountry past a placid lake. Stop at the information panels to learn about the coal that was mined here for a century. Twist your way through Cedar Canyon, whose dramatics start to include dried black lava that solidified 5000 years ago. About 17 miles from Cedar City, **3 roadside pull-offs** entice with southerly views over Zion National Park. Soon after the Zion viewpoint is the turnoff for Hwy 148 and **4 Cedar Breaks National Monument** (p78). Stretch your legs on a short walk to see the surprisingly sculpted hoodoos, which look delightfully similar to Bryce Canyon's but see far fewer visitors. Carry on to a scenic point above **5 Navajo Lake**, which has its only drainage through lava tubes and sinkholes on the lake floor. Located 5 miles further east, the **6 Duck Creek Visitor Center** provides information for nearby trails and fishing in the adjacent pond and stream. The ever-expanding log-cabin town of **7 Duck Creek Village** has some services, including a few restaurants. About 7 miles east of Duck Creek, a passable dirt road runs 10 miles to **8 Strawberry Point**, an incredibly scenic overview of red-rock formations and forestlands.

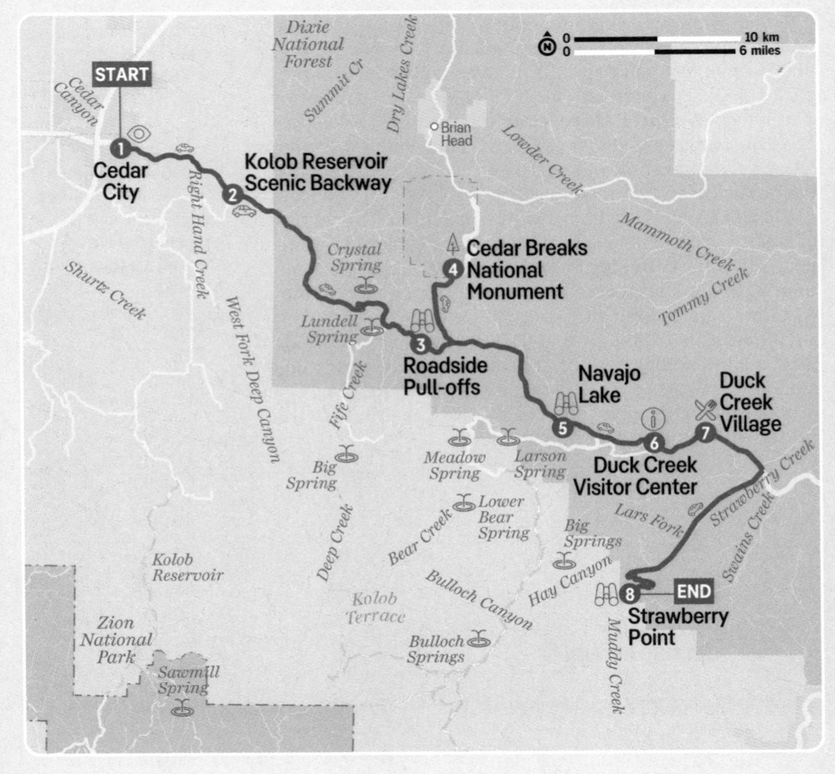

ST GEORGE

Nature looms large around St George, though many visitors just speed past on their way to the national parks. The region has some great hikes, history and even a ghost town to explore.

Nicknamed 'Dixie' for its warm weather and southern location, St George has long attracted winter residents, spring breakers and retirees. Brigham Young, the second president of the Mormon church, was one of the first snowbirds, and his winter home is now open as a museum in the interesting and small historic downtown core that spans a few blocks.

For travelers, the abundant and affordable accommodations are what make St George an oft-used stop between Las Vegas and Salt Lake City – or en route to Zion National Park after a late-night flight. The downtown district has some atmospheric dining spots and cool coffee shops, while chains and large stores congregate along I-15.

St George

TOP TIP

St George is about an hour's drive from Zion's south entrance and 30 minutes from the Kolob Canyons Visitor Center. There are closer bases to both parts of Zion National Park, but if you're a budget traveler, accommodations prices in St George are some of the lowest in the region.

GERALD PEPLOW/SHUTTERSTOCK ©

St George

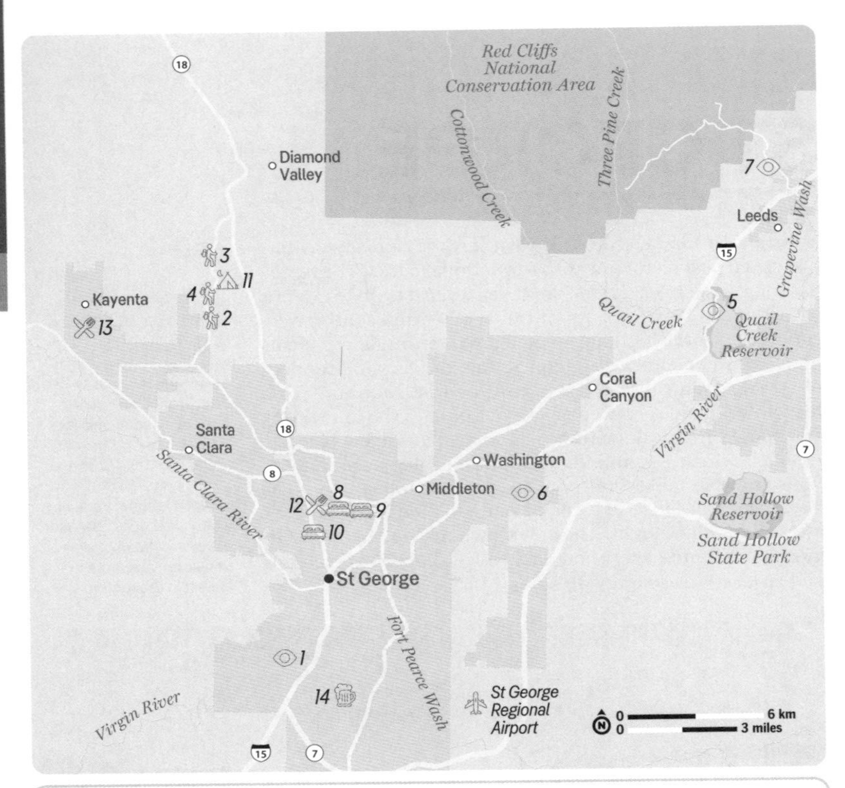

ACTIVITIES
1 Bloomington
2 Jenny's Canyon Trail
3 Petrified Dunes Trail
4 Pioneer Names Trail
5 Quail Creek State Park
6 Shinob Kibe Mesa
7 Silver Reef

SLEEPING
8 Best Western Coral Hills
9 Chalet Motel
10 Inn on the Cliff
11 Snow Canyon Campground

EATING
12 Painted Pony
13 Xetava Cafe

DRINKING & NIGHTLIFE
14 Silver Reef Brewing Co.

Hiking & History at Snow Canyon State Park

A QUIETER SLICE OF SOUTHERN UTAH

Located 11 miles northwest of St George, **Snow Canyon State Park** is an 11.5-sq-mile sampler of southwest Utah's famous land features, without the crowds. Red and white swirls of sandstone flow like lava, and actual cooled lava lies broken like sheets of smashed marble. Easy trails that are perfect for kids lead to tiny slot canyons, cinder cones, lava tubes and fields of undulating slickrock. The park was named after Utah pioneers Lorenzo and Erastus Snow, not frozen precipitation, but it does occasionally snow here.

Climbing, St George

Snow Canyon State Park has more than 38 miles of hikes, and trails loop off the main road. **Jenny's Canyon Trail** is an easy half-mile round-trip to a short slot canyon, and the 1.2-mile **Petrified Dunes Trail** leads to remarkable Navajo sandstone formations. Wind through a cottonwood-filled field and past ancient lava flows to a 200ft arch on **Johnson Canyon Trail** (2-mile round-trip). The short crescent-shaped **Pioneer Names Trail** rambles past a canyon wall where 1880s Mormon settlers wrote their names in wagon-axle grease.

Cycling is popular on the main road through the park – it's a 17-mile loop from St George (where you can rent bikes). The park also has great **rock climbing**, with bolted sport routes and traditional climbs across six separate areas.

Summers are blazing hot. Visit in the early morning or come in spring or fall. Snow Canyon has a scenic 31-site **campground**; about half the sites have electrical and water hookups. The entry fee is $15 per vehicle or $5 if you're cycling or walking into the park.

JENPENG/SHUTTERSTOCK ©

Jenny's Canyon Trail

BEST PLACES TO EAT & DRINK IN & AROUND ST GEORGE

Painted Pony
Beautifully plated gourmet comfort foods (eg bacon-wrapped duck and sage-smoked quail) in a bright downtown space. $$$

Xetava Cafe
Organic, locavore burgers, salads and brunch served in a stunning red-rock setting near Snow Canyon. $$

Silver Reef Brewing Co.
Laid-back taproom pouring pints among the beer tanks in an industrial park south of town.

WHERE TO STAY IN ST GEORGE

Inn on the Cliff
Soak in sweeping views of St George from the cliffside pool and hot tub or your private balcony. $$

Chalet Motel
Good-value motel with a friendly welcome, updated decor and bathrooms, and kitchenettes. $$

Best Western Coral Hills
Dated but clean rooms within walking distance of downtown restaurants, cafes and historic sites. $$

SPECIAL DELIVERY

Atop a handful of hills around St George are huge 50ft concrete arrows that once helped deliver the mail.

In the 1920s the US government constructed these **navigation arrows** to guide pilots transporting airmail in the days before radio navigation, allowing them to eyeball their way across the country. The arrows were placed every 10 miles, painted bright yellow and lit by oil lamps at night.

A branch of the transcontinental 'Pony Express of the Sky' ran from Salt Lake City to Los Angeles, and you can still climb the hills and visit three of these arrows around St George: in Bloomington, near Quail Creek State Park and on the Shinob Kibe mesa.

Spirit of Silver Reef

DISCOVERING SILVER IN SANDSTONE

Northeast of St George, the 19th-century ghost town of **Silver Reef**, once the largest town in southern Utah, is the only place in North America where silver was ever found within sandstone, drawing in miners ready to strike it rich but ultimately going bust. By 1879 Silver Reef had about 2000 residents, who frequented the mile-long Main St. A few of the original buildings remain intact, including the 1878 Wells Fargo building, which houses a **museum** with exhibits on mining and life in the town. When the price of silver dropped in the mid-1880s, it was the death knell that gradually closed the mines over the next two decades.

Jail, Silver Reef ghost Town

ORCHID LADY/SHUTTERSTOCK ©

Outside the museum, two rock-lined loop trails meander past the foundations of the once-thriving saloons, hotels, restaurants and dance halls that are nearly in the backyards of the encroaching subdivision. The foundations and walls are sparse and require some imagination, but the quiet desert setting is sublime. The Cosmopolitan Restaurant (next to the museum) has been reconstructed, and the small jail, removed when Silver Reef was abandoned and sent off to a nearby town to start a second life as an icehouse and granary, is back in its rightful place near a saloon (which was sometimes used as a courtroom).

The museum has limited opening hours (10am to 3pm Thursday to Saturday and Monday). You can walk the trails even when the buildings are closed, but the museum provides the necessary context to fully enjoy your visit.

GETTING AROUND

You'll need a car to get around St George. The town lies about 41 miles (up to an hour's drive) from Zion National Park's south entrance, 34 miles (30 minutes) from the Kolob Canyons' entrance on I-15, and 57 miles (50 minutes) from Cedar City.

St George Regional Airport is southeast of town and has a handful of connections to Phoenix, Salt Lake City and Denver.

St George
Valley of Fire State Park
Lost City Museum
Lake Mead Visitor Center
Lake Mead National Recreation Area
Hoover Dam

Beyond St George

Two hours on I-15 is all that stands between Las Vegas and Utah, but hop off the interstate to uncover Nevada's true nature.

Las Vegas is usually the most convenient airport location for the majority of travelers flying in to visit Zion National Park, and although Sin City is far from a naturalist's vision of the United States, geological treasures can be found on its doorstep, reachable as day trips or by taking a slower scenic route to St George. The two most intriguing stops are polar opposites: the otherworldly rock formations of Valley of Fire State Park and the topaz waters of Lake Mead, filled by the Hoover Dam.

The sparse, small towns along the quiet state highways don't offer much beyond the basics, with limited accommodations and food options. Stay in Vegas or Boulder City for more choices.

TOP TIP

Nevada's lower elevation means that temperatures there soar earlier in the year compared with Utah. Shade is rare; be prepared when hiking.

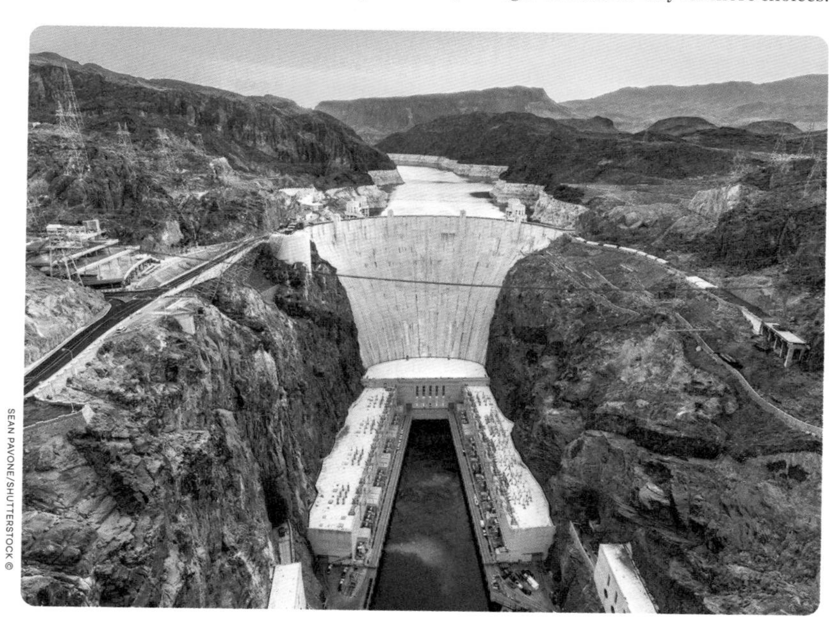

SEAN PAVONE/SHUTTERSTOCK ©

Hoover Dam (p87)

Valley of Fire State Park

ERIC POULIN/SHUTTERSTOCK ©

RESCUING NATIVE HISTORY

Visitors don't linger long in the tiny town of Overton, Nevada, east of Valley of Fire State Park, but it's worth making a stop here at the **Lost City Museum**.

Constructed in 1935, the museum showcases Native American artifacts taken out of archaeological sites before they were submerged by Lake Mead, including baskets, pottery and even shells that were traded from the California coast.

Within the museum itself are some excavated ruins, and visitors can climb down into a recreated Ancestral Puebloan pit house near the museum entrance.

On Another Planet at Valley of Fire State Park

A UNIVERSE AWAY

Valley of Fire State Park is a masterpiece of Southwest desert scenery, containing over 62 sq miles of red Aztec sandstone fractured and eroded by wind and water over thousands of years into colorful slot canyons and out-of-this-world rock formations. Established in 1935, Valley of Fire was Nevada's first state park, and it has played a starring role in many movies, including *Star Trek Generations*, *When Fools Rush In* and *Total Recall*.

A number of hikes run through the park. The **Seven Wonders Loop** takes in the best parts, circling through the evocatively named Fire Wave, Pastel Canyon, White Domes and the remnants of the set from the 1965 film *The Professionals*. The undulating drive to get to the trailhead along Mouse's Tank Rd gives a good taste of the beauty to come, and you might spot bighorn sheep. Elsewhere, don't miss the fascinating petroglyphs and petrified trees. Bring plenty of water and hike early; there's precious little shade. The park shuts at sunset, making evening visits problematic, and hiking trails are closed from June to October because of the heat.

Get maps and information at the visitor center, which also has

WHERE TO STAY & EAT BEYOND ST GEORGE

Boulder Dam Hotel
This grand column-fronted Dutch Colonial–style hotel in Boulder City has welcomed illustrious guests since 1933. **$$**

North Shore Inn at Lake Mead
This Overton motel isn't anything special, but it is the closest non-campsite to Valley of Fire. **$$**

Cablp
Overton stop for gourmet Italian ice, top-notch pizzas and more from a native New Yorker. **$**

a small exhibit on the park's history and geology. Two campgrounds have first-come, first-served sites and shaded tables, grills, water and showers.

Valley of Fire is an hour's drive from Las Vegas or an hour and 45 minutes from St George.

Finding Water in the Desert

THE COUNTRY'S LARGEST RESERVOIR

Even those who question the USA's commitment to damming the great rivers of the West have to marvel at the engineering and architecture of the **Hoover Dam** over the Colorado River. Completed in 1936, the dam, towering over Black Canyon in the bone-dry Mojave Desert, created the enormous **Lake Mead**, with its 550 miles of shoreline. The 726ft-high Hoover Dam was built by thousands of men who migrated to the area at the height of the Great Depression. The graceful, art-deco-style curve of the dam contrasts superbly with the stark landscape that surrounds it. The excellent **Lake Mead Visitor Center**, halfway between Boulder City and Hoover Dam, off Hwy 93, is a great place to start your explorations of the area. From here, North Shore Rd winds around Lake Mead and makes for a scenic drive.

The **Lake Mead National Recreation Area**, the biggest in the country, is a popular boating, swimming and weekend camping destination. While most visitors come for the water, the area has a handful of hiking trails too. At **Grapevine Canyon** near Lake Mohave, a quarter-mile jaunt takes you to a petroglyph panel. Longer routes include the **Historic Railroad Tunnel Trail** along an old train line with five tunnels that link the Lake Mead Visitor Center to Hoover Dam. The **Arizona Hot Spring Trail**, the most challenging hike in the area, follows a 3-mile trail down 800ft to a set of hot springs in a slot off Black Canyon.

THE END OF LAKE MEAD?

Decades of drought and increasing water demands have dropped the level of Lake Mead precipitously. In 2022 the lake hit historic lows, at just 30% capacity, less than 150ft away from becoming a 'dead pool,' when the reservoir is so low that water cannot flow downstream from the dam.

As the shoreline recedes, the NPS has closed beaches and boat ramps, and a white 'bathtub ring' shows where the water level once was. The vanishing lake is dredging up boats, including a WWII-era Higgins landing craft, and even the bodies of drowned swimmers from many years prior.

Lake Mead

GETTING AROUND

You'll need a car to travel to Valley of Fire State Park and around Lake Mead.

BRYCE CANYON NATIONAL PARK & SOUTHERN UTAH

HIKING THROUGH HEAPS OF HOODOOS

Famous for its otherworldly sunset-colored spires punctuated by tracts of forest, Bryce Canyon National Park is one of the planet's most exquisite geological wonders.

The high altitude of Bryce, which hugs the eastern edge of an 18-mile plateau, sets it apart from Utah's other national parks. Repeated freezes and thaws have eroded the small park's soft sandstone and limestone into a landscape that's utterly unique: sandcastle-like pinnacles known as hoodoos, jutted fins, and huge amphitheaters filled with thousands of pastel daggers.

Dotted along the scenic drive that skirts the rim of the Paunsaugunt Plateau is a series of dramatic viewpoints from which to marvel at the powerful forces that forged this remarkable landscape, while hiking trails descend through 1000ft amphitheaters into a maze of fragrant juniper and high-mountain desert. At sunrise and sunset, the golden-red spires shimmer like trees in a magical stone forest, creating a hypnotic and Tolkien-esque place that is surely inhabited by nimble elves and mischievous sprites.

The ethereal formations spill outside of the national park's boundary and into Red Canyon to the west. These hiking trails see far fewer visitors, granting a more peaceful experience among the vibrantly colored monoliths. South-central Utah stuns with its sheer diversity and density of unique geology. The slot canyons are a particular treat, and this region is thought to have the most and the longest of anywhere in the world. Kanab – this area's largest town, with a population of just 5000 – makes an excellent base camp.

Opposite: Thor's Hammer, Bryce Canyon National Park (p98); Inset: Scenic Hwy 12 (p114)

THE MAIN AREAS

BRYCE CANYON NATIONAL PARK
World's highest concentration of hoodoos.
p94

GRAND STAIRCASE-ESCALANTE NATIONAL MONUMENT
Huge expanse of remote hikes and 4WD roads.
p111

KANAB
Western movie town still spinning tales.
p123

Find Your Way

You need a private vehicle to explore this region of Utah to the fullest. It's possible to see Bryce Canyon as a day trip from Zion National Park, but it deserves a dedicated itinerary.

Bryce Canyon National Park, p94

Let your imagination run wild as you visit the planet's epicenter of hoodoos (unusual 'fairy chimneys' shaped by erosion).

Kanab, p123

Once a favorite filming location for Hollywood Westerns, this laid-back town has three national parks on its doorstep, plus plenty of trailheads of its own.

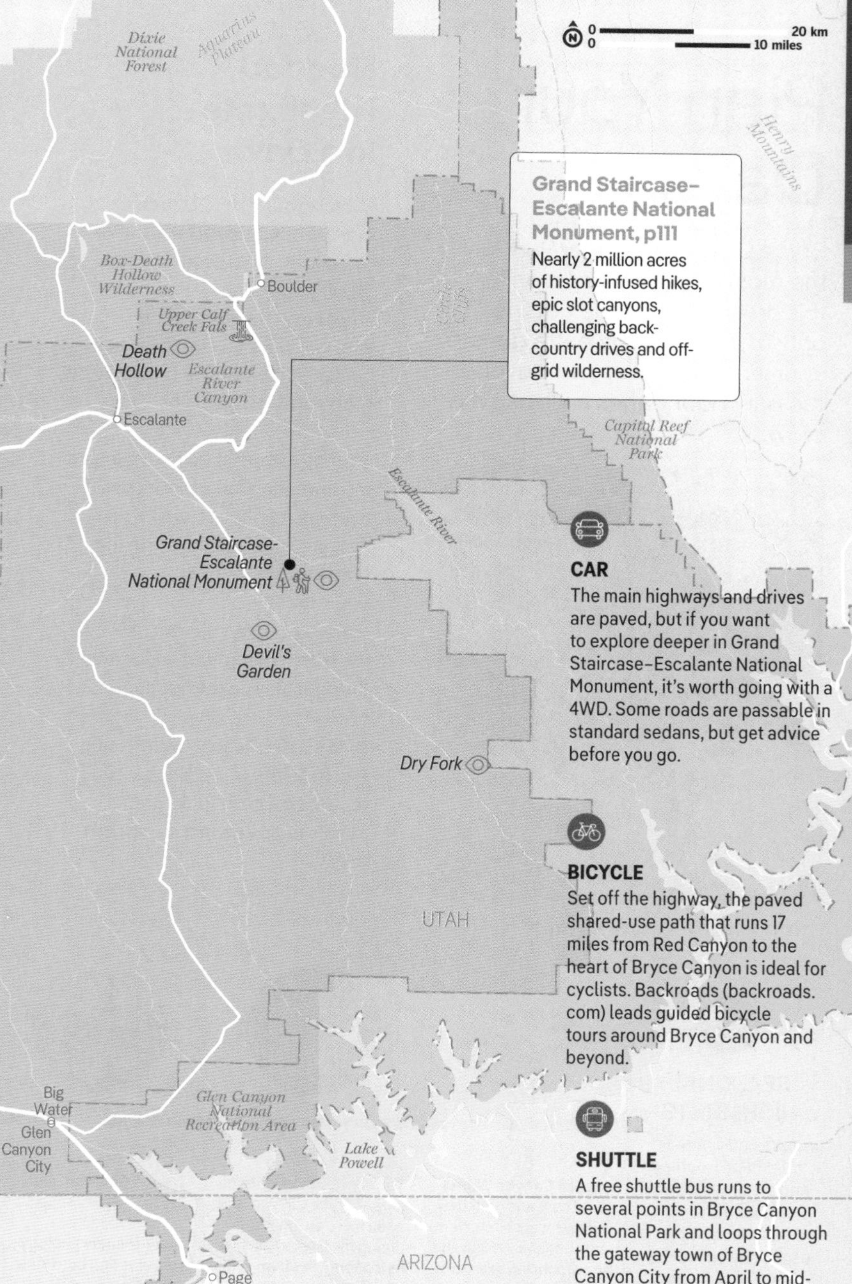

Grand Staircase–Escalante National Monument, p111

Nearly 2 million acres of history-infused hikes, epic slot canyons, challenging back-country drives and off-grid wilderness.

CAR

The main highways and drives are paved, but if you want to explore deeper in Grand Staircase–Escalante National Monument, it's worth going with a 4WD. Some roads are passable in standard sedans, but get advice before you go.

BICYCLE

Set off the highway, the paved shared-use path that runs 17 miles from Red Canyon to the heart of Bryce Canyon is ideal for cyclists. Backroads (backroads.com) leads guided bicycle tours around Bryce Canyon and beyond.

SHUTTLE

A free shuttle bus runs to several points in Bryce Canyon National Park and loops through the gateway town of Bryce Canyon City from April to mid-October. Private vehicles are still allowed in the park when the shuttle is running.

Plan Your Days

Bryce Canyon National Park is the most obvious attraction in this area but certainly not the only one. Find some extra days in your itinerary to explore beyond the park boundaries and lose the crowds.

PAT TR/SHUTTERSTOCK ©

Wall Street, Navajo Loop Trail (p98)

Hoodoo Highlights in a Day

- Start your visit to **Bryce Canyon National Park** (94) by cruising the **Scenic Drive** (p104) from Rainbow Point and stopping at the major overlooks on your way back toward the visitor center. Refuel with lunch at **Bryce Canyon Lodge** (p98).

- Head to Sunset Point to glimpse the towering eroded hoodoos of Bryce Amphitheater and then descend into the canyon on the **Navajo Loop** (p98).

- Back at higher elevations, stroll the **Rim Trail** (p100) and watch the light play on the hoodoos.

- At sunset, head to west-facing **Paria View** (p101). Stick around for **stargazing** (p101) or the ranger-led **evening program** (p99).

SEASONAL HIGHLIGHTS

April and October offer ideal weather and are arguably the best months to visit. During the summer, especially on holiday weekends, the park gets crazy busy.

FEBRUARY

Bryce Canyon Winter Festival puts on snowy high-elevation fun, from cross-country skiing and snowmobiling to archery and snow sculpting.

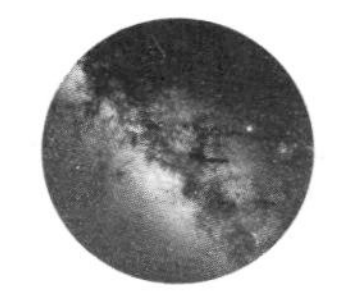

JUNE

You can see thousands of stars at Bryce Canyon, and even more are on display during the **Bryce Canyon Astronomy Festival**, with Salt Lake Astronomical Society's huge telescopes.

JULY

During **GeoFest**, join Bryce Canyon rangers for guided hikes, family-friendly geology programs and bus tours with a geologist.

ALBERTOGONZALEZ/SHUTTERSTOCK ©, KRISTI BLOKHIN/SHUTTERSTOCK ©, PIERRE LECLERC/SHUTTERSTOCK ©

A Long Weekend Around Bryce Canyon

- Leave the crowds behind with a morning hike on the **Fairyland Loop** (p96). The 700ft elevation change is sure to wake you up.

- For an easy, family-friendly nature walk, leave the main park entrance and drive east on Hwy 12 to **Mossy Cave** (p107).

- Grab lunch in **Tropic** (p107) and then explore the picture-perfect colors of the sandstone chimneys and petrified geysers in **Kodachrome Basin State Park** (p108).

- The next day, seek out the slots of **Willis Creek** (p110) and get your head back in hoodoo country with a hike or mountain bike ride in **Red Canyon** (p107).

Beyond Bryce

- If you have the right wheels and know-how, leave the paved roads of the national park behind and venture onto the roller-coaster backways of **Grand Staircase–Escalante National Monument** (p111).

- Lace up your hiking boots for an awesome adventure into the **Dry Fork slot canyon** (p121), one of many activities along historic **Hole-in-the-Rock Rd** (p120).

- Return to civilization in **Kanab** (p123). Try your luck getting a permit for the **Wave** (p126) or settle for 'next best' at **Wire Pass** and **Buckskin Gulch** (p128).

- Day trip to the **North Rim of the Grand Canyon** (p129), squeezing in short hikes, scenic drives and vertigo-inducing viewpoints.

AUGUST

Kanab lives for the annual **Western Legends Roundup**, with concerts, cowboy poetry, a Longhorn cattle drive and more.

SEPTEMBER

September is still hot, but days are clear, rivers remain warm and leaves begin to change.

OCTOBER

Experience Bryce Canyon, Zion and Horseshoe Bend on a trail run during the three-day **Grand Circle Trailfest**.

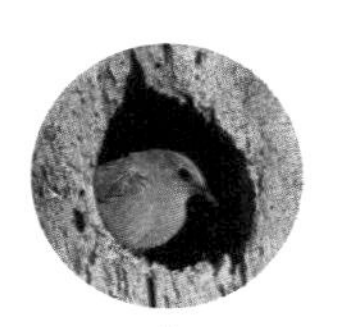

DECEMBER

Join the longest-running citizen science project in the world for the **Annual Christmas Bird Count** at Bryce Canyon.

BRYCE CANYON NATIONAL PARK

The sight of Bryce is nothing short of otherworldly. Yes, you're still in the desert, but it's the wonderful power of water that sculpted this soft sandstone and limestone into alien formations that tickle the imagination. Though it's the smallest of Utah's national parks, Bryce Canyon stands among the most prized.

Despite its name, Bryce is not actually a canyon but rather the eastern edge of an 18-mile plateau. (A canyon is formed by flowing water.) The Pink Cliffs mark the top step of the Grand Staircase, a giant geologic terrace reaching to the Grand Canyon in Arizona. Trails leave from the rim and descend thousands of feet into the maze of stunningly sculpted high-mountain desert.

Its high altitude means Bryce has cooler temperatures than other Utah parks. Clean, dry air also means excellent visibility, reaching all the way into the Andromeda Galaxy 2.5 million light-years away.

Bryce Canyon

TOP TIP

If you're visiting from April to mid-October, avoid adding to traffic congestion and ride the free shuttle into the park. The shuttle goes as far as Bryce Point. Buses arrive roughly every 15 minutes from 8am to 8pm (to 6pm in April, the first two weeks of May, September and October).

JENIFOTO/SHUTTERSTOCK ©

Mossy Cave Trail (p107)

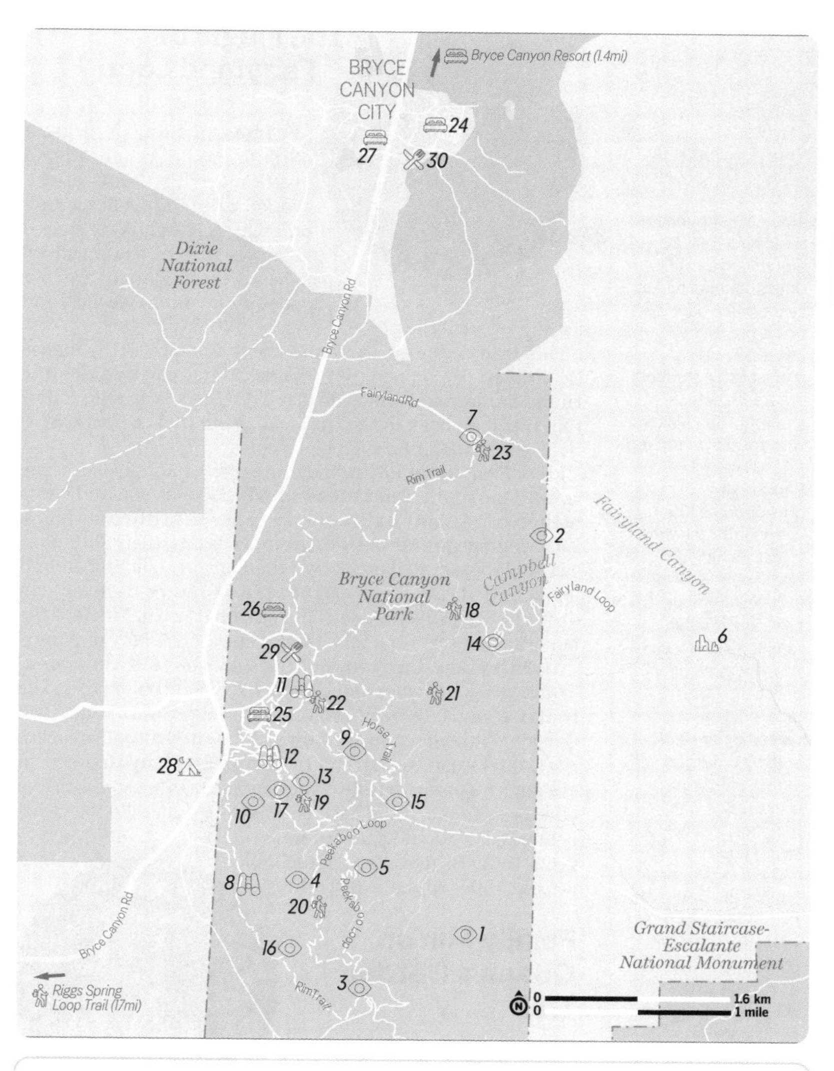

HIGHLIGHTS
1 Alligator
2 Boat Mesa
3 Bryce Point
4 Cathedral
5 Fairy Castle
6 Fairyland Canyon
7 Fairyland Point
8 Inspiration Point
9 Queen Victoria
10 Silent City
11 Sunrise Point
12 Sunset Point
13 Thor's Hammer
14 Tower Bridge
15 Two Bridges
16 Wall of Windows
17 Wall Street

ACTIVITIES & TOURS
18 Fairyland Loop Trail
19 Navajo Loop Trail
20 Peekaboo Loop Trail
21 Queen's Garden Trail
22 Rim Trail
23 Under-the-Rim Trail

SLEEPING
24 Bryce Canyon Grand Hotel
25 Bryce Canyon Lodge
26 North Campground
27 Ruby's Inn
28 Sunset Campground

EATING
29 Bryce Canyon General Store
30 Ebenezer's Barn & Grill

SEEING STARS IN BRYCE CANYON

Amateur astronomers are in for a treat at Bryce Canyon. All Utah's national parks are certified dark-sky parks, but Bryce offers the widest range of star-studded programs, activities and events for visitors who are astro-curious.

The National Park Service puts on some 100 astronomy programs a year, including an Astronomy Festival in June, full-moon hikes and regular ranger talks. Check the park's calendar online (nps.gov/brca/planyourvisit/calendar.htm) and stop by the visitor center when you arrive to see what's happening while you're there.

The park is open 24 hours. Time your visit for the new moon, when the skies are darkest, and watch as the Milky Way shimmers all the way to the horizon.

The Magic of Fairyland Loop

A HIKE ON THE QUIET SIDE

Fairyland Loop is a great 8-mile day hike and a good workout, with 1900ft of elevation gain. Unlike Bryce Amphitheater, Fairyland is spared the crowds. It is difficult primarily because it meanders in and out of the hoodoos, down into washes, and up and over saddles.

This trail begins at Fairyland Point and circles the majestic cliffs of flat-topped, 8076ft Boat Mesa, emerging on the rim near Sunrise Point. The last 2.5 miles of the loop follow the Rim Trail back to the trailhead. Note that the park shuttle doesn't stop at Fairyland.

From **Fairyland Point**, the route dips gradually below the rim. To the south, **Boat Mesa** stands between you and views of the park. A short walk leads past ancient bristlecone pines, some clinging precariously to the ragged cliffs, their 1000-plus-year-old roots curled up like wizened fingers. Looping around hoodoos that rise like castle turrets and towers, the trail soon drops to the canyon floor and a seasonal wash. Much of the north-facing terrain holds its snowpack until May or June.

At **Fairyland Canyon**, 600ft below your starting point, towers of deep-orange stone stand like giant totem poles. The trail rises and falls before traversing a ridge toward Campbell Canyon. Zigzagging up and down, the trail eventually reaches a seasonal wash on the floor of **Campbell Canyon**. Keep an eye out for **Tower Bridge**, which connects three spires to two windows. To reach the base of the formation, take the clearly marked dead-end spur from the wash.

From Tower Bridge, it's a 950ft climb over 1.5 miles to the Rim Trail.

Family Fun on Queen's Garden Trail

ROCK OF ROYALTY

Good for kids, **Queen's Garden Trail** is the easiest route into the canyon. It makes a gentle descent over sloping erosional fins

Hoodoos, Queen's Garden Trail

WHERE TO STAY IN BRYCE CANYON NATIONAL PARK

Bryce Canyon Lodge
Charmingly rustic 1920s lodge; cabins are a better pick than the generic motel-style rooms. **$$**

North Campground
Large campground close to showers, laundry, the general store and the visitor center. **$**

Sunset Campground
First-come, first-served 102-site campground; shadier than North Campground but has fewer amenities. **$**

and passes elegant hoodoo formations but stops short of the canyon floor. Queen's Garden Trail is not a loop but an in-and-out hike. If you decide to go further, add on the **Queen's Garden Connecting Trail**, part of the Queen's Garden–Navajo Loop Combination Trail (p103).

From **Sunrise Point**, follow signs to the trailhead off the Rim Trail. Views of the amphitheater as you descend are superb. A maze of colorful rock spires extends to Bryce Point, and deep green pines dot the canyon floor beneath undulating slopes seemingly tie-dyed pink, orange and white. As you drop below the rim, watch for the stark and primitive bristlecone pines, which are thought to be about 1600 years old. These ancient trees' dense needles cluster like foxtails on the ends of the branches.

After a series of switchbacks, turn right and follow signs to the Queen's Garden Trail. The short spur from the main trail passes through a tunnel and emerges among exceptionally beautiful hoodoo castles in striking colors amid the pines. After looping around a high wall and passing through two more tunnels, bear right and follow signs to **Queen Victoria**. The trail's namesake monarch peers down from a white-capped rock, perched atop her throne.

Queen's Garden Trail

CALM IN THE CANYON

Peter Densmore, park ranger at Bryce Canyon, shares his recommendations for finding solitude in the park.

The Rim Trail
One of the park's easiest hikes, the Rim Trail follows the canyon edge as it connects Bryce Canyon's popular viewpoints. While these viewpoints can become crowded, a short walk on the trail is a great way to get some space. The section from Bryce Point to Inspiration Point is my favorite.

When to Visit
Visitation peaks April through October, with spikes on major holidays, but August is often quieter. A winter visit requires packing more clothes, but the vivid contrast of snow on red rocks makes it a favorite season for a hardy few.

WHERE TO STAY IN BRYCE CANYON CITY

Ruby's Inn
This gargantuan hotel complex is your one-stop shop for accommodations, activities, groceries and more. **$$**

Bryce Canyon Grand Hotel
The large, clean rooms are a step up from other hotels clustered outside the park entrance. **$$**

Bryce Canyon Resort
Definitely more motel than resort, but has good-value kitschy rooms 4 miles from the park. **$$**

WINTER IN BRYCE CANYON

With an average elevation of 8000ft, Bryce Canyon is a high-altitude park that is blanketed by snow in winter. The snowcaps on the formations are stunning, and the cycle of freezing and thawing water is responsible for shaping the hoodoos. Most roads are plowed, while others are designated for **cross-country skiing** and **snowshoeing**.

The best cross-country skiing and snowshoeing trails are on the Paria Ski Loop, the Rim Trail and Fairyland Rd. Rangers lead free two-hour snowshoeing hikes – and even hikes in the snow during the full moon.

Rent snowshoes and cross-country skis from **Ruby's Inn** in Bryce Canyon City, which also has miles of groomed trails.

CHRISTOPHER MOSWITZER/SHUTTERSTOCK ©

Bryce Canyon Amphitheater (p100)

Return to the rim the way you came or link with the Navajo Loop Trail via the Queen's Garden Connecting Trail, which drops to the canyon floor.

Hoodoo Circuit on the Navajo Loop

CITY OF STONE

Ready for a leg burner? The steep 1.3-mile **Navajo Loop Trail** is short but spectacular. From the trailhead at Sunset Point, you drop right into the canyon beneath towering hoodoos that dwarf hikers.

Before you set off, check with rangers to see whether the Wall Street side of the loop is open; it's often closed because of rockfall. Rangers strongly recommend hiking the loop clockwise to avoid a steep descent through Wall Street, a notorious ankle-buster. To lengthen your hike by 30 minutes to an hour, you can add on the Queen's Garden Trail (p96).

From **Sunset Point**, follow signs for the Navajo Loop Trail. The trail drops immediately into a switchback and then forks about 300ft ahead. Take the left fork, which leads past **Thor's Hammer**, Bryce Canyon's most iconic rock formation, down a long slope to the canyon floor. Entering the canyon, follow

WHERE TO EAT IN & AROUND BRYCE CANYON NATIONAL PARK

Bryce Canyon Lodge
The park's only restaurant; standard American menu with nice regional additions like elk chili. **$$**

Bryce Canyon General Store
Grab-and-go pizza, sandwiches and ice cream, plus a good selection of drinks, including Utah craft beer. **$**

Ebenezer's Barn & Grill
Big dinners of grilled meat and all the fixins come with live country music. **$$**

the sign on your left to see **Two Bridges**, a pair of small water-carved arches.

At the canyon floor, turn right to continue the loop. **Wall Street** features 100ft walls that reveal only a sliver of sky above, keeping the narrow canyon shady and cool out of the sun. The giant Douglas fir trees towering between the walls are more than 750 years old.

To the left of the Wall Street trail, the rock formations of **Silent City** loom large. If the spur trail through the tunnel on your left is open, take a quick jaunt to look down on these eerie pinnacles. The trail finishes with a steep ascent and some 30 switchbacks that lead to the rim.

Hiding Out on Peekaboo Loop

HOODOO, I SEE YOU

An ideal half-day hike, the **Peekaboo Loop Trail** sees the most variety of terrain and scenery in Bryce, with 1560ft of elevation change. The Peekaboo Loop Trail is also a horse trail, so expect to see occasional riders. If you don't want to navigate around horse droppings, choose another route, but the views here are among the park's best.

Peekaboo Loop Trail

HANNATOR/SHUTTERSTOCK ©

From **Bryce Point**, follow signs to the Peekaboo Connecting Trail east of the parking area. Bear left at the fork and descend 1.1 miles, passing through mixed conifers and swooping out along a gray-white limestone fin beneath the Bryce Point overlook. Further down the trail, hoodoo columns take on a bright-orange hue. After passing through a human-made tunnel, look for the **Alligator** in the white rock ahead. As you work your way down the switchbacks, watch for the **Wall of Windows**, which juts above the hoodoos atop a sheer vertical cliff face perpendicular to the canyon rim.

At the loop trail junction, bear right. As you pass beneath healthy fir and spruce trees, you'll spot a few blackened snags. They're victims of lightning, not forest fires. Look for ancient bristlecone pines too. An inch of these trees' trunks represents a century of growth.

Climbing a saddle, you rise to eye level with the hoodoo tops before dropping over the other side to the cluster of delicate red spires at **Fairy Castle**. Just past the turnoff for the Navajo Loop, the trail climbs again to spectacular views of

PEEKABOO ON HORSEBACK

See Bryce Canyon from the saddle on a guided tour of Peekaboo Loop. **Canyon Trail Rides**, the park's official concessioner, has a corral near Bryce Canyon Lodge and offers two- and three-hour rides on horses and mules through the hoodoos from April through October. Seeing the sights from this angle promises another perspective, even if you've already ticked many of the hikes off your list, and the 'cowboy' guides add amusing commentary, telling stories and pointing out rock formations along the way.

Horse owners are also allowed to bring their own stock into the park, but only in certain areas and at specific times. None of the park's backcountry campgrounds are suitable for stock animals.

RANGER PROGRAMS AT BRYCE CANYON NATIONAL PARK

Hoodoo Geology Talk
This hoodoo FAQ will give you the answers you seek; daily at 11am at Sunset Point.

Rim Walk with a Ranger
Hour-long interpretive hike from Sunset Point at 2pm, Memorial Day to Labor Day.

Evening Program
A grab bag of topics is up for discussion in the auditorium of Bryce Canyon Lodge.

Silent City and passes beneath the **Cathedral**, a majestic wall of buttress-like hoodoos. The rolling trail skirts the Wall of Windows, threads through a tunnel and switchbacks down. As you approach the Bryce Point Trail, take the spur on the right to the lush green rest area near the horse corral for a cooldown or picnic before climbing out of the canyon.

A Full View of Bryce on the Rim Trail

Thor's Hammer

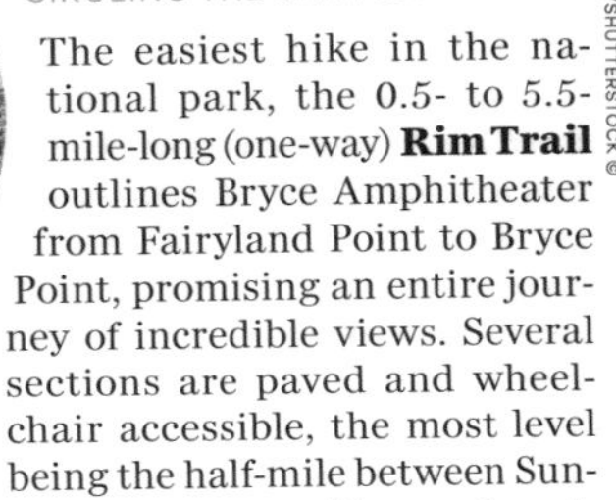

CIRCLING THE CANYON

The easiest hike in the national park, the 0.5- to 5.5-mile-long (one-way) **Rim Trail** outlines Bryce Amphitheater from Fairyland Point to Bryce Point, promising an entire journey of incredible views. Several sections are paved and wheelchair accessible, the most level being the half-mile between Sunrise Point and Sunset Point. In other spots you'll ascend moderately steep, wooded rises to seek shade beneath the pines, watch wildlife or delight in vibrant displays of spring wildflowers. The colors in the rock pop out most when lit by the morning or afternoon sun.

When the park shuttle is running (April to mid-October), you can easily take it to any one point and return from another instead of backtracking to your car. You can join the Rim Trail anywhere along its 5.5-mile route. Note that shuttle buses don't stop at Fairyland.

Remember that Bryce sits atop a sloping plateau. The north end of the Rim Trail is lower than the south end, so it's downhill from Bryce Point to Fairyland Point, though the trail rises and falls in a few spots.

From **Bryce Point** to **Inspiration Point**, the route skirts the canyon rim atop white cliffs, revealing gorgeous formations, including the **Wall of Windows**. After passing briefly through trees, it continues along the ridge top to the uppermost level of Inspiration Point, 1.3 miles from Bryce Point. The leg to **Sunset Point** drops 200ft in 0.75 miles, winding its way along limestone-capped cliffs. Below the rim, **Silent City** rises in all its hoodoo glory.

At **Sunset Point**, you may wish to detour along the Navajo Loop Trail (p98) for a taste of the canyon. You can reemerge on the Rim Trail further ahead by adding the Queen's Garden Trail. Otherwise, stay the course and look for **Thor's**

WHY I LOVE BRYCE CANYON NATIONAL PARK

Lauren Keith, writer

"Even if you've seen photos of it before, nothing quite prepares you for the sight of Bryce Amphitheater as more hoodoos come into view with every step.

My body never lets me stay up too late, so on this trip I set an alarm for 4am to squeeze in as much stargazing as I could before sunrise. I walked through pitch-black forest to Sunrise Point, switched my flashlight off and let the darkness settle. After 20 minutes, I thought I saw a cluster of stars, but they were at ground level and coming toward me. Soon some fellow stargazers appeared and our little constellation swapped stories until the sun came up."

WILDLIFE TO LOOK OUT FOR

Utah Prairie Dog
These burrowing rodents pop up from their colony between the visitor center and Bryce Canyon Lodge.

Uinta Chipmunk
Don't feed these cute striped critters that often hang around picnic areas and overlooks.

Pronghorn
Fastest land animal in the western hemisphere; likely the largest you'll spot in the park.

The Amphitheater from Inspiration Point

Hammer as you continue the 0.5-mile stroll along a paved path to **Sunrise Point**, the most crowded stretch of trail in the entire park. The views are worth it.

Past Sunrise Point, crowds thin as the trail climbs 150ft toward North Campground. Fork left at the Fairyland Loop Trail junction, unless you'd like to follow the moderately difficult, 3-mile round-trip spur into the canyon (950ft elevation loss) to see the window-laced **China Wall** and **Tower Bridge**, twin arches between chunky rock spires. Otherwise, watch for these features from the Rim Trail.

Topping out near North Campground, the path ambles across gently rolling hills on the forested plateau before rejoining the canyon rim at Fairyland Point, 2.5 miles from Sunrise Point.

EVEN MORE VIEWPOINTS IN BRYCE

Paria View
Two miles off the main road, this is *the* place to come at sunset. Most of the hoodoo amphitheaters at Bryce face east and are best viewed at sunrise, but Paria View looks west.

Inspiration Point
Sits lower than Bryce Point and provides much the same view, but Silent City is most compelling from here. The hoodoos feel closer, and you can make out more details on the canyon floor. It's a great place for stargazing.

Multiday Hikes in Forests & Meadows

THE BEAUTY OF BRYCE'S BACKCOUNTRY

If you seek solitude, head into the backcountry of Bryce Canyon for a multiday adventure. Only 1% of visitors venture into the park's remote areas. You won't walk among many

COMMON TREES IN BRYCE CANYON

Bristlecone Pine
Among the planet's oldest living organisms; the most ancient in the park is 1600 years old.

Ponderosa Pine
One of the tallest trees in the Southwest, growing to 200ft; found throughout the park.

Limber Pine
Slow-growing, high-elevation species with branches so pliable they can be tied into knots (but don't).

hoodoos here, but you will pass through forests and meadows with distant views of rock formations.

Backcountry permits are required and can be booked in advance on recreation.gov for trips during the busy months of March through November or purchased at the visitor center if spaces are still available. Permits for December through February are available on a walk-in basis. Campsites are assigned as part of your permit.

Under-the-Rim Trail

KELLY VANDELLEN/SHUTTERSTOCK ©

Bryce Canyon has black bears, mountain lions, coyotes, snakes and other wildlife that might be around backcountry campsites. You must have a bear canister or rent one (for free) from the visitor center. If you bring your own canister, a ranger will inspect it. Water sources in the backcountry aren't reliable, and water from them needs to be filtered before drinking.

Most backcountry trails are covered with snow from late October to March or April. Even in May, snowpack sometimes obscures sections of trail. June and September are ideal times to hike, while in July and August you'll have to contend with thunderstorms.

Both of Bryce's backcountry routes are strenuous, with lots of elevation change. The 23-mile **Under-the-Rim Trail**, south of Bryce Amphitheater, skirts beneath cliffs, wanders through amphitheaters and walks amid pines and aspens. The 11-mile stretch between Bryce Point and Swamp Canyon is one of the hardest and most rewarding. The 8.8-mile **Riggs Spring Loop Trail** goes from the tip of the Paunsaugunt Plateau, then descends beneath the spectacular Pink Cliffs through spruce, fir and aspen and on through ponderosa pines to a desert habitat of sagebrush and scrub oak. Fit hikers could finish it in a day, negating the need to get a permit and campsite.

AWAY FROM THE CROWDS

In the heat of high season, every parking lot is jam-packed, but it's still possible to find a little quiet in Bryce Canyon.

Fairyland Loop
Has views that make you feel as though you've landed on the moon.

Dixie National Forest
The land surrounding the national park sees fewer visitors but still has amazing hiking and hoodoos.

Stargazing
Even the most popular parts of the park clear out at night as the Milky Way comes out to play.

GETTING AROUND

During the busy season from April through October, free buses shuttle passengers around the park. Visitors are still allowed to drive into Bryce Canyon when the shuttle is running. The shuttle has 15 stops, nine of which are in the park; it also stops at some hotels in Bryce Canyon City outside the park entrance. A private vehicle is the only transportation option from fall through spring.

Cycling is a great way to get around the park, and you can bike to every major trailhead. The paved multiuse path is perfect for families. It goes through the park to Inspiration Point and connects with the Red Canyon Bicycle Trail, which ends 15.5 miles from the visitor center.

HIKING THE QUEEN'S GARDEN–NAVAJO LOOP COMBINATION TRAIL

The most popular route in the park, the fairly gentle Queen's Garden–Navajo Loop Combination Trail hits Bryce's signature features in a relatively short amount of time, despite the sometimes steep grade. The full loop is 2.9 miles (two to three hours) and can get quite busy, so consider an early-morning hike to avoid the crowds. It's possible to do this trail clockwise or counterclockwise (starting from Sunset Point), but the National Park Service recommends going clockwise.

Start at **1 Sunrise Point** and follow the Queen's Garden Trail down below the rim. Follow signs for the **2 Queen's Garden Connecting Trail**, which descends to the garden of spires and follows the canyon floor. A major advantage of taking this trail is that it provides extra time at the bottom of the Bryce Amphitheater, where tall pines provide shade and offer perspective on oversized hoodoos. Head back to the rim on either side of the **3 Navajo Loop Trail**. The final push is steep, polishing off your trek by going up multiple switchbacks, but you're rewarded with dramatic views, cool staircases and close proximity to the hoodoos. **4 Wall Street**, on the western side of the loop, is the more dramatic of the two ascents but is often closed because of fallen rocks. If it's closed, ascend to the rim via the Two Bridges side of the Navajo Loop Trail. Before you top out on the rim, detour right a short distance to see **5 Thor's Hammer**, one of the park's most famous formations. Exit the amphitheater at **6 Sunset Point** and stroll back to Sunrise Point along the **7 Rim Trail**, gazing into the canyon for yet another angle of the hoodoos.

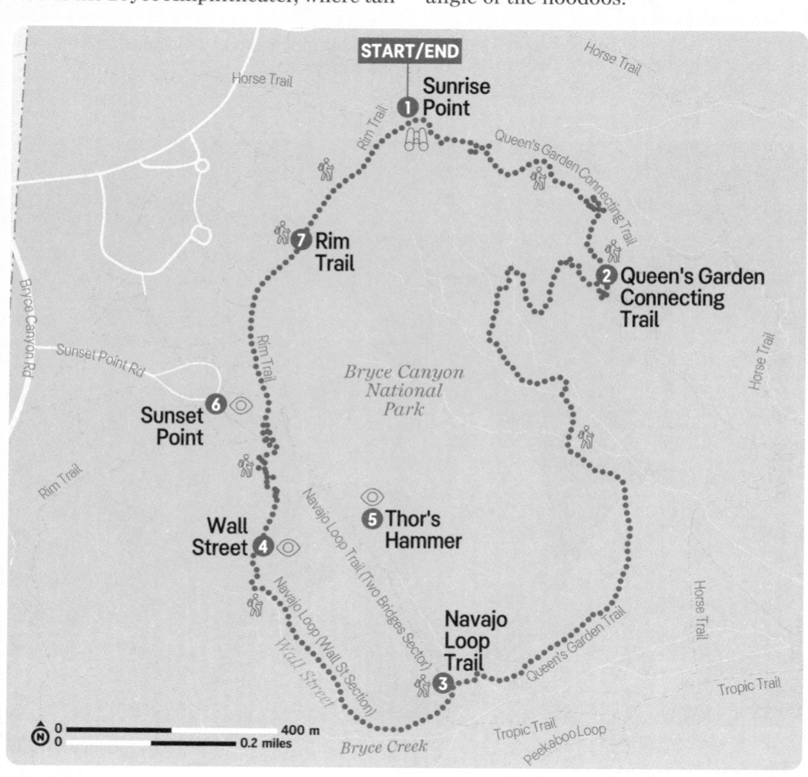

ROAD TRIP

Hoodoo Highlights from Bryce Canyon Scenic Drive

Spanning the length of the park, this route hits all the high points. The Scenic Drive winds south for 17 miles and roughly parallels the canyon rim, climbing from 7894ft at the visitor center to 9115ft at Rainbow Point at the road's end. Because most of the viewpoints are on the eastern side, it's best to hightail it all the way to Rainbow Point and then make your way slowly back.

1 Rainbow Point & Yovimpa Point

On a clear day, you can see more than 100 miles from Rainbow Point. Giant sloping plateaus, tilted mesas and towering buttes jut above the vast landscape. On the northeastern horizon look for the Aquarius Plateau – the top step of the Grand Staircase – rising 2000ft higher than Bryce.

At the other end of the parking lot, another short, paved, wheelchair-accessible trail leads to Yovimpa Point, one of the park's windiest spots. The southwest-facing view reveals more forested slopes and less eroding rock.

The Drive: Heading north, you pass overlooks nearly every mile. One of the best stops at this end of the park, the Agua Canyon Overlook eyes two large formations of precariously balanced, top-heavy hoodoos.

AARON J HILL/SHUTTERSTOCK ©

Rainbow Point

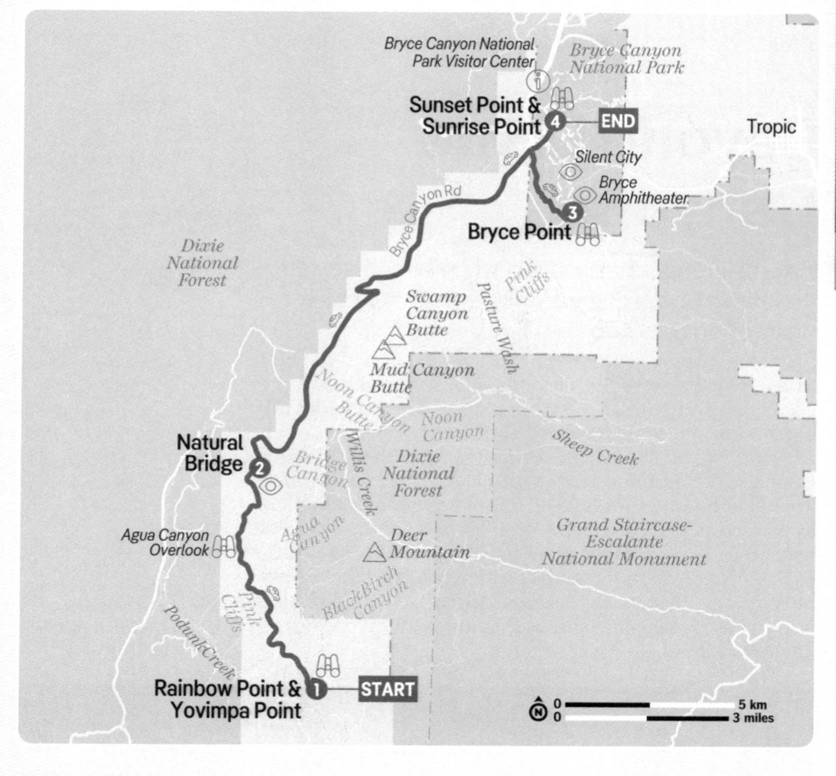

2 Natural Bridge

The parking lot at Natural Bridge is the biggest since Rainbow Point, and with good reason: a stunning span of eroded, red-hued limestone juts from the edge of the overlook. Though called a bridge, it's technically an arch. A bridge forms when running water, such as a stream, erodes the rock. In this case, the freezing and thawing of water inside cracks and crevices, combined with gravity, shattered the rock to create a window formation.

The Drive: Continue north for about 10 miles and turn right on Bryce Point Rd.

3 Bryce Point

Perhaps the best viewpoint in the park, the stretch of landscape seen from Bryce Point is gasp-worthy. You can walk the rim above Bryce Amphitheater for awesome views of Silent City, an assemblage of hoodoos so dense, gigantic and hypnotic that you'll surely begin to see shapes of figures frozen in the rock. Follow the path to the actual point, a fenced-in promontory that juts over the forested canyon floor 1000ft below, allowing a broad view of the hoodoos.

The Drive: Back on the main drive, turn right. Look for parking around Bryce Canyon Lodge.

4 Sunset Point & Sunrise Point

Views into Bryce Amphitheater at **Sunset Point** are as good as they get, but don't expect solitude. It's at the core of the park, near campgrounds, the lodge and all visitor services. Aside from great views of Silent City, this point is known for Thor's Hammer, a big square-capped rock balanced atop a spindly hoodoo.

Walk for 10 minutes along the paved Rim Trail to **Sunrise Point**. This southeast-facing spot offers great views of hoodoos, the Aquarius Plateau and the Sinking Ship, a sloping mesa that looks like a ship's stern rising out of the water.

Beyond Bryce Canyon

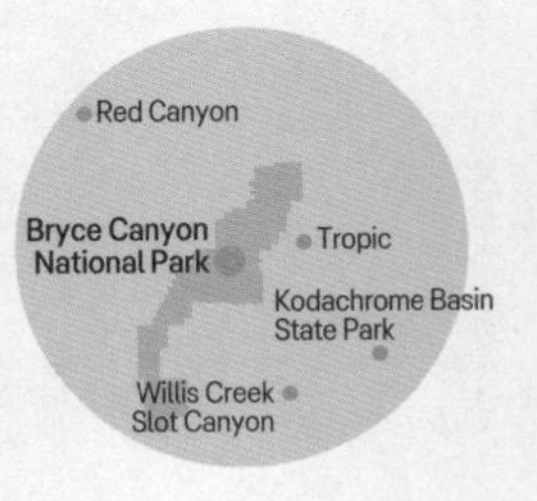

Hikers and hoodoo hunters who haven't gotten their fill in Bryce Canyon will find plenty more distractions outside the park.

Along Hwy 12 west of Bryce, scenic Dixie National Forest covers almost 2 million acres, with endless opportunities for hiking, biking and camping in red-rock country.

Even if you aren't in this area for the activities, you might come for the accommodations if places closer to the park are full or beyond your budget. Campgrounds and RV villages abound in both directions on Hwy 12 from the road that leads into Bryce Canyon National Park. To the east of the park entrance, the tiny town of Tropic was founded in 1891 by Mormon pioneers and has a wider variety of – and more atmospheric – sleeping options than Bryce Canyon City, plus a few restaurants and cafes.

TOP TIP

Ride into the national park on the Red Canyon Bicycle Trail, a paved multiuse trail that starts at Thunder Mountain trailhead.

PAUL BRADY PHOTOGRAPHY/SHUTTERSTOCK ©

Highway 12 near Red Canyon

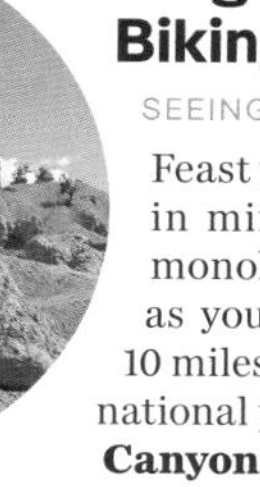

Thunder Mountain Trail

MEGANOPIERSON/SHUTTERSTOCK ©

Hiking & Mountain Biking Red Canyon

SEEING RED

Feast your eyes on Bryce Canyon in miniature: impressive ocher monoliths rise up the roadside as you drive along Hwy 12, just 10 miles west of the turnoff into the national park. The aptly named **Red Canyon**, part of Dixie National Forest, provides easy access to these eerie, intensely colored formations. In fact, you have to drive through two blasted-rock arches to continue along the highway.

Make your first stop the **Red Canyon Visitor Center**, which has informative displays and trail maps. Several moderately easy hikes begin from here, such as the 0.5-mile **Pink Ledges Trail**, which starts near the 1928 Podunk Guard Station that was once used by US Forest Service employees, and the short and sweet 0.3-mile **Hoodoo Trail** that wanders by this area's most iconic formations.

For a longer and more challenging hike with incredible hoodoo views, walk across the highway to the trailhead for **Golden Wall**. It's infinitely quieter than Bryce, so you might have this hike and the hoodoos all to yourself. It forms a small loop with the **Castle Bridge Trail** or a longer 5-mile loop with the **Buckhorn Trail**.

Mountain bikers should take their wheels to **Thunder Mountain Trail**, one of the best in the region. The single-track route covers nearly 3000ft of elevation change through switchbacks and climbs. Use the paved Red Canyon Bicycle Trail to make it a loop. Outfitters around Bryce Canyon City rent mountain bikes if you don't have your own.

BUTCH CASSIDY COUNTRY

Nearly every place in southern Utah claims a connection to Butch Cassidy (1866–1908), the Old West's most famous bank and train robber.

As part of the Wild Bunch, Cassidy (originally named Robert LeRoy Parker) pulled 19 heists from 1896 to 1901. A short drive east of the Red Canyon Visitor Center is the 8.9-mile **Cassidy Trail**, the route the outlaw supposedly fled down after a brawl at a dance in the nearby town of Panguitch.

This area was also the main filming location for 1969's *Butch Cassidy and the Sundance Kid*.

Channelling Nature at the Mossy Cave Trail

WATER IN ALL SEASONS

One of the easiest hikes in Bryce Canyon National Park has its trailhead outside the main entrance. The 0.8-mile round-trip **Mossy Cave Trail** is a low-elevation excursion to a year-round waterfall that's a summertime treat and a frozen winter spectacle. In 1892, Mormon pioneers completed a two-year

ON THE OUTLAW TRAIL

Butch Cassidy is also said to have hidden out among the remote canyons that are now in Capitol Reef National Park. The Cassidy Arch (p186), an excellent hike to a lofty canyon-top viewpoint, bears his name.

WHERE TO STAY AROUND RED CANYON

Red Canyon Campground
Limestone formations and ponderosa pines surround 37 scenic no-reservation sites with showers and drinking water. **$**

Panguitch House
Century-old red-brick home with big breakfasts and hosts ready with advice on area adventures. **$**

Canyon Base Camp
Tipis, yurts and log cabins spread across multiple locations along Hwy 89. **$**

BEST PLACES TO STAY IN TROPIC

Stone Canyon Inn
Cabins, bungalows and even elevated treehouses in a Wild West setting backed by Technicolor sunsets. $$$

Bullberry Inn
Farmhouse-style inn with a handful of rooms; breakfast is prepared with organic ingredients plucked from the garden. $$

Bryce Trails B&B
Tidy, homey rooms named after Bryce Canyon formations and hiking trails; 1 mile from Main St. $$

Bryce Country Cabins
Well-designed pine cabins with small porches lining Tropic's Main St. $$

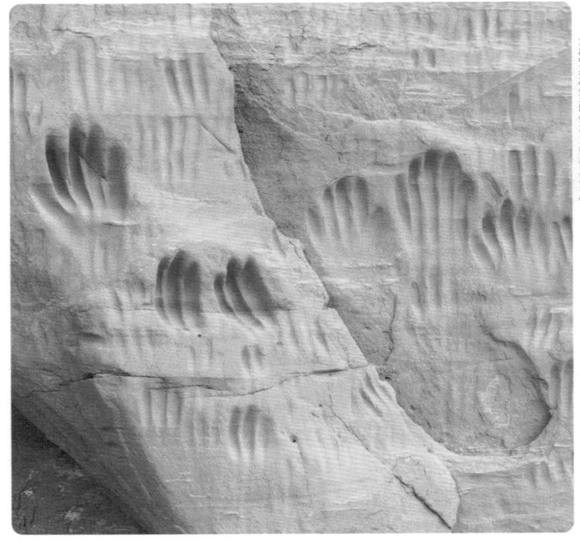

PAUL MAGUIRE/SHUTTERSTOCK ©

Indian Cave, Kodachrome Basin State Park

effort to build a canal, called Tropic Ditch, which diverted water from the East Fork of the Sevier River for agriculture and the definitely misnamed town of Tropic. The laborers used natural channels that the water already flowed through when it rained, and water still courses through it today, cascading over the small waterfall at the end of this hike.

The trailhead is east of the entrance to Bryce Canyon, signposted off Hwy 12 at Mile 17. **Tropic**, population 500, is 4 miles further south on Hwy 12 and has a decent selection of places to stay and eat for a town of such small size.

Cameras at the Ready at Kodachrome Basin State Park

A KODAK MOMENT

Petrified geysers and dozens of red, pink and white sandstone chimneys – some nearly 170ft tall – resemble everything from a sphinx to a snowmobile at **Kodachrome Basin State Park**. Its rainbow of hues and photogenic landscape led a National Geographic Society expedition to name it after Kodak's popular color film in 1948.

Most sights can be explored from the hiking and

WHERE TO EAT IN TROPIC

Stone Hearth Grille
This upscale restaurant at Stone Canyon Inn is the best dinner option in the area. $$$

IDK BBQ
Food truck turned roadside eatery specializing in beef brisket and pulled pork. Add a cobbler cone for dessert. $

Pizza Place
Wood-fired pizzas piled high with fresh ingredients. Don't forget to order the famous breadsticks. $

mountain biking trails. The moderately easy, 3-mile round-trip **Panorama Trail** gives the best overview. Take the side trails to **Indian Cave**, where you can check out the handprints on the wall, and **Secret Passage**, a short hike through a narrow slot canyon. **Angel Palace Trail** (1.5-mile loop, moderate) has great desert views from on high. The 1.7-mile **Sentinel Trail** affords spectacular vistas of Grand Staircase–Escalante National Monument.

Red Canyon Trail Rides offers one- and two-hour adventures on horseback through Kodachrome Basin.

The park has three campgrounds and a range of amenities for overnighters, including a laundromat and a generator that runs from noon to 4pm. **Kodachrome Basin Campground** has 37 well-spaced sites that are close to the hiking trails. Flush toilets and hot showers are available. **Bryce View Campground** comprises 11 reservable sites with fire rings, vault toilets and water taps. Enjoy great sunset views from here. The 13 sites of **Arch Campground** are on the eastern side of the park and some have hookups for RVs. All sites have fire rings and picnic tables.

Two **bunkhouses** that sleep six are also available; they are BYOB (bring your own bedding) and do not have running

NATALIA BRATSLAVSKY/SHUTTERSTOCK ©

Kodachrome Basin State park

DRIVING COTTONWOOD CANYON ROAD

Sculpted red-sandstone monoliths, beige and yellow arches and charcoal-gray peaks: **Cottonwood Canyon Road** unfolds as a striking geology lesson right outside Kodachrome Basin State Park.

The first 9 miles of road to the park are paved. The remaining 37 miles can be driven in a 2WD in dry conditions, but stop at the **Cannonville Visitor Center** for advice before you go.

After Kodachrome Basin, the road continues south, weaving among stark white pinnacles that contrast with the red hoodoos that make up the **Cockscomb**, a distinctive, long, narrow fold in the earth's crust. The landscape morphs from jagged rock into coal-colored dirt hills before the road reaches the pastoral Paria Valley and Hwy 89 beyond.

ROCK LAYERS OF KODACHROME BASIN STATE PARK

Carmel Formation
An inland sea deposited white stripes of gypsum in red cliffs 180 million years ago.

Henrieville Sandstone
It's hard to see within the park, but Grosvenor Arch about 11 miles south is made from this layer.

Tropic Shale
Found in the highest parts of the park's formations; contains fossils of marine life.

A GEODESIC GOODNIGHT

Bubble domes and canvas tents are bringing a touch of luxe to the landscape around Bryce Canyon.

Opened in 2022, family-run **Bryce Glamp & Camp** pampers guests in its 10 gorgeous geodesic domes that feel like a home away from home, with kitchenettes, plush mattresses and outdoor gas firepits on 6 secluded acres near Kodachrome Basin.

North of the national-park entrance, **Under Canvas Bryce Canyon** (also opened in 2022) has staked up safari-style canvas tents with wood floors, private bathrooms, and organic bath products. By night, gather around the firepit for complimentary s'mores.

For a slightly closer-to-nature experience, **Wander Camp** has rustic but cozy tents without plumbing or electricity south of Tropic.

water. Bathrooms are in the nearby laundromat.

The visitor center sells snacks and souvenirs and also rents e-bikes and mountain bikes that you can ride inside or outside the park.

Kodachrome Basin State Park lies off Hwy 12, 9 miles south of Cannonville and 26 miles southeast of Bryce Canyon National Park. Visit in the morning or afternoon, when shadows play on the red rock.

Splashing in Willis Creek Slot Canyon

FAMILY-FRIENDLY FUN

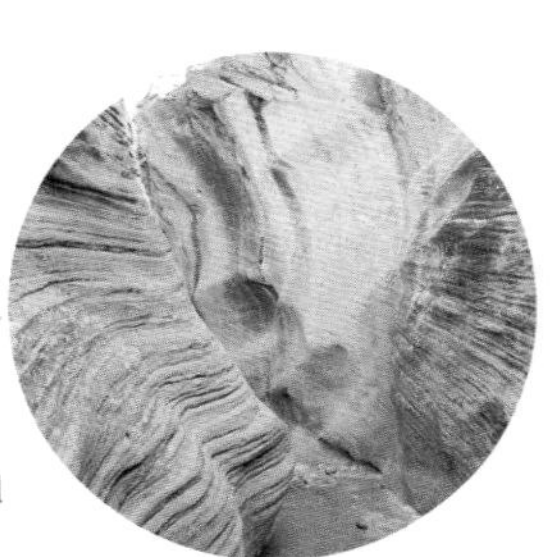

Willis Creek slot canyon

SARAH GOODRICH/SHUTTERSTOCK ©

Willis Creek is a wonderful slot-canyon hike that's accessible to young and old. It's actually more like four little slot canyons, as you alternate between open and narrow sections along a seasonal creek. Easy access, an almost level canyon floor and a gentle, shallow stream make this a great family route. Willis Creek is a particularly good summer hike, thanks to the cooling water and high canyon walls that provide shade from the sun, but remain aware of the weather. Do not enter any slot canyon if storms threaten, and note that the road to the trailhead might be impassable when wet.

Unlike most slot canyons in the wider area, the cliffs around Willis Creek are light beige, not red. The trail starts 3 miles south of Cannonville on Skumptah Rd (access via Cottonwood Canyon Rd). The trail is also used by horse riders, who have the right of way.

Across the road from the parking lot, follow the well-worn path through ponderosa pines down the hill and proceed left, down canyon. In less than five minutes, the serpentine walls rise around you. There's no trail per se; you're just wandering from bank to bank following Willis Creek. The narrows open up after about half a mile, and this is where many people turn around, but it's worth continuing.

Once you hike around, not slide down, the 11ft pour-off, the canyon walls grow taller. At times, cliffs tower 200ft above, only 6ft apart. Tight and narrow sections alternate until you reach the confluence with Sheep Creek, the end of this half-day hike.

GETTING AROUND

You need a car to get around the area surrounding Bryce Canyon.

GRAND STAIRCASE–ESCALANTE NATIONAL MONUMENT

Grand Staircase-Escalante
National Monument

Grand Staircase–Escalante National Monument (GSENM) is one of the largest parks in the Southwest with some of the least visited – yet most spectacular – scenery, including impossibly narrow slot canyons, rippled slickrock and pink dunes. Its name refers to the 150-mile-long geological strata that begin at the bottom of the Grand Canyon and rise in stair steps 3500ft to Bryce Canyon. The striped layers of rock reveal 260 million years of history, as well as still-surviving evidence of human habitation by the Ancestral Puebloans and the Fremont culture.

First-time visitors might find it difficult to figure out how to approach GSENM, which covers more than 2800 sq miles and is larger than the state of Delaware. The monument has no entrance stations, so you might not even know when you're in it. Tourist infrastructure is minimal and limited to towns on the monument's edges.

TOP TIP

GSENM has four visitor centers: in the towns of Cannonville and Escalante on the monument's northern side and in Kanab and Big Water on its southern side. Stop by for details on hikes and road conditions. Much of the monument is explored from 4WD roads that become impassable when wet.

COREY LYNCH/SHUTTERSTOCK ©

Cosmic Ashtray (p120)

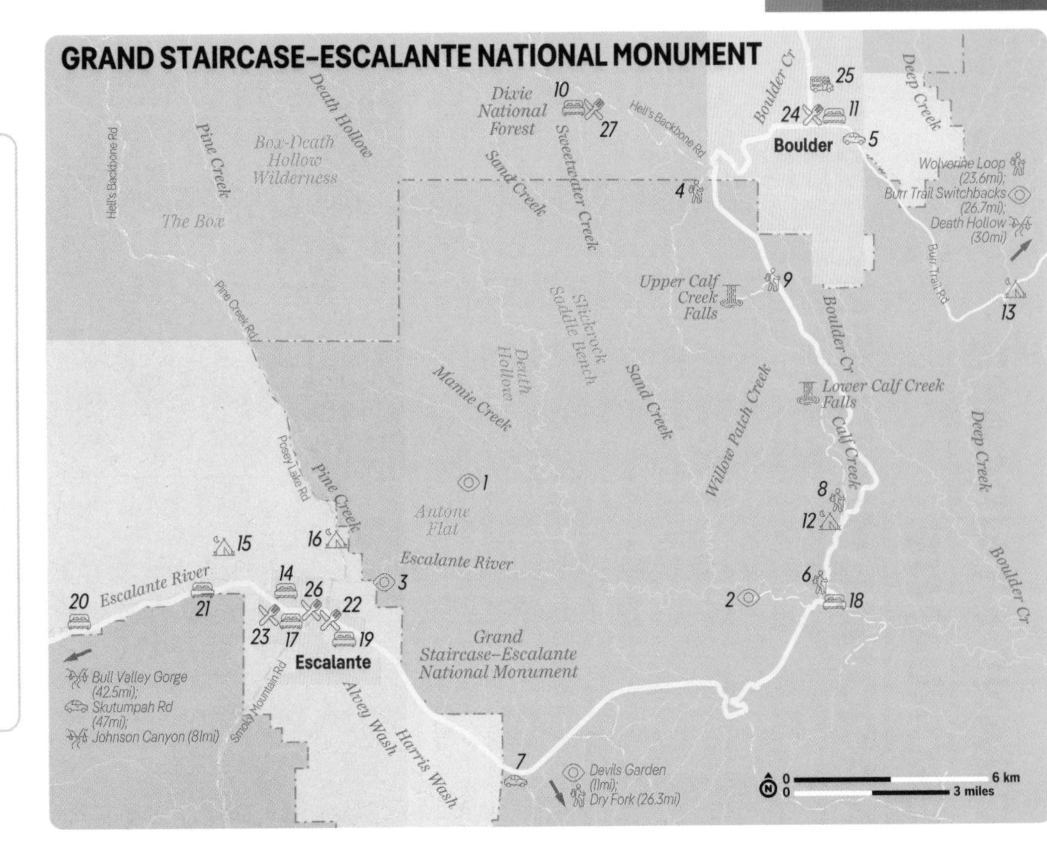

HIGHLIGHTS
1 Antone Flat
2 Escalante Natural Bridge
3 Pine Creek

ACTIVITIES & TOURS
4 Boulder Mail Trail
5 Burr Trail
6 Escalante Natural Bridge Trail
7 Hole-in-the-Rock Road
8 Lower Calf Creek Falls Trail
9 Upper Calf Creek Falls Trail

SLEEPING
10 Boulder Mountain Guest Ranch
11 Boulder Mountain Lodge
12 Calf Creek Recreation Area Campground
13 Deer Creek Campground
14 Escalante Escapes
15 Escalante Petrified Forest State Park Campground
16 Escalante Yurts
17 Inn of Escalante
18 Kiva Kottage
19 Rainbow Country Bed & Breakfast
20 Slot Canyons Inn
21 Yonder Escalante

Coyote Natural Bridge, Coyote Gulch

Into the Water on the Escalante Natural Bridge Trail

ARCHES AROUND ESCALANTE

Be ready to get your feet wet on the 4.4-mile round-trip hike on **Escalante Natural Bridge Trail**. You'll crisscross a stream seven times before reaching a huge natural bridge and an arch beyond. The Escalante River hike is not as demanding as Lower Calf Creek Falls (p119), and it allows (read: requires) you to play in the water.

The trail is 13 miles south of Boulder or 15 miles east of Escalante. Park at the trailhead by the Hwy 12 bridge over the Escalante River, just west of the Calf Creek Recreation Area. Water sandals are best for the alternating sandy and wet conditions. Biting flies can be bothersome in early summer.

Descend and cross the **Escalante River**. Walk through cottonwoods and then an exposed sagebrush and sand valley. Trees appear again when you get closer to the second river crossing, and the cliff walls close in before the third. After another full-sun stint, **Escalante Natural Bridge** appears off to the left. The 130ft-high sandstone arch with a 100ft span is best viewed from the fourth crossing at 1.8 miles.

Continue and look up and left for the rock alcove that has the remnants of a small **Native American granary**. You'll ford the river three more times before you get to **Natural Arch** up on the skyline to the southwest. The day hike ends at this point, but you can continue on this trail for a total of 15 miles and end up at a trailhead back in Escalante town.

POLITICS OF GSENM

Since its creation by President Bill Clinton in 1996, Grand Staircase–Escalante National Monument has been a source of controversy, pitting environmentalists against industry. The 1.8 million acres of GSENM made it the second-largest national monument in the country, after Misty Fjords in Alaska, when it was established.

GSENM was thrust back into the headlines in 2017 when President Donald Trump ordered the monument to be reduced by 47%, to just over 1 million acres. The battle headed to the courtroom, where it remains, but on his first day in office in 2021, President Joe Biden called for a review of the changes and later that year restored GSENM's original boundaries.

WHERE TO CAMP AROUND ESCALANTE & BOULDER

Calf Creek Recreation Area Campground
Campground surrounded by canyons with 13 popular, nonreservable sites near the Lower Calf Creek trailhead. $

Escalante Petrified Forest State Park Campground
This 20-site, reservable campground has water, picnic tables, firepits and restrooms with hot showers. $

Backcountry Camping
Dispersed backcountry camping is widely available in GSENM, but you need a (free) permit. $

ROAD TRIP

Highway 12 Scenic Drive

Arguably Utah's most diverse and stunning route, Hwy 12 Scenic Byway winds through rugged canyon land on a 124-mile journey west of Bryce Canyon National Park and ends near Capitol Reef, making for an incredible journey from Zion to Bryce and beyond. The section between the towns of Escalante and Torrey traverses a moonscape of sculpted slickrock, crosses narrow ridgebacks and climbs over high hills.

1 Red Canyon

A sign near the intersection of Hwy 89 and Hwy 12 welcomes you to this 'All-American Road.' Before you hightail it to the hoodoos of Bryce Canyon, stop at the Red Canyon Visitor Center (p107) to get a small taste of the topography on the short hiking trails.

The Drive: Continue east on Hwy 12, driving through two arches blasted open in the 1920s for motor traffic. Turn right on Hwy 63, which leads to the Bryce Canyon entrance.

2 Bryce Canyon National Park

A highlight of southern Utah, this national park (p94) puts on a big geologic show. Hit up the viewpoints along Scenic Dr (p104) and lace up your boots to hike among the hoodoos on Queen's Garden Trail (p96) or the quieter Fairyland Loop (p96).

The Drive: Leave Bryce Canyon on Hwy 63, turning right on Hwy 12. Continue your journey east, savoring the colorful rocks and epic high-desert scenery.

BENEMALE/SHUTTERSTOCK ©

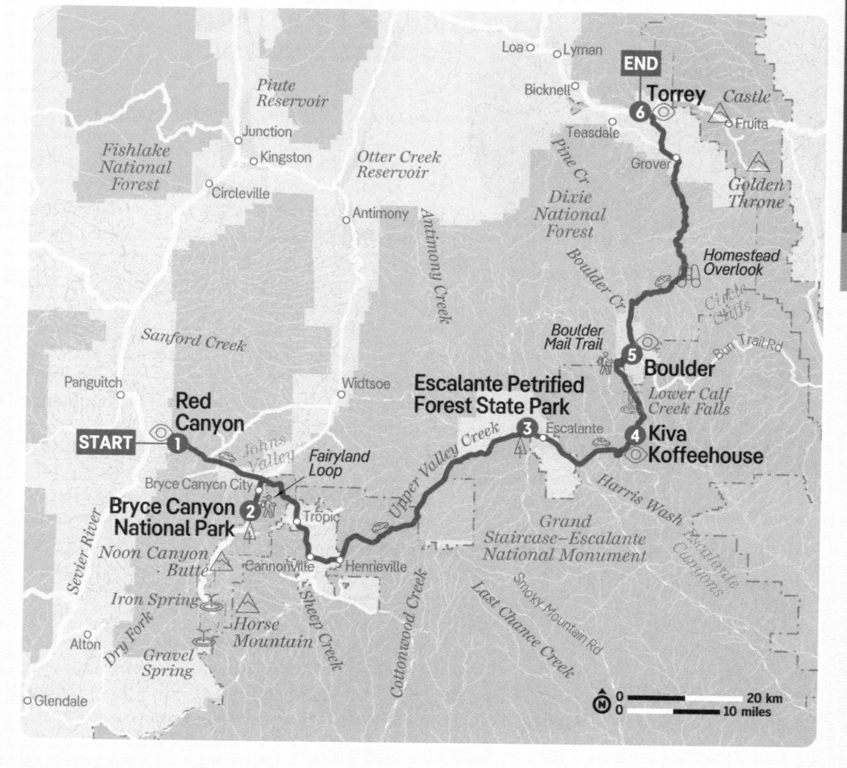

3 Escalante Petrified Forest State Park

Keep the colors bright with a stop at this state park northwest of Escalante. Take the 1-mile hike through lava flows to see thousands of pieces of petrified wood that are millions of years old.

The Drive: On your way east out of town, stop at the roadside info panel at the intersection with Hole-in-the-Rock Rd (p120) that explains the history of the 'longest shortcut.'

4 Kiva Koffeehouse

Take a super-scenic coffee break at Kiva Koffeehouse, set in a round structure built directly into the cliffside. Floor-to-ceiling glass windows wseparated by giant timber beams overlook the expansive canyons beyond. Stretch your legs on the hiking trails around Escalante River, such as Lower Calf Creek Falls (p119), which leads to southern Utah's highest waterfall.

The Drive: Let the car climb up the high and narrow Hogback, a ridge with views for miles, before cruising down into Boulder.

5 Boulder

Until 1940, this isolated outpost received its mail by mule, and it's still so remote that the federal government classifies it as a 'frontier community.' The 16-mile Boulder Mail Trail (p116) traces the historic supply and postal route.

The Drive: Continue onward, stopping at Homestead Overlook about 11 miles outside of town, which sits at nearly 9400ft, the highest point of this drive.

6 Torrey

The unforgettable Hwy 12 comes to an end in tiny Torrey, the gateway town to Capitol Reef (p198). Turn right on Hwy 24 to head to the national park.

Box-Death Hollow

DANITA DELIMONT/SHUTTERSTOCK ©

Backpacking the Boulder Mail Trail

MAIL BY MULE

The 16-mile one-way **Boulder Mail Trail** follows the historic Boulder–Escalante mail route around rugged Box-Death Hollow. Detouring into the slickrock wilderness area provides an interesting extra day's adventure. A free permit is needed for overnight hikes and can be picked up at any visitor center, information kiosk or trailhead register. Beware: poison ivy abounds along the creek banks.

This historic trail was once the supply and mail route between Boulder and Escalante. Much of it is unmarked or follows cairns. Most people do the one-way trip in two days, but a third day allows you to add in some cross-country wandering and further explore Death Hollow.

This hike has serious ups and downs. You start at the **Boulder landing strip**, off Hell's Backbone Rd outside Boulder at 6800ft, and end at the Upper Escalante River trailhead, less than a mile outside Escalante at 5800ft. Arrange a hiker shuttle to and from the trailhead, or just back to your car from the endpoint. Take detailed maps and check with rangers for current conditions. Don't start late: you'll want plenty of light for the final descent.

A mile-long 4WD road leads from the parking lot to the sign marking the start of the Boulder Mail Trail and the flats atop **New Home Bench**. From there, it's 450ft down to the **Sand Creek** drainage, where cottonwoods offer shade and there's water year-round. Next, it's a 400ft trudge back up to the Slickrock Saddle Bench before making the precipitous 900ft drop into **Death Hollow**, a gorgeous riparian canyon named for mules lost on the steep trip down. Death Hollow has several springs at the point where the Mail Trail traverses the canyon. Several campsites lie within 0.25 miles of where the trail meets the creek here.

A strenuous 800ft ascent out of Death Hollow kicks things off on day two. The trail then crosses to a slickrock plateau, descends to the usually dry **Mamie Creek**, and along and over a cracked sandstone formation resembling a giant cerebellum. At **Antone Flat** you come into open country, where a chalky-white slickrock draw may hold water in deep pockets.

After another 900ft slickrock descent, you climb down to **Pine Creek**. The creek's west bank is private, so follow its east bank to the **Escalante River**. To the west, the canyon

BEST PLACES TO STAY IN & AROUND BOULDER

Boulder Mountain Lodge
An ideal place for day-hikers who want to return to high-thread-count sheets, plush terry robes, spa treatments and an outdoor hot tub. $$

Boulder Mountain Guest Ranch
This giant log lodge is in a peaceful 168-acre wilderness west of town with trails, a waterfall and outfitter-led hikes and activities. $$

Kiva Kottage
Two cushy hideaway rooms at the Kiva Koffeehouse with jetted tubs, fireplaces and stellar views; 14 miles south of Boulder. $$

WHERE TO EAT IN BOULDER

Hell's Backbone Grill
This southern Utah must-eat has garnered regional fame as a pioneer in sustainable Southwestern food. $$

Magnolia's Street Food
Rolls filling farm-to-table burritos inside an old Blue Bird school bus. $

Sweetwater Kitchen
Yearly changing Southwestern-flavored menu that uses mostly locally sourced, organic ingredients. $$$

opens, and the trail swings south through the brush, meeting a 4WD road and the Upper Escalante Canyon trailhead.

Must-Do Drive: Burr Trail

LEAVING THE PAVEMENT BEHIND

The most immediately gratifying, dramatic drive in the area, **Burr Trail** is a comprehensive introduction to southern Utah's geology. You pass cliffs, canyons, buttes, mesas and monoliths – in colors from sandy white to deep coral red. Sweeping curves and steep ups and downs add to the attraction. It heads east from Boulder as a paved road, crosses Grand Staircase–Escalante National Monument's northeastern corner and, after 30 miles, arrives at Capitol Reef National Park, where the road becomes loose gravel. The first section can also be done as a challenging road bike ride.

Enter GSENM from Boulder. The seven-site **Deer Creek Campground** has first-come, first-served spaces beside a year-round creek beneath tall trees. There's no potable water, but it does have toilets. Just past the Deer Creek trailhead, look for the towering vertical red-rock slabs of **Long Canyon**. At 11 miles, keep an eye out for an unmarked pullout on the road's left side. You'll see the opening for a side **slot canyon**

CHRIS CURTIS/SHUTTERSTOCK ©

Singing Canyon, Burr Trail

MORE ACTIVITIES IN BOULDER & ESCALANTE

Hell's Backbone Ranch & Trail
Head across the slickrock plateaus or up the forested mountain on a horseback ride.

Escape Goats
Hikes around local slot canyons and herbal tours that teach about traditional medicinal plants. Also runs hiker shuttles.

Excursions of Escalante
For canyoneering trips, Excursions is the best; it offers hiker shuttles and guided photo hikes too.

Boulder Outdoor Survival School
Learn how to survive in this forbidding wilderness. The school operates multiday courses in GSENM, with subjects including primitive living and hunter-gathering.

WHERE TO EAT IN ESCALANTE

Mimi's Bakery & Deli
French-inspired bakery with made-from-scratch pastries, freshly baked artisan bread and delicious quiche. $

Georgie's Outdoor Mexican Cafe
Fill up on burritos, tacos, quesadillas and flavored lemonades at this friendly food truck with outdoor tables. $

Big Bubba's
Hearty portions of barbecue and burgers; the baked beans draw visitors from miles around. $

(nicknamed Singing Canyon) north across a scrubby wash.

Driving out of Long Canyon, stop at the crest for views of the sheer **Circle Cliffs**, which hang like curtains above the undulating valley floor. Still snowcapped in summer, the Henry Mountains rise above 11,000ft on the horizon.

On the right is a turnoff for **Wolverine Loop**, a 25-mile, 4WD road that circles south through an area riddled with scrubland, canyons and cliffs. Several hiking trails lead off from there, and the area is popular with mountain bikers. Continuing on Burr Trail, you cross the plateau of **White Canyon Flat** before the pavement ends and the road meets the giant, angled buttes of the 100-mile Waterpocket Fold in Capitol Reef, the feature that blocked 19th-century settlers' passage west. Trailhead access to Muley Twist Canyon (p191) is nearby.

Just ahead, the **Burr Trail Switchbacks** follow an original wagon route through the fold. You can continue onto Notom-Bullfrog Rd and north to Hwy 24 or south to Glen Canyon. But if you plan to turn around and return to Boulder, first drive the switchbacks – the magnificence and scale of the landscape will blow your mind.

WHAT'S IN A NAME?

Grand Staircase-Escalante is a mouthful, but its long name and large area hint at the region's deep history.

The Grand Staircase consists of sedimentary rock layers that extend from the bottom of the Grand Canyon to the top of Bryce Canyon, showing off over 600 million years of geological history – more than anywhere else on the planet. In 1870, geologist Clarence Dutton described this area as a huge staircase and gave the 'steps' rich names: Chocolate Cliffs, Vermilion Cliffs, White Cliffs, Gray Cliffs and Pink Cliffs.

'Escalante' comes from Silvestre Vélez de Escalante, a Spanish Franciscan missionary who came upon the Grand Canyon in 1776 while scouting for a route from Santa Fe to California.

A Desert Oasis at Upper Calf Creek Falls

BRING YOUR BATHING SUIT

Upper Calf Creek Falls

JEREMY CHRISTENSEN/SHUTTERSTOCK ©

The short (2.2-mile round-trip) but steep and strenuous **Upper Calf Creek Falls Trail** leads down slickrock and through a desert moonscape to two sets of pools and waterfalls that appear like a mirage at the hike's end. Soaking your feet in a moss-covered pool while canyon wrens and mountain bluebirds dart about seems like an impossible dream when you first start your descent. The upper hike might not be as well known or dramatic as Lower Calf Creek Falls, but stick with it and you'll be rewarded with unexpected beauty. The quarter-mile unmarked dirt road to the trailhead is outside of Boulder, on the north side of Hwy 12 between mile markers 80 and 81.

Start at the rim, which overlooks all of **Calf Creek Canyon** and the **Straight Cliffs** beyond. From there, the trail descends 550ft down steep white Navajo sandstone

WHERE TO GLAMP IN ESCALANTE

Escalante Yurts
Splurge-worthy comfortable and spacious yurts on a tranquil 20-acre property north of town. **$$$**

Yonder Escalante
Vintage Airstreams, sleek cabins with panoramic windows and a drive-in movie theater with nightly screenings. **$$$**

Escalante Escapes
Nine thoughtfully designed tiny homes on 4 acres with enough space to sleep six. **$$$**

littered with dark volcanic boulders. Follow the cairns down until the incline levels off. The rock becomes more stratified and colorful just about the time you get a glimpse of treetops in the inner canyon to the west.

Shortly after, you'll come to a fork. Follow cairns down to the left and you'll reach the **lower pool** of the upper trail, a vegetation-covered oasis beneath an 86ft waterfall. Follow the path up to the right for the **upper pools**, where water cascades through shallow potholes and ponds before falling over the rim. Swim if it's warm, look over the canyon edge and appreciate the isolation.

WHAT ARE SLOT CANYONS?

Slot canyons are an iconic feature of Utah's landscape, and it's thought that this state has more than anywhere else in the world.

Slot canyons are formed when water erodes the sandstone or other sedimentary rock into a narrow channel. Water often continues to flow through slot canyons, and they are extremely dangerous places to be when there's even a hint of rain in the forecast.

The towering walls can reach hundreds of feet high, creating a microhabitat that's shaded for much of the day and far cooler than the surroundings. All of Utah's national parks except Bryce contain slot canyons – the Narrows (p54) in Zion National Park is the most famous.

Easy Outing at Lower Calf Creek Falls

SOUTHERN UTAH'S HIGHEST WATERFALL

Lower Calf Creek Falls Trail wanders through a canyon past Native American sites to an impressive waterfall and pool. Lower Calf Creek Falls' beauty is no secret – it can get packed on warm weekends and holidays. Its accessibility – right off Hwy 12 between Escalante and Boulder – makes it a perfect stopover. Though it doesn't climb much, the trail has long sandy stretches that can take a lot out of you. Carry plenty of water. You can fill your bottles at the trailhead.

Lower Calf Creek Falls

Park at the **Calf Creek Recreation Area** (day use $5) and campground, between mile markers 75 and 76 on Hwy 12. As you work your way toward the creek, you pass honeycombed rocks and Navajo sandstone domes, an 800-year-old **Native American granary**, a box canyon where calves were once herded (hence the name Calf Creek), **prehistoric Fremont pictographs** and lush green wetlands. Bring binoculars to get a better view.

Past the last bend, the trail ends in an amphitheater of rock with a 126ft-tall **waterfall** whose thin stream cascades into a large pool. The sandy shore and extended knee-deep wading area before the deeper drop-off make this a favorite for families. The sandy walk out is as strenuous as the walk in, so pace yourself.

WHERE TO GET GROCERIES & SUPPLIES AROUND GSENM

Hills & Hollows
Groceries and organic snacks are available at this Boulder spot year-round; winter hours are limited.

Griffin Grocery
Escalante's only full-selection grocery store; closed Sundays.

Escalante Mercantile
Well-stocked natural grocer with organic products, sandwiches and pastries in Escalante.

EVEN MORE SLOT CANYONS IN GSENM

Zebra Slot
Long hike across open desert scrubland to a short slot canyon that gets its name from its pink and red striped walls.

Tunnel Slot
Accessed from the same trailhead as Zebra Slot, Tunnel is dark and often full of water.

Brimstone Gulch
A shadowy slot canyon with dark stone walls that's less than 3ft wide for much of its length; often added on to a hike after Peekaboo and Spooky Gulch.

LARS BENTRUP/SHUTTERSTOCK ©

Devils Garden, Hole-in-the-Rock Road

Exploring Hole-in-the-Rock Road

IN THE WAGON RUTS OF HISTORY

The history is wilder than the scenery along **Hole-in-the-Rock Road**. From 1879 to 1880, more than 200 pioneering Mormons followed this route on their way to settle southeastern Utah. When the precipitous walls of Glen Canyon on the Colorado River blocked their path, they blasted and hammered through the cliff, creating a hole wide enough to lower their 80 wagons through, a feat honored by the road's name today. The final part of their trail lies submerged beneath Lake Powell.

The road is passable by ordinary passenger cars when dry, except for the last 7 miles, which always require 4WD. Even if you don't drive the entire route, at least visit **Devils Garden**, 12 miles in. Here, rock fists, orbs, spires and fingers rise to 40ft above the desert floor. It's a sandy but fairly short walk from the parking lot to the formations.

About 26 miles in, turn left for **Dry Fork**, with the most well-known slot-canyon day hikes on the road. While there are no facilities, **dispersed camping** is permitted with a free backcountry permit.

ICONIC ROCK FORMATIONS AROUND GSENM

Cosmic Ashtray
Rock bowl filled with bright-orange sand reached by a challenging 8.3-mile hike with no marked trail.

Grosvenor Arch
Rare stone double arch that looms 150ft overhead near Kodachrome Basin State Park.

The Toadstools
Late-afternoon light best shows the shape and depth of these rock features east of Kanab.

The last 7 miles are so rugged that they can take almost as long to traverse as the first 50. The road stops short of the actual Hole-in-the-Rock, but hikers can trek out and scramble down past the 'hole' to Lake Powell in less than an hour.

Hiking the Slot Canyons of Dry Fork

CURVING THROUGH THE CLIFFS

GSENM is famous for its sculpted slot canyons, spillways of brightly colored, weathered rock, and the three slots on this route are some of the most visited in the monument. Expect to encounter pools of water in some. From Hwy 12, drive 26 miles down Hole-in-the-Rock Rd to Dry Fork Rd (Rte 252), turn left and then drive 1.7 miles to the parking area, bearing left at all intersections. The last section of this road may be really rough, in which case you should park and walk the final half-mile to the trailhead parking lot.

The path can be tough to follow, so look for rock cairns and download a trail map before you go. From the parking area, the trail switchbacks steeply down the slickrock, and you find yourself alternately sidestepping and pitching forward. Head toward the reddish-brown dirt hills with little vegetation to the north to reach the bottom of **Coyote Gulch** wash. Follow it north, and when you emerge into an opening, **Dry Fork** slot canyon is immediately to the west. You can walk for miles between undulating orange walls with only a few small boulder step-ups.

Double back to Coyote Gulch and head downstream (east), keeping your eyes peeled for the first slot on the left, **Peekaboo**. You'll have to climb up a 12ft handhold-carved wall (much easier if you're tall or not alone); from there, the slot tightens dramatically and passes under several arches. You may have to navigate some water, and scrambling is required to get to the end. Hikers have climbed up and over Peekaboo to sneak up behind Spooky Gulch, but it requires good orienteering skills or it's easy to get lost.

Retrace your steps to the main wash. A half-mile further downstream, veer left and hike through the sandy wash to **Spooky Gulch**, which is even narrower. The 0.3-mile slot is less technically challenging, but impassable for larger hikers. When you've finished exploring, turn back and return to the trailhead from here.

Dry Fork Slot Canyon

SLOT CANYON SAFETY

Check the Weather Forecast
Do not enter a slot canyon if there's a chance of rain in the vicinity or upstream. Flash floods arrive swiftly and with terrifying force, pushing logs, rocks and debris through the tiny spaces. The summer monsoon season often brings afternoon thunderstorms that unleash buckets of rain in a short amount of time.

Research Your Route
Stop by visitor centers to check conditions and read reviews on apps such as AllTrails to see recent reports from fellow hikers.

SAFE TRAVEL IN GSENM

Drive the Right Vehicle
Many roads through the monument are rough and unpaved, and towing fees are astronomical.

Cell Service Is Unreliable
Download maps before you go, and let someone know where you're headed and for how long.

Check with Rangers
Before you venture into the wilderness, stop by a visitor center for advice and free backcountry permits.

MORE 4WD ADVENTURES

Hell's Backbone Road
Loops a gravel-strewn 48 miles off Hwy 12 between Boulder and Escalante. The original mule mail route crosses the rugged Box-Death Wilderness area. The highlight is a single-lane track atop an impossibly narrow ridge.

Smoky Mountain Road
A challenging 78-mile dirt and gravel road between Escalante and Big Water visitor center. The prime destination is Alstrom Point, a plateau-top vantage with stunning views that include Lake Powell.

Spencer Flat Road
Undulates for 3 miles over gravel and sand through desert, slickrock formations and canyons.

Cliffs, Johnson Canyon Road

Driving Skutumpah & Johnson Canyon Roads

THROUGH CLIFFS AND CANYONS

Together, Skutumpah and Johnson Canyon Rds comprise Grand Staircase–Escalante National Monument's westernmost route. Paved **Johnson Canyon Rd** trundles north for 16 miles to intersect **Skutumpah Rd** (pronounced *scoot*-em-pah). This extremely rutted dirt route (4WD recommended, and sometimes required) continues for 35 miles to Cannonville on Hwy 12. Driving south to north provides the best perspective.

Start out in scenic **Johnson Canyon**, which has distant views of the coral-colored Vermilion Cliffs. About 6 miles along, you'll see the crumbling wooden buildings of the old ***Gunsmoke* set**, where the TV Western was filmed. Soon after, the landscape changes color as the White Cliffs appear to the east.

After 11 miles, take the right fork for Skutumpah Rd. If you don't have the time or the right vehicle to tackle Skutumpah Rd, carry on via the 15-mile Glendale Bench Rd, a much easier 2WD dirt track that leads west to Glendale and Hwy 89.

Numerous old side roads shoot off Skutumpah Rd, so pay attention and keep to the main road. The Gray Cliffs rise to the north and you pass through pastureland before reaching the trailhead for **Lick Wash**. It's 8 miles round-trip on this trail, turning around at Park Wash junction. Uneven stones line part of the way and it can be broiling hot in the canyon, but it's worth doing just the first section to see the scenery.

The road gets steep and rocky before **Bull Valley Gorge**. Stop at the wide spot in the road and walk left along the gorge rim. After about 50ft, look back at the debris beneath the 'bridge' you're about to drive across. Exploring the gorge itself requires rock climbing skills.

Soon after, on the road north, is the trailhead parking lot for Willis Creek (p110), an easy slot-canyon hike. The dramatic Pink Cliffs are the last thing you see before the sharp descent to the valley intersection with Cottonwood Canyon Rd (p109), just south of Cannonville.

GETTING AROUND

Driving a high-clearance 4WD vehicle allows you the most access around GSENM because many roads are unpaved and only occasionally bladed. (Most off-the-lot SUVs and light trucks are not high-clearance vehicles.) Heed all warnings about road conditions. Remember to buy gasoline whenever you see it.

Some outfitters in towns around the monument offer hiker shuttles and 4WD rentals.

KANAB

Vast expanses of rugged desert surround the remote outpost of Kanab. Look familiar? Hundreds of Western movies were shot here. Founded by Mormon pioneers in 1874, Kanab was put on the map by John Wayne and other gun-slingin' celebs in the 1940s and '50s. Just about every resident had something to do with the movies from the 1930s to the '70s. You can still see a couple of movie sets in the area and hear old-timers talk about their roles.

Kanab sits at a major crossroads near Zion and Bryce Canyon and makes a good base for exploring the southern side of GSENM – one of the monument's four visitor centers is here – and Paria Canyon–Vermilion Cliffs formations such as the Wave. Kanab has a great selection of B&Bs and lodgings, and its dining scene offers impressive creativity for such a tiny town.

Kanab

TOP TIP

Budget extra time for Kanab. Tons of trailheads, dinosaur tracks, Hollywood history and fascinating natural features are all near this town, as are three national parks (Zion, Bryce Canyon and Grand Canyon). The delightful staff at Kane County Information Center can assist with your adventure plans.

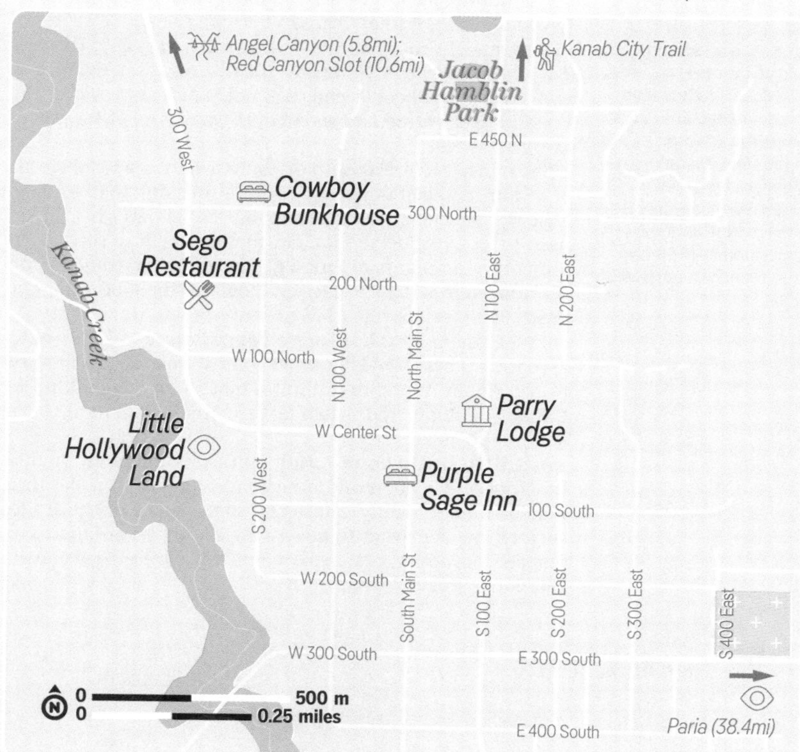

BEST PLACES TO STAY & EAT IN KANAB

Purple Sage Inn
A former Mormon polygamist's home that later became a hotel where Western author Zane Grey stayed. Now it's a B&B with exquisite antique details. $$

Cowboy Bunkhouse
Budget shared and private rooms with a communal feel in the former 1960s county hospital. $

Sego Restaurant
If Kanab is aspiring to be the next Sedona, this boutique hotel-restaurant will fast-track things. The small sharing plates of regional new American cuisine range from foraged mushrooms to pork belly and watermelon. $$

KIT LEONG/SHUTTERSTOCK ©

Little Hollywood Land

Kanab on Screen

READY, SET, ACTION

From *Stagecoach* to *Planet of the Apes*, Kanab has been a favorite filming location since the 1930s. During Kanab's Hollywood heyday, **Angel Canyon** became the site of scores of movies and TV shows, including *The Lone Ranger*, Disney's *The Apple Dumpling Gang* and *The Outlaw Josey Wales*. The cliff ridge above Best Friends Animal Sanctuary is where the Lone Ranger reared and shouted 'Hi-yo Silver!' at the end of every episode.

The movie set at **Paria** (pa-*ree*-uh), where many Westerns were filmed, burnt down in 2006. A 5-mile dirt road leads to a picnic area and an interpretive sign that shows what the set used to look like. Hike 1.5 miles further north to see the rudimentary remnants of **Paria ghost town** and cemetery on the other side of the Paria River. Floods in the 1880s rang the death knell for the 130-strong farming community.

Built in the 1930s, the historic **Parry Lodge** was once movie central. Stars stayed here, and you still can too. From April to November, it shows a nightly history of filmmaking in Kanab at 6:30pm and then a feature film at 7pm in the barn behind the lodge.

At **Little Hollywood Land**, you can wander through a bunkhouse, a saloon and other buildings used in Western movies filmed locally, and learn some tricks of the trade, such as low doorways to make movie stars seem taller. The displays have seen better days, but this classic roadside attraction is free to visit.

GETTING AROUND

Kanab's small downtown is walkable, but you need a car to get any further.

Beyond Kanab

Coral Pink Sand Dunes State Park
Kanab
Wire Pass
The Wave
Buckskin Gulch

Explore miles of weathered, swirling slickrock and unbelievably photogenic slot-canyon systems that can be hiked for days along Hwy 89.

The 112,500-acre Paria Canyon–Vermilion Cliffs Wilderness Area spans the state line between Utah and Arizona and contains some of the Southwest's most famous geologic sights, including the Wave, a natural rock formation striped in mesmerizing bands of red, orange and white. Little known before Microsoft launched Windows 7 in 2009, the Wave was featured as a desktop wallpaper, causing a spike in visitors. Numbers are now strictly controlled and the permits are highly prized.

Kanab is also within day-tripping distance of the lesser-visited but equally spectacular North Rim of the Grand Canyon, which takes four hours to reach by car from the South Rim but only 1¾ hours from southern Utah.

TOP TIP

Apply for and download permits while you have cell service because there's often no signal (or it's unreliable) at the trailheads.

The Wave, Coyote Buttes North (p126)

Shifting Gears at Coral Pink Sand Dunes State Park

A SEA OF SAND

Restless winds move giant Sahara-like sand dunes across the 3730-acre **Coral Pink Sand Dunes State Park**. For lovers of the strange, it's worth the 20-mile trip off Hwy 89 to see the shocking pink-orange hills, the result of eroding Navajo sandstone that's rich in iron oxide. The park is home to the endemic Coral Pink Sand Dunes tiger beetle, one of the rarest insects in the country. Its tiny geographical range is just a 7-mile portion of the park.

Some 90% of the dunes are open to ATV riders, and Coral Pink ATV Tours runs guided trips, including some at sunset. The entire area is open to walkers, and the visitor center rents sand boards and sleds for you to cruise down the dunes.

The park has a 30-site **campground** with toilets and hot showers, but the same winds that shift the dunes can make tent camping unpleasant. Reservations are essential from May to September, and on weekends when off-roaders come to play.

VISITING PIPE SPRING NATIONAL MONUMENT

A vital source of water for desert flora and fauna, the Ancestral Puebloans, the Paiute, and the Mormons who followed them into this stark country, **Pipe Springs** is now a monument to the history of the people who persisted in this landscape. Rangers lead tours of Winsor Castle, a fort built by Mormons in the 1870s, and museum exhibits tell the story of the Kaibab Paiute and modern Paiute culture.

The monument's namesake spring still flows – you can fill up a bottle in the museum with its water. Pipe Spring is on the Kaibab Reservation on the Arizona side of the border, 21 miles from Kanab.

Volunteering at Best Friends Animal Sanctuary

GOTTA PET THEM ALL

Surrounded by more than 33,000 mostly private acres of red-rock desert 5.5 miles north of Kanab, **Best Friends Animal Sanctuary** is the largest no-kill animal-rescue center in the country. Sign up for a tour of the facility that lets you meet some of the more than 1600 horses, pigs, dogs, cats, birds and other critters under its love and care.

You can volunteer, take a dog on a walk and even have a sleepover with one of the adoptable animals. The affiliated accommodations at **Best Friends Roadhouse** in Kanab go beyond pet-friendly to pet-focused, with dog washing stations, a dog park and cubbies for snuggling.

Say Hello to the Wave

THE SOUTHWEST'S MOST COVETED HIKE

The Wave, a geologic formation that's part of the **Coyote Buttes North** area, is one of the most iconic features of the region, and a lucky set of hikers can take on the magical 6.4-mile round-trip hike among swirling, striped slickrock. In the last decade the Wave's popularity has exploded, leading the Bureau of Land Management to require permits for hik-

GUIDES & RESOURCES FOR PARIA CANYON–VERMILION CLIFFS WILDERNESS AREA

Paria Contact Station
This seasonal information center can provide important weather and road updates; 44 miles east of Kanab.

Paria Outpost & Outfitters
Hiker shuttles, guided treks and photo workshops, plus space for tent camping or hanging a hammock.

Dreamland Safari
Hikes with naturalist tour guides to gorgeous backcountry sites and slot canyons reached by 4WD.

ers to see it. A maximum of 64 people per day are allowed to visit, and all permits are issued by lottery: one that takes place months in advance, and the other two days ahead of time. All permits are day-use only; you cannot stay overnight.

Both lotteries must be entered online or through the recreation.gov app – the in-person day-before lottery in Kanab was discontinued in 2022. For the **advance lottery**, you can apply at any time during a particular month for the chance of getting a permit four months in the future. For example, if you want to hike the Wave in April 2025, the lottery opens on December 1, 2024, and closes on December 30. The lottery is drawn on January 1, 2025, and all applicants are contacted with their results. It costs $9 to enter the lottery, and the fee is not refunded if your application is unsuccessful. If you get a permit, you must pay an additional $7 per person (and per dog). The advance lottery awards permits to 48 people or 12 groups, whichever comes first during the drawing process.

Enter the **daily lottery** two days before you want to hike, between 6am and 6pm. You must use the recreation.gov phone app and be located in a geofenced area that spans from the eastern entrance of Zion National Park through Kanab and Big Water, UT, and south into Fredonia and Page, AZ. Successful applicants are notified at 7:15pm and have until 8am the next day to open the app, claim the permits and pay the additional fees. Hikers must also attend a safety briefing the day before the hike. The daily lottery issues the remainder of the permits to 16 people or four groups.

Permits are issued every day of the year, but be aware that hiking is not always safe or possible. Thousands of people apply for both lotteries and the chances of winning a permit are slim – some sources say about 4%. Fortunately, the area has plenty else to do if you aren't one of the chosen ones.

Coyote Buttes North is a remote backcountry area that is undeveloped wilderness. The road to get to the trailhead for the Wave is unpaved and rarely maintained. Hikers in a 2WD

TIPS ON WINNING THE LOTTERY

Gather a Group
Apply as a group and have every member of the group submit their own applications. This method costs more but improves your odds. The maximum group size is six. Don't list other members of the group as alternatives on one permit; this disqualifies their applications.

Enter Multiple Dates
The advance lottery allows you to include three dates for the month you want to hike.

Apply in Winter
Fewer people visit in December, January and February, increasing your odds.

VWAGNER/SHUTTERSTOCK ©

The Wave, Coyote Buttes North

THE WAVE ALTERNATIVES

Coyote Buttes South
You have to enter a similar lottery – and only 20 permits are available per day – but they are less in demand. Having a 4WD vehicle and experience driving in deep sand are required to reach this remote area.

Wire Pass
Popular slot-canyon day hike (p128) that starts at the same trailhead as the Wave.

Lick Wash
Slot with more solitude; after a mile-long squeeze, the narrows open up into a wider scenic canyon.

Slot canyon, Buckskin Gulch

high-clearance vehicle can often reach the trailhead, but 4WD is better and might be required when the road is wet. The hike requires some wayfinding, so be sure that everyone in your group is up for the challenge.

Tour companies, such as Kanab-based **Dreamland Safari**, offer guided trips to the Wave for permit-holders and are a good option if you don't have the right vehicle to tackle the bumpy road. Guides can also point out formations and features along the route that you might otherwise miss, including dinosaur tracks.

Hiking Wire Pass & Backpacking Buckskin Gulch

WORLD'S LONGEST SLOT-CANYON SYSTEM

Wire Pass (3.4-miles round-trip) is a great slot-canyon day hike. You descend a sandy wash to where the gorge becomes a slot canyon, narrowing to shoulder width in places. You'll scramble down a few boulder-choked sections and under logs jammed 50ft overhead before reaching a wide alcove with what was likely an ancient granary ledge. Look for the **petroglyph panel** at the far end.

Wire Pass dead-ends at the confluence with **Buckskin Gulch**, the planet's longest slot canyon. Stop here (1.2 miles along) or continue exploring the Buckskin slot canyon as far north or south as you like. At times, there may be water in one or both of the canyons. The parking lot is 8 miles south along House Rock Valley Rd and shares a trailhead with the Wave. Day-use permits are required and cost $6. Buy one in advance on recreation.gov or pay in cash at the trailhead. Cell service is unreliable, so don't count on purchasing a permit on your phone once you're there.

For a longer trip, backpackers can continue from Wire Pass through Buckskin Gulch to the **White House** trailhead for a 21-mile journey over two days. This route isn't for the faint of heart. The canyon has few sources of drinking water, and dangers include rattlesnakes, potential flash floods, deep mud and quicksand. Rock obstructions could require rope to descend safely, and you might have to swim through stagnant pools of cold water. Permits for overnight use are required ($5, in addition to the $6 day fee) and are limited to 20 people per day.

On the Edge at the Grand Canyon's North Rim

A SOLITARY STUNNER

The remote, wild and forgotten **North Rim** is far less developed and sees far fewer visitors than its southern counterpart, but arguably it's Grand Canyon plus. The elevation is a little higher, the temperatures are a little cooler, the trails are a little steeper and the views might really be a little bigger. Because this section gets more rain and snow, erosion has chewed deeper into the North Rim, creating mazes of side canyons while leaving sky islands and temples towering above the Colorado River.

The North Rim is an easily doable day trip, 81 miles south of Kanab on Hwy 89A, but beware of its long seasonal closure. At these altitudes (8000ft), the winter snows shut things down between October 15 and May 15 – and possibly longer.

Get your bearings at the small but informative **visitor center** and then put it all in perspective with the view from **Bright Angel Point**, a spectacular viewpoint at the end of the knife-edge ridge. Spend the rest of the morning hiking through meadows and aspen on the **Widforss Trail**, which concludes at a dramatic overlook. Although it's a relatively popular day hike, people disperse quickly, and you likely won't see more than a few other explorers. In the afternoon, drive out to **Point Imperial** – at 8819ft, the highest viewpoint in Grand Canyon National Park – soak up the view and then backtrack and continue on to **Cape Royal Point** to the south. Strategically located at the southernmost tip of the North Rim, high above the great westward turn of the Colorado River, Cape Royal takes in almost every major part of the Grand Canyon with expansive views.

TAKING THE MOUNTAIN BIKE TO TILTED MESA

Still under construction at the time of research but slated to open in summer 2023, **Tilted Mesa** is made up of 13 miles of single-track mountain biking trails across 400 acres on three mesas. These tracks are best for intermediate or advanced riders, though some trails fall on the easier side of intermediate – unfortunately, beginners are out of luck. The ride takes you through patches of juniper and piñon with views of the valleys below.

To find the trailhead, take Hwy 89 east of Kanab. After 9.3 miles, turn right onto Kane County Rd 3200. Drive south for 1 mile and head left at the fork. After 300ft, turn right (uphill) for the parking lot.

GETTING AROUND

A 4WD vehicle is best for accessing many trails and necessary for more remote adventures. Expect washboard surfaces, washed-out roadbeds, deep wallows of sand and mud. Don't attempt to drive on clay-surface roads when the rain turns them into a quagmire, and never attempt to cross a flash flood – it may look only a few inches deep, but that's assuming the road surface is still where it's supposed to be.

ARCHES, CANYONLANDS & SOUTHEAST UTAH

WONDERS OF WIND AND WATER

Experience earth's beauty at its most elemental in this rocky and rugged desert corner of the Colorado Plateau.

Beyond the few pine-clad mountains, there's little vegetation to hide the impressive handiwork of time, water and wind in southeast Utah. Thousands of red-rock curves dot Arches National Park, a cauldron of geologic wonders that includes balanced rocks, a swath of giant rock fins and one span that's so photogenic it's emblazoned on Utah license plates. A stone's throw across the highway is equally stunning Canyonlands National Park, a maze of plateaus, mesas and sheer-walled river gorges as forbidding as it is beautiful.

Moab, whose northern tip is barely 3 miles from the Arches Visitor Center, is one of the most adventure-loving towns in the US, with as much four-wheeling, white-knuckle river rafting and outfitter-guided fun as you can handle. It's also the mountain biking capital of the country, thanks to the surrounding desert slickrock that makes a perfect 'sticky' surface for knobbly tires. Moab makes every activity you can dream of accessible, no matter your appetite for adrenaline. At the end of the day, you can bed down at a local campsite, a retro roadside motel or a high-thread-count hotel.

Moab and its two national parks can sometimes feel overwhelmed in the April to October busy season, but it's not hard to lose the crowds while looking for Ancestral Puebloan rock art and dwellings in miles of isolated and undeveloped lands in this southeastern corner of the state.

Inset: Hell's Revenge (p159); Opposite: Double O Arch (p142)

THE MAIN AREAS

ARCHES NATIONAL PARK
Earth's highest density of rock arches.
p136

CANYONLANDS: ISLAND IN THE SKY DISTRICT
Plateau-top perch above river-carved canyons.
p146

MOAB
Activity-filled town with something for every traveler.
p154

CANYONLANDS: NEEDLES DISTRICT
Desert solitude among the pinnacles.
p168

Find Your Way

As in the rest of Utah, the distances between the national parks, trailheads and other worthy sights and activities are vast so having a car is essential for getting around.

Arches National Park, p136

Giant sweeping arcs of sandstone frame snowy peaks and desert landscapes while whimsical rock formations give a taste of Mother Nature's magic.

Moab, p154

Get ready to play in southeast Utah's adventure base camp, where any activity is possible in the surrounding canyons, mountains, deserts and rivers.

Canyonlands: Island in the Sky District, p168

Look thousands of feet down over the plateau edge to see the ribbon of river responsible for this spectacular scene.

Tower Arch
Sand Dune Arch
Fiery Furnace
Delicate Arch
Arches National Park
Double Arch
Moab
Colorado River
Colorado River
Upheaval Dome
Island in the Sky
Aztec Butte
Canyonlands National
La Sal

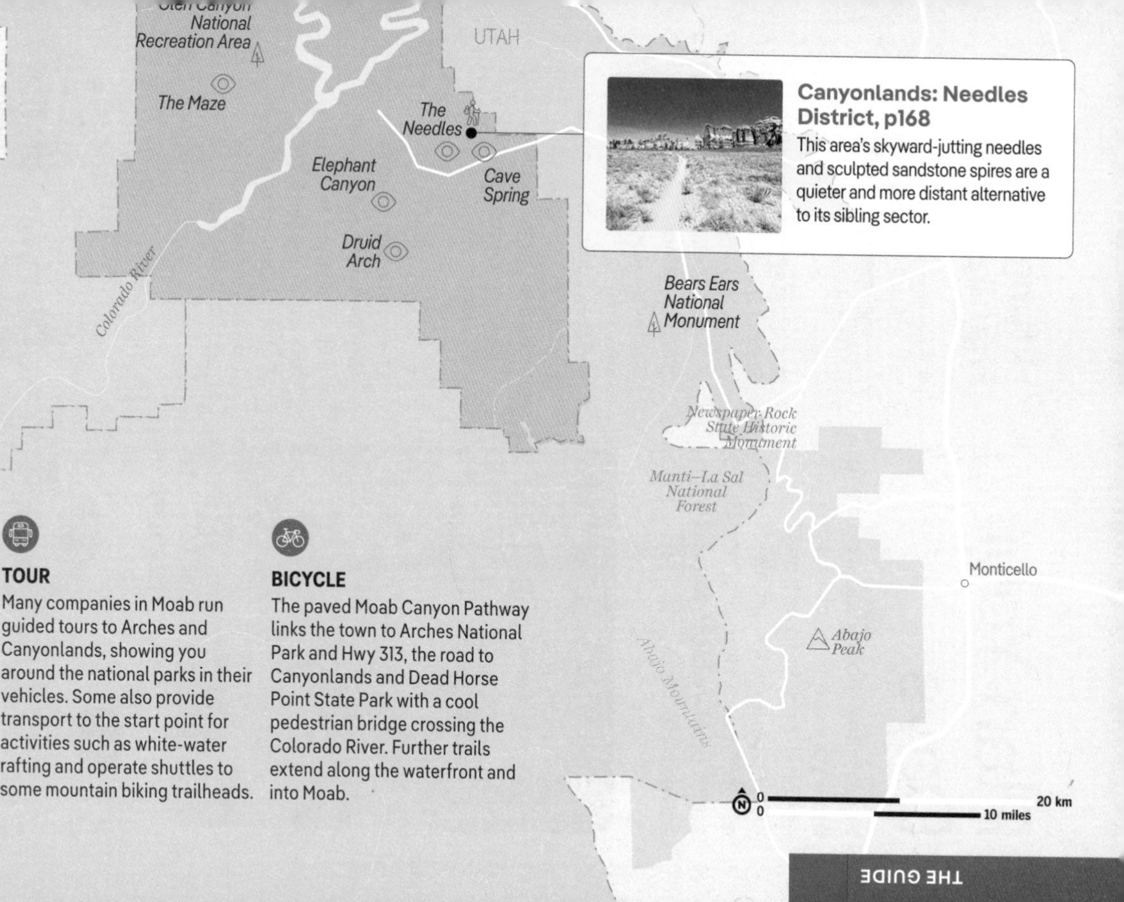

Canyonlands: Needles District, p168

This area's skyward-jutting needles and sculpted sandstone spires are a quieter and more distant alternative to its sibling sector.

CAR

A car is a necessity to visit all the nooks and crannies of this corner of Utah. Having a high-clearance 4WD vehicle – and the requisite experience to drive it – means you can get off the beaten track, accessing remote trailheads and backroads beyond Moab.

TOUR

Many companies in Moab run guided tours to Arches and Canyonlands, showing you around the national parks in their vehicles. Some also provide transport to the start point for activities such as white-water rafting and operate shuttles to some mountain biking trailheads.

BICYCLE

The paved Moab Canyon Pathway links the town to Arches National Park and Hwy 313, the road to Canyonlands and Dead Horse Point State Park with a cool pedestrian bridge crossing the Colorado River. Further trails extend along the waterfront and into Moab.

Plan Your Days

Moab is the most logical place to base yourself to pack in as much national-park time as possible. Don't overlook the smaller towns of Monticello, Blanding and Bluff, south on Hwy 191, to extend your adventure.

MARGARET.WIKTOR/SHUTTERSTOCK ©

Balanced Rock Trail (p144)

Hitting the Highlights

- If you have just a day or two, base yourself in **Moab** (p154) and start early to explore **Arches National Park** (p136).
- Take the **scenic drive** (p144) along the park's main road, stopping to stretch your legs on short hikes such as **Park Avenue** (p144), the **Windows** (p137) and **Balanced Rock** (p144).
- Admire **Delicate Arch** (p138) from afar and investigate the Native petroglyphs and historic 20th-century wood cabin near the trailhead.
- Hop across the highway to **Canyonlands' Island in the Sky District** (p146), soaking in the spectacular scene from the expansive **Grand View Point** (p151) and the mysterious **Upheaval Dome** (p149).

SEASONAL HIGHLIGHTS

Crowds flock to southeast Utah from spring to fall and Arches has implemented a timed entry system from 7am to 4pm between April 1 and October 31. Moab loves a party and throws them regularly.

JANUARY

Winter dusts the arches and canyons with powdered-sugar **snow**. Campgrounds and trails are quiet but freezing cold.

MARCH

Take off on two wheels during the **Skinny Tire Festival**, with rides in scenic locations around Moab, including the parks.

APRIL

In the lead-up to Easter, thousands of Jeeps and their drivers rock up in Moab for **Jeep Safari**.

JULIA MCHUGH/SHUTTERSTOCK ©, VANDATHAI/SHUTTERSTOCK ©, OGLETREE PHOTOGRAPHY/SHUTTERSTOCK ©

Stacking Up the Arches

- With more time, conquer the longer hikes in Arches, Canyonlands and beyond. Bag a bounty of arches in **Devils Garden** (p142) and mark your calendar in advance to snag a coveted permit for **Fiery Furnace** (p140).

- Wake up for sunrise at **Mesa Arch** (p150) at Island in the Sky and get out of town to admire **Corona Arch** (p162).

- Drive south to **Canyonlands' Needles district** (p168), stopping to ponder the petroglyphs at **Newspaper Rock** (p173) on the route to the park entrance, before beholding a thousand years of Native and cowboy history on the **Cave Spring Trail** (p169).

More in Moab & Beyond

- Moab dishes up an impossible-to-choose-just-one buffet of activities – gorge yourself. Get wet on a wild **white-water rafting trip** (p157) on the Colorado or a multiday river adventure through the canyons.

- Ride the roller-coaster of roads on a **mountain bike** (p156) or in a **4WD vehicle** (p159), or stick to the paved but equally stunning **Colorado River Scenic Byway** (p167) and **La Sal Mountain Loop** (p165).

- Head further afield to plunge into the past at lesser-visited sites that showcase Native history and living heritage, such as **Bears Ears National Monument** (p173), **Hovenweep National Monument** (p175) and **Monument Valley** (p177) on the Arizona state line.

MAY

In years of good rain, **wildflowers** bloom in a rainbow of colors, especially swaths of orange globe mallow along the highways.

JULY

Moab is filled with free festivals, including a summer **concert** and **film series** on Friday nights in Swanny Park.

AUGUST

Moab Music Festival features world-class classical, jazz and Latin musicians and even has full floating concerts on the Colorado River.

NOVEMBER

Enjoy folk music, jam sessions and demos accompanied by food, drinks and art at **Moab Folk Festival**.

ARCHES NATIONAL PARK

Giant arcs of sandstone frame snowy peaks and desert landscapes at Arches National Park, home to 2000 rock arches, the highest density of anywhere on Earth. You'll lose all perspective on size at some, such as the thin and graceful Landscape Arch – among the largest in the world – which stretches 306ft across. A scenic drive through the heart of the park makes the spectacular arches accessible to all. Arches has many short trails, but is geared more toward drivers than hikers, with most of the main sights close to paved roads.

This wildly popular park saw 73% more visitors between 2011 and 2021, hitting a high of 1.8 million, leading officials to implement a timed entry system. If you're planning to visit between 7am and 4pm from April through October, you must reserve an hour-long entry window on recreation.gov, which costs $2 and does not include the park entry fee.

TOP TIP

Services are limited inside Arches. The park doesn't have anywhere to buy food or any non-camping accommodations. Cell phones usually do not work beyond the visitor center. Come prepared: bring supplies for a picnic if you're planning to stay for the full day. Download maps and apps before you arrive.

ADAM SPRINGER/SHUTTERSTOCK ©

Delicate Arch (p145)

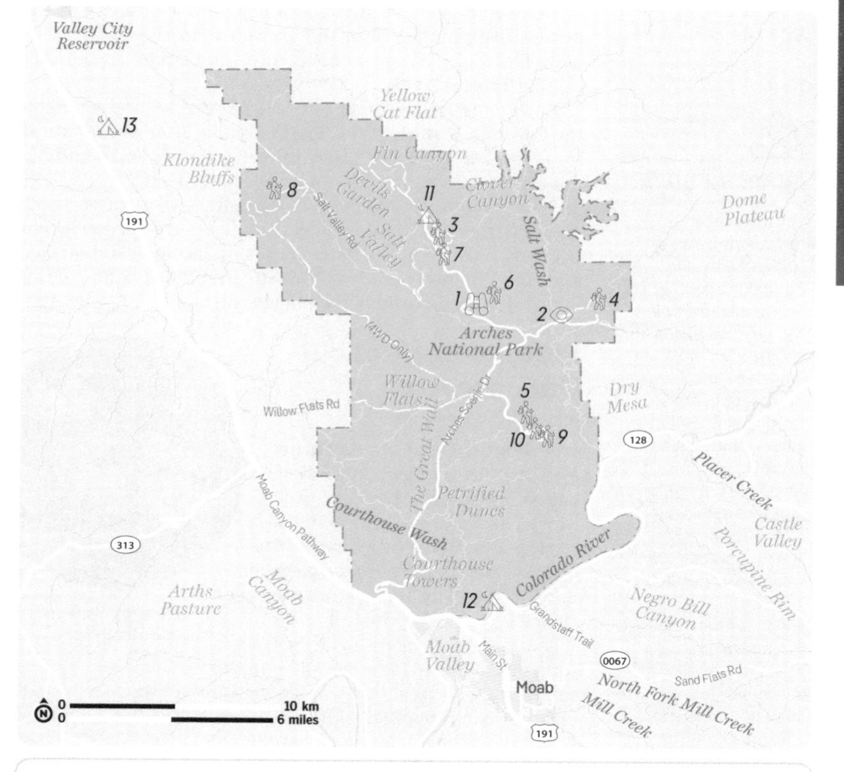

HIGHLIGHTS
1 Fiery Furnace Viewpoint
2 Wolfe Ranch

ACTIVITIES
3 Broken Arch
4 Delicate Arch
5 Double Arch
6 Fiery Furnace
7 Sand Dune Arch
8 Tower Arch
9 Windows Primitive Loop
10 Windows Trail

SLEEPING
11 Devils Garden Campground
12 Goose Island Campground
13 North Klondike Campground

Windows on a Sandstone World

SEEING DOUBLE

North Window

The **Windows Trail** is an easy 1-mile loop that gently climbs to three massive photogenic arches: North Window, South Window and Turret Arch. It's hard to grasp the immensity of these gigantic marvels until you're beside them.

This hike is one of the busiest in the park, but you can leave some of the crowds behind by returning on the longer **Windows Primitive Loop**, with a beautiful back view of the two windows. The primitive trail is less obvious and doesn't have as many trail markers.

The path forks about 500ft from the lot. Take the left fork and head to the **North Window**, which measures 51ft high and 93ft wide and frames the distant desert. A spur trail (part of the Windows Primitive Loop) heads to the **South Window**, sitting higher from the ground than the North Window. The main Windows Loop trail then circles to the castle-like **Turret Arch**.

For a bonus arch, head back to the parking lot and set off on the 0.6-mile **Double Arch Trail**. Double Arch is the tallest in the park at 112ft and you're allowed to walk and scramble underneath the arch (but not on the arch itself).

The National Park Service considers parts of these trails 'barrier free,' and some wheelchair users can access them with assistance. Double Arch Trail has a hard-packed surface and the Windows trail is flat for the first 300ft before arriving at stone steps and other uneven surfaces.

AN ARCH IS BORN

The magnificent formations in Arches National Park and throughout southern Utah are created by the varying erosion of sandstone, mudstone, limestone and other sedimentary layers. When water freezes and expands in cracks, it forms fins: thin, soaring, wall-like features. When portions of the rock break away underneath, an arch results.

These formations are forever in flux and they all eventually lose to gravity, breaking and disappearing. The most recent notable collapse happened in 2008, when 71ft-wide Wall Arch thunderously fell to the ground overnight. As you stroll beneath these monuments to nature's power, listen carefully, especially in winter and you may hear spontaneous popping noises – it's the sound of the future forming.

Picture-Perfect Delicate Arch

HIKING TO A UTAH ICON

You've seen **Delicate Arch** before: it's the unofficial state symbol, stamping nearly every Utah tourist brochure and gracing license plates. While two **viewpoints** provide perspective (and an easier hike) from below, the best way to experience the arch is close up.

Petroglyphs, Wolfe Ranch

The trail to Delicate Arch may seem interminable on the way up, but the rewards are so great that you'll quickly forget the toil, provided you wear rubber-soled hiking shoes and drink a quart of water along the way – there is zero shade. This hike is the most popular long trail at Arches and it's best tackled early in the day, when you'll feel less like an ant under a magnifying glass.

From the parking lot, take the short, easy walk to **Wolfe Ranch**, a one-room cabin built in 1907. Cross the footbridge over Salt Wash for a look at a small **petroglyph panel**. Likely carved by the Ute after 1600 CE, the markings show people on horseback. The trail is wheelchair-accessible to this point.

Past the panel, the path climbs a series of small switchbacks, soon emerging onto a long, steady slickrock slope. This hill is visible from the trailhead, where you'll see tiny figures trudging up the slickrock like pilgrims.

Delicate Arch remains hidden as the trail skirts behind a narrow slickrock ledge. As you round the final corner, a broad sandstone amphitheater opens up below, with Delicate Arch crowning its rim, framing the 12,700ft La Sal Mountains in

WHERE TO CAMP IN & AROUND ARCHES

Devils Garden Campground
The only place to stay inside the park. Extremely popular; book months in advance. $

Goose Island Campground
These first-come, first-served BLM campsites, the closest to the park entrance, fill by morning. $

North Klondike Campground
Opened in 2022; few facilities (no toilets), but close to top-notch mountain biking trails. $

the distance. Circle the rim to the base of the arch, which sits atop a saddle that drops precipitously on either side.

Sand Dune & Broken Arches

AN ARCHES ASSORTMENT

This varied walk leads through rock fins, cool sand dunes and slickrock, giving a taste of Fiery Furnace for those who aren't able to get a permit. It's a good spot for kids, especially Sand Dune Arch, but savvy adult hikers might find it too tame. Even though the hike is short, there's precious little shade along the trail, so bring plenty of water and come early in the day.

From the Sand Dune Arch parking area, follow the trail through deep sand between narrow stone walls that are the backmost fins of Fiery Furnace (p140). In less than a quarter of a mile, you'll arrive at 30ft-wide **Sand Dune Arch**, which looks something like a poodle kissing a polar bear.

From here, you can go left to return to your car or go right across open grassland en route to 60ft **Broken Arch**. At the next fork (the start of the loop trail), grasses give way to piñon and juniper along a gentle climb to Broken Arch, which despite its name isn't broken – yet. The treat here is the walk

DAN SEDRAN/SHUTTERSTOCK ©

Sand Dune Arch

AWAY FROM THE CROWDS

Even in a national park that sees thousands of visitors a day, it's possible to find sections of solitude in Arches.

The timed entry system introduced in 2022 has helped manage the traffic, but visiting outside of these times (7am to 4pm from April through October) is bound to be quieter still, plus arriving early or late also means you won't be hiking in the blazing sun. Visitor numbers usually peak around Memorial Day (late May) and Labor Day (early September).

Arches' more challenging hikes, such as the Devils Garden Primitive Trail (p142), are less visited, as are the trailheads off dirt roads, such as Tower Arch (p143).

RANGER PROGRAMS AT ARCHES NATIONAL PARK

Patio Talk
Head to the visitor center at 10am daily for a free talk from a ranger.

Evening Program
Hour-long session starting at 9pm on varying topics at the Devils Garden Campground Amphitheater.

Windows Guided Walks
Interpretive hike around the Windows area. Free and no reservation required; check online for timings.

OUTSTANDING ARCHES

Karen Garthwait, Acting Public Affairs Specialist at Arches, has worked at the national park for more than a decade. These are some of her favorite features.

Double Arch
Over 100ft high, this arch in the Windows section is the park's tallest. You can see it from your car, but it's worth the half-mile walk to stand beneath and gaze up in wonder.

Baby Arch
Most arches aren't labeled on the park map. This one near the Courthouse Towers is a great reminder to keep an eye out for hidden treasures.

Delicate Arch
The park's most famous feature. I recommend the easy Lower Viewpoint walk; the long hike up is like climbing 50 flights of stairs.

MARAP/SHUTTERSTOCK ©

Tapestry Arch

through the arch atop a slickrock ledge, taking photos from both sides and admiring the often snow-capped La Sal Mountains in the background.

You can return to the parking lot or complete the loop through Devils Garden Campground. Dedicated arch hunters should tack on **Tapestry Arch**, accessible from a short spur trail.

Finding Your Way Through Fiery Furnace

ARCHES' LABYRINTH

So named because of its spectacular rock formations that glow red and orange in the sunset, the narrow sandstone maze of Fiery Furnace has no marked trails and provides an extra level of adventure for hikers. Because of the extreme nature of wayfinding here (online maps and GPS do not work well because of the high canyon walls), as well as sections that require jumping across ledges and shimmying through

GEOLOGY WORDS TO KNOW

Fin
Wall of sedimentary rock that remains after surrounding surfaces have been eroded away.

Desert Varnish
Drip-like red or black mineral coating on rock surfaces; petroglyphs are often carved into it.

Tafoni
Water-caused weathering that etches honeycomb or Swiss-cheese-like formations into the rock.

crevices, permits are required – the only hike in Arches where they are mandatory.

Permits come in two flavors: ranger-led ($16 per person) or self-guided ($10 per person). Purchase them on recreation.gov a week in advance, but be quick – they sell out within minutes. Ranger tours cover 2 miles and last 2½ hours.

The National Park Service recommends that people hiking Fiery Furnace for the first time go on a ranger-guided tour or with someone who has been before. If you get a self-guided permit, you can have a group of up to six people and all members of the hiking party must watch an educational video and listen to an orientation talk before setting off on the hike.

Permits must be picked up the day before or the day of the hike at the Arches Visitor Center, which opens at 7:30am. Make sure you leave enough time to drive from the visitor center to the trailhead, which takes 30 to 45 minutes. Permit holders do not have to get timed-entry tickets to the park.

If you don't manage to snag a hiking permit, you can still survey the scene from the Fiery Furnace viewpoint (p145).

QUOTH THE RAVEN

One of the most common wildlife sightings in Arches National Park is of the majestic common raven (*Corvus corax*). Ravens are some of the smartest birds in the world, thanks to their large brains and they are able to problem-solve, imitate and communicate about distant finds.

These birds have more than 30 types of call, which you might hear echoing off the sandstone walls. In addition to the standard calls you might expect, ravens can also mimic sounds from their surroundings, including human speech.

Keep an eye – and an ear – out for this species around the park.

JON G. FULLER/VWPICS/ALAMY STOCK PHOTO ©

Fiery Furnace

TYPES OF ARCHES & OPENINGS

Freestanding Arch
Independently standing formations; the most popular arches in the park fall into this category.

Cliff Wall Arch
Next to rock walls and cliffs; often hard to spot unless you're standing below it.

Non-Arch Opening
To qualify as an arch, the rock must have an opening of at least 3ft in one direction.

DEVIL OF A TIME: HIKING DEVILS GARDEN

At the paved road's end, 19 miles from the visitor center, Devils Garden trailhead marks the beginning of a hike that passes eight arches. Most people only go 1.3 miles to Landscape Arch, a gravity-defying, 306ft-long behemoth that's the largest in North America. Further along, the trail gets less crowded as it grows rougher and steeper.

From the **1 Devils Garden trailhead**, the route passes through large rock fins before an offshoot trail heads to **2 Tunnel Arch** and **3 Pine Tree Arch**. Back on the main path, the long and thin **4 Landscape Arch** appears. Beyond this arch, the trail becomes more difficult, sometimes requiring scrambling and route-finding, so some hikers choose to turn back. The path climbs through and then over a rock fin, reaching a spur trail to **5 Partition Arch** and low-to-the-ground **6 Navajo Arch**. Back on the main route, continue gaining elevation and lofty views before dropping down and around the backs of the fins to **7 Double O Arch**, where a much larger arch sits atop a smaller one. Add on a side trip to **8 Dark Angel**, a 150ft rock column standing on its own. For an extra dose of adventure, those confident in their wayfinding skills should head back toward Double O Arch and then set off on the **9 Primitive Trail**. This route wiggles through fins and is marked by cairns, but it's helpful to have a map pre-downloaded. If you're not arched-out, head to the quiet **10 Private Arch** before working your way down fins and back onto flat ground. Soon you'll reconnect with the main trail near Landscape Arch, which leads back to the trailhead.

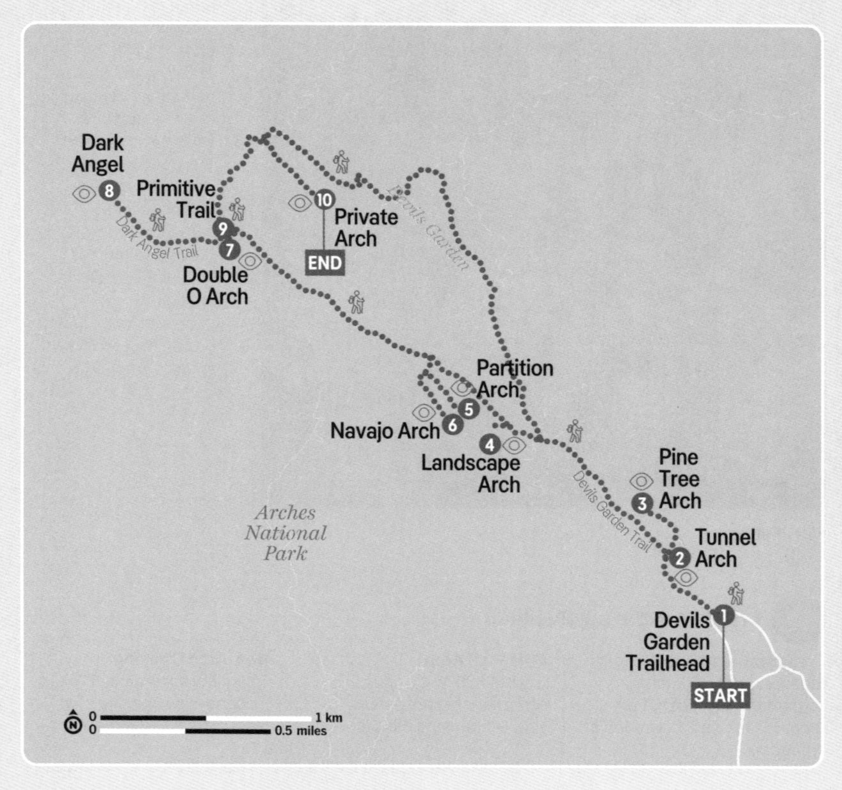

Ups & Downs Around Tower Arch

GETTING OFF THE BEATEN TRACK

On the park map but not signposted from the main road, **Tower Arch** is in the Klondike Bluffs section of Arches National Park, accessible on a dirt road (Salt Valley Rd) that's suitable for standard sedans in dry conditions. Most visitors never come to this remote corner, but this area had the only vehicle access to the park when it first opened. There's still an unmanned entrance, but you won't save any time getting into Arches this way.

The 3.5-mile out-and-back hike to Tower Arch, almost certainly the least-visited trailhead in the park, ascends steeply up the Klondike Bluffs for a short segment, allowing you to catch your breath and views at the top. The route carries on through a flat wash and then climbs up through deep sand to the rock fins and arches. To your left (southeast), look out for the **Marching Men**, a phalanx of huge rock pinnacles lined up in formation. The hike curves around and soon arrives at the namesake arch, where you can scramble up a short distance for a snack and a photo.

If you have the right vehicle, you can take the rough 4WD-only road around the back, shortening the hike to Tower Arch to just a quarter of a mile.

This trail has few signs but is marked with occasional cairns, so it's helpful to have a map pre-downloaded.

Tower Arch

LIVING SOIL

Signs around Arches National Park implore hikers to watch their step and not 'bust the crust.' Cryptobiotic crust, also known as biological soil crust, covers and protects desert soils, literally gluing sand particles together so they don't blow away.

Cyanobacteria, one of earth's oldest life forms, start the process by extending mucous-covered filaments into dry soil. Over time, these filaments and the sand particles adhering to them form a thin crust that is colonized by algae, lichen, fungi and mosses.

This crust stores rainwater and reduces erosion. Unfortunately, the thin crust is easily fragmented under heavy-soled boots and tires. Once broken, the crust takes 50 to 250 years to repair itself.

GETTING AROUND

Driving is the best and easiest way to get around Arches National Park. There is no shuttle system or public transport. Some companies in Moab run bus tours through the park.

Admiring the Arches on a Desert Drive

Hitting all the highlights, this paved drive on the park's main road visits Arches' strange forms and flame-colored desert landscapes. The route is packed with photo ops and short walks to arches and iconic landmarks. We've included the six best stops here, but geology nerds and eager hikers have plenty more viewpoints and information panels to pick from, which are well-signed along the road from the visitor center.

1 Park Avenue

You might not need to stretch your legs yet, but hop out of the car to stroll Park Avenue – or at least visit the viewpoint. While it doesn't have any arches on display, it's a good geological showcase. At the end of the hike (or from the road as you drive onward), look for the Three Gossips, a towering rock trio sharing a secret.

The Drive: Go on for 5.5 miles, stopping as you'd like at the scenic viewpoints.

2 Balanced Rock

Balanced Rock, a 3600-ton boulder as big as a naval destroyer, teeters on a spindly pedestal that shoots from the ground like a fist. The 15-minute loop trail helps you grasp its actual size (128ft to the top of the rock) and provides a good look at the forces of erosion at work. There is wheelchair access to the viewpoint.

The Drive: Turn right onto Windows Rd, which ends at two trailheads.

GMELAND/SHUTTERSTOCK ©

Park Avenue

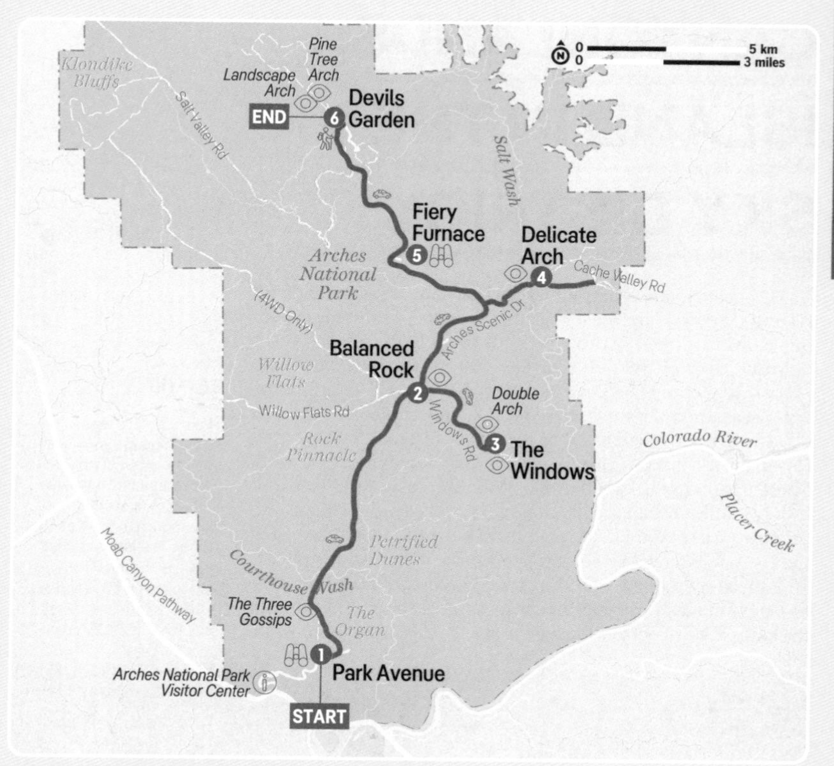

3 The Windows

Get up close to the arches on this short trail to a rock fin with two ginormous openings (p137). From a separate trailhead across the parking lot, you can clamber around the base of Double Arch.

The Drive: Head back to the park's main road and turn right. After 3 miles, turn right at the intersection with Delicate Arch Rd.

4 Delicate Arch

Delicate Arch (p138) is an unofficial state symbol of Utah. A 3-mile hike leads to it; otherwise, two viewpoints further along the road allow a glimpse. The Lower Viewpoint is an easy 150ft walk, or you can bear left for a moderately strenuous 0.5-mile hike and 200ft ascent to the better Upper Viewpoint.

The Drive: Return to the main road, turning right. After 2.5 miles, turn right at signs for Fiery Furnace.

5 Fiery Furnace

A permit is required to hike Fiery Furnace (p140), but the viewpoint is open to all. A short walk between split-rail fences leads to the overlook of giant fins of Entrada sandstone. At sunset, they resemble flames in a furnace.

The Drive: Follow the main road to its end, where it loops near the Devils Garden trailhead.

6 Devils Garden

The Devils Garden trail (p142) takes in a huge number of arches. Tunnel Arch and Pine Tree Arch are closest to the parking lot, or a moderately easy walk goes to Landscape Arch, the span of which is longer than a football field.

CANYONLANDS: ISLAND IN THE SKY DISTRICT

Canyonlands National Park
Islands in the Sky District

A 527-sq-mile vision of ancient Earth, Canyonlands National Park is Utah's largest – and least visited – national park. Vast serpentine canyons tipped with white cliffs loom high over the Colorado and Green Rivers, their waters 1000ft below the rim rock. Skyward-reaching needles and spires, deep craters, swirling tie-dye mesas and majestic buttes dot the landscape.

The two rivers form a Y that divides the park into four separate districts, inaccessible to one another from within the park. Cradled atop the Y, Island in the Sky is the most developed and visited district because of its proximity to the town of Moab and the entrance to Arches National Park, both about 30 miles from the visitor center. You'll comprehend space in new ways atop the appropriately named Island in the Sky. This 6000ft-high flat-topped mesa drops precipitously on all sides, providing some of the longest, most enthralling vistas of any park in southern Utah.

TOP TIP

Make sure you leave enough time if you want to visit the other districts of Canyonlands. From Island in the Sky, it's a two-hour drive south to the Needles (p168). The Maze district (p201) is the most remote and requires 4WD and self-sufficiency. Many travelers stay for at least three days.

STEVEN MILNE/ALAMY STOCK PHOTO ©

Green River Overlook (p149)

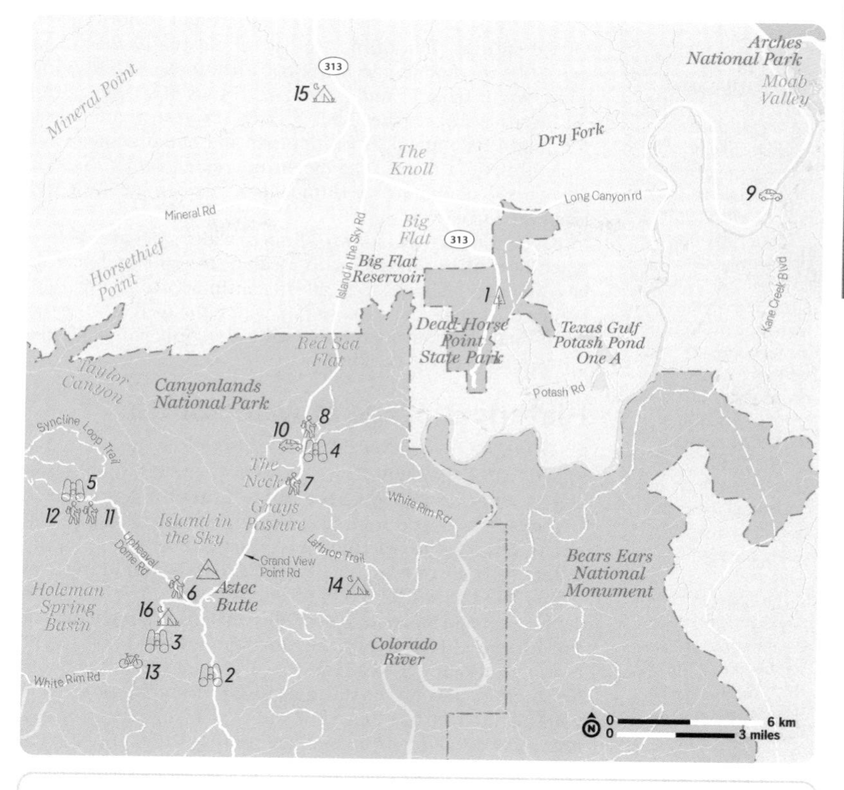

SIGHTS
1 Dead Horse Point State Park
2 Grand View Point
3 Green River Overlook
4 Shafer Trail Viewpoint
5 Upheaval Dome Viewpoint

ACTIVITIES
6 Aztec Butte Trail
7 Lathrop Trail
8 Neck Spring
9 Potash Rd
10 Shafer Trail
11 Syncline Loop
12 Upheaval Dome
13 White Rim Rd

SLEEPING
14 Airport Campground
15 Horsethief Campground
16 Willow Flat Campground

Desert Stream at Neck Spring

PLANTS, ANIMALS AND PEOPLE OF CANYONLANDS

Sego Lily, Neck Spring Trail

One of Canyonlands' few loop trails, **Neck Spring** is good for solitude seekers. Despite its proximity to the visitor center, this trail attracts few hikers, perhaps because it doesn't take in the panoramic vistas that are the signature of Island in the Sky, but this stream canyon is a magnet for wildlife and fills with wildflowers in springtime as one of the plateau's rare water sources. Look for the remnants of pioneer ranching along the way. Ranchers and the Native Americans here before them, used the narrow bridge of land (the Neck) as a natural corral and animal trap, building fencing along this thin strip to close in the entire mesa.

Following the sign in the Shafer Canyon Overlook parking

area, the hike crosses the road and descends Taylor Canyon to two springs. The initial trail is an old roadbed built in the 1800s by ranchers to bring livestock to water. Hitching posts, water troughs and pipes are still visible. Descending slightly, the trail reaches Neck Spring. If you stay quiet here, you might see mule deer, chipmunks and bighorn sheep approaching for a drink. The moisture creates a microhabitat that's an ideal climate for Gambel oak, maidenhair fern and Fremont barberry.

Leaving the alcoves, start to climb to white sand hills before reaching **Cabin Spring**, with a cabin, troughs and corrals near the site. A short, steep ascent continues over sandstone. Follow the cairns to the mesa top, where the trail crosses the main road and continues half a mile along the rim of Shafer Canyon back to the parking lot.

QUIET IN CANYONLANDS

It's not too difficult to avoid crowds in Canyonlands: Utah's biggest national park is also its least visited.

About 780,000 travelers came to Canyonlands in 2022, accounting for less than 1% of all national-park visits across the country. Crowds tend to cluster at the easy-to-reach overlooks, such as Grand View Point, but it's incredibly simple to go on a hike and rarely see another soul.

The Island in the Sky district brings in the most visitors, so try the Needles (p168), the Maze (p201) and Horseshoe Canyon (p200) for a more off-grid experience, but make sure you're prepared for the trip away from it all.

Historic Storage at Aztec Butte

HIKING TO AN ANCESTRAL PUEBLOAN GRANARY

Shortly after the turnoff on Upheaval Dome Rd, the moderate 1.4-mile round-trip **Aztec Butte Trail** climbs slickrock to stellar views and an ancient granary ruin. (Despite the name, the structure was built by Ancestral Puebloans, not the Aztecs.) It's the only archaeological site at Island in the Sky.

This short ascent of a Navajo sandstone dome yields stellar views; it's a steep hike over slickrock to the top. Parts of this hike require going up and down high ledges that might require scrambling. Wear rubber-soled shoes or hiking boots for traction. Stay on the trails, as fragile cryptobiotic crust is widespread atop the dome. In summer, bring plenty of water and wear a wide-brimmed hat because the exposed butte offers no shade.

A little more than a quarter mile from the parking area, a spur trail leads to a **granary** built around 1200 to 1300 CE, tucked below an overhang on the butte's northern side. Native people stored food and medicine in this structure, sheltered from the elements. Head back to the main trail and carry on to Aztec Butte. Use the cairns and switchbacks to follow the route up. The butte levels off at the top, revealing birds-eye views and endless sky. Circle the top of the butte to soak in the sights before returning back the same way to the parking area.

MORE NATIVE SITES

Canyonlands has some of the most evocative Native American history of Utah's national parks. Don't miss the petroglyph-filled Newspaper Rock (p173) or the 'Louvre of the Southwest' in Horseshoe Canyon (p200).

WHERE TO CAMP IN & AROUND CANYONLANDS

Willow Flat Campground
The 12-site Willow Flat campground has vault toilets but no water or hookups. **$**

Dead Horse Point State Park
Two campgrounds for RVs and tents, plus nine glamping yurts with wraparound decks. **$$**

Horsethief Campground
BLM-run spot with no-reservation sites atop a mesa in a piñon-juniper forest. **$**

Upheaval Dome: History's Mystery

A GEOLOGIC MARVEL

Was Upheaval Dome created by salt or something from outer space? Scientists disagree over how the feature formed. Some suggest it's a collapsed salt dome, while more recent research posits that it was the site of a meteorite strike some 60 million years ago. Scope out the geologic drama on the moderate **Upheaval Dome Trail**, which leads to two overlooks that gaze out at the 3-mile-wide crater.

It's an easy 0.3 miles one way to the first overlook. From the parking area, climb to the fork in the trail, bear right and ascend the slickrock to the **viewpoint**. If you find yourself on switchbacks, you've made a wrong turn. To reach the second overlook, return to the fork in the trail and bear right, descending over slickrock before clambering to a final steep ascent. From here, you have a broader panorama of the surrounding landscape. The afternoon light is magnificent and this viewpoint adds only 1 mile to the trip.

Hikers up for a strenuous trek can take the **Syncline Loop**, a difficult 8.1-mile hike around the dome (but doesn't have views of it). It's the district's most challenging route and most park rescues happen on this trail, so make sure you're prepared for steep switchbacks, scrambling through boulder fields and navigating with few markers. Tackle it clockwise for more shade in the afternoon.

TUPUNGATO/SHUTTERSTOCK ©

Upheaval Dome

WHO WERE THE ANCESTRAL PUEBLOANS?

The Ancestral Puebloans were a Native people who lived across the Four Corners region (modern-day Utah, Colorado, New Mexico and Arizona) from as far back as the 12th century BCE. They farmed and built a variety of homes and communal spaces, such as pit houses, ceremonial underground kivas and multiroom and multistory complexes tucked under cliff faces.

Prime examples of their impressive architecture can be found at Mesa Verde National Park in southwestern Colorado. Their modern descendants include the Pueblo, Hopi and Zuni.

Ancestral Puebloans have been referred to as Anasazi, a Navajo word that's sometimes translated as 'ancient enemies.' Some Pueblo people today consider this word derogatory. The Hopi call them Hisatsinom, which means ancient people.

WHERE TO SEE CANYONLANDS' BEST VIEWS

Grand View Point
A humble name belies the park's best overlook at the end of the paved road.

Green River Overlook
Get a glimpse of one of Canyonlands' great carvers; less busy than some other viewpoints.

Shafer Trail Viewpoint
Watch as Jeeps and 4WD vehicles navigate the hairpin turns that unfurl down the canyon.

ROAD TRIP

Cruising Island in the Sky

From the visitor center, the paved road through the Island in the Sky district leads past numerous overlooks and trailheads, ending after 12 miles at Grand View Point, one of the Southwest's most sweeping views, rivaled only by the Grand Canyon and nearby Dead Horse Point State Park. This scenic drive takes in the best of the viewpoints and short hikes in this part of the national park.

1 Shafer Canyon Overlook

About 0.5 miles south of the visitor center, pull off to the left at the Shafer Canyon Overlook, where you can peer down 1500ft. Watch as Jeeps snake down the switchbacks of Shafer Trail, once used by cattle ranchers and later by the Atomic Energy Commission to truck uranium to Moab for processing.

The Drive: A quarter-mile ahead, you'll cross the Neck, where the ridge narrows to 40ft across – eventually this strip will erode away, further isolating the mesa. Drive on for another 5.5 miles.

2 Mesa Arch Trail

This easy 0.6-mile round-trip hike is worth every step. The 27ft-long arch perched right on the cliff edge makes a beautiful frame for the distant La Sal Mountains and it's particularly popular at sunrise when its underside glows a fiery red.

The Drive: Head south, turning right on Upheaval Dome Rd. Follow it for 5 miles until the parking lot at its end.

DEAN FIKAR/SHUTTERSTOCK ©

Mesa Arch

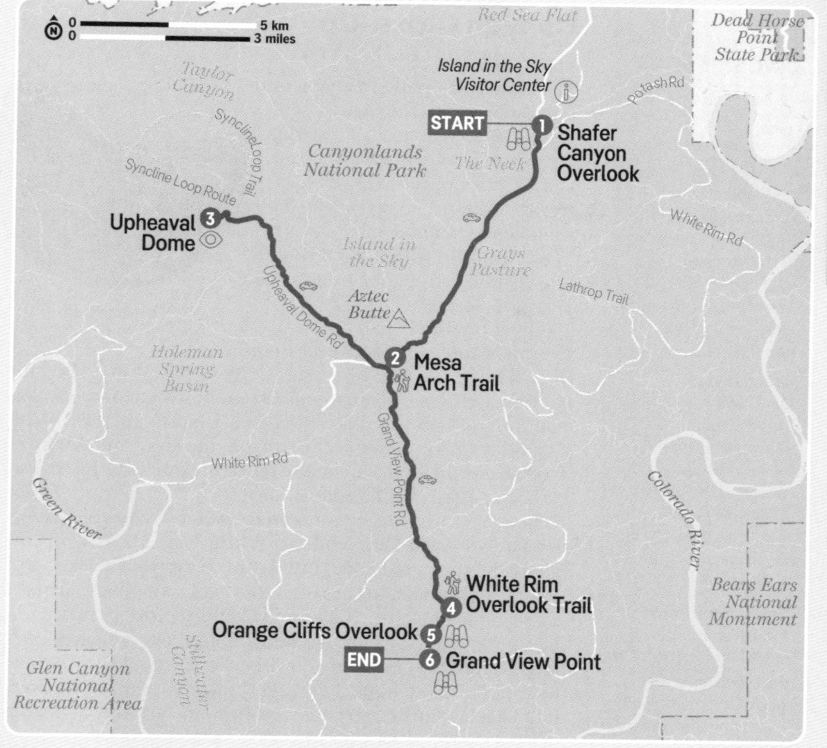

3 Upheaval Dome

Can you solve the Island in the Sky's geologic mystery? While most of this district has systematic layers of rock, Upheaval Dome jumbles them. Was this caused by 'salt bubbles' that deformed the rocks or from the impact of a meteor? Hike the steep quarter-mile to a viewpoint and decide for yourself.

The Drive: Return to the main park road, turning right to continue heading south.

4 White Rim Overlook Trail

Enjoy your packed lunch at the picnic tables around the parking lot before setting off on this 1.8-mile round-trip trail that skirts the canyon edge before peering down into the depths. This east-facing overlook has a similar vantage point as Grand View but fewer visitors.

The Drive: Continue driving south for 1 mile.

5 Orange Cliffs Overlook

This turnoff offers views west to the Henry Mountains, the last-charted mountain range in the Lower 48. The Orange Cliffs lie southwest, beyond the Maze district of Canyonlands. At sunset, the canyons glow orange in the waning light.

The Drive: Carry on until the end of the road, which loops in a parking lot.

6 Grand View Point

The name says it all: Grand View is one of the Southwest's most sweeping and beautiful scenes. Hundred-mile views are easily earned by walking the short distance to the cliff edge, but for more of a leg stretch, set off on the easy 1.8-mile round-trip stroll to the overlook for a better look at the massive mesa underfoot.

CANYON CONTEMPLATION

Cadence Cook is the District Interpreter at Canyonlands' Island in the Sky. These are her favorite viewpoints in the national park.

Green River Overlook
This viewpoint showcases stunning views of Green River and the vast wilderness of the Maze district. Light in these canyons is best in the morning.

Grand View Point
A short walk leads to stunning views toward the south, east and west. From here you'll see myriad canyons and beautiful red-rock layers. Check at the visitor center to see whether any ranger talks are happening here.

Big Spring Overlook
This viewpoint in the Needles district is a great spot to see unique geologic features including hoodoos and terraced canyons.

Canyon Close-Up

CLIFFS AND THE COLORADO RIVER

Lathrop Trail

The **Lathrop Trail** is a longer and quieter hike into the canyon, with stellar views. For an easier stroll, you can hike out and back to the rim (5 miles round-trip, 158ft of elevation change). Trekkers up for a challenge can hike all the way to White Rim Rd (p152), for a round-trip distance of nearly 12 miles and 1721ft of elevation change.

Follow the level sandy path through the grasslands. It passes over undulating slickrock marked by cairns. Canyon views start here, including a glimpse of a gorgeous bend in the Colorado River. The trail returns to sandy paths and twists along the canyon rim. Soak in the views of the canyon, the river and **Airport Tower**, a 700ft-high sandstone butte so named for its resemblance to an air traffic control tower.

The trail then descends steep switchbacks to a boulder-strewn wash that leads to White Rim Rd. Hikers can follow the spur road down into Lathrop Canyon, a descent of 1600ft. It's possible to backpack this trail, camping overnight at one of the four sites at **Airport Campground** or further in the Gooseberry/Lathrop at-large camping zone, which doesn't have designated sites and allows backpackers to choose their own spot in a low-impact area. Permits are required for overnight backcountry trips and are in high demand in spring and fall. Reserve your permit on recreation.gov.

Driving & Biking through Canyonlands' Backcountry

MAKING A GETAWAY

White Rim Rd

Canyonlands has hundreds of miles of unpaved roads, inviting mountain bikers and drivers with high-clearance 4WD vehicles and off-grid know-how into the park's hidden and more remote corners. Blazed by

RANGER PROGRAMS AT CANYONLANDS NATIONAL PARK

Geology Talk
Remember all the rock layers after this lesson at Grand View Point; 10am and 10:30am daily.

Patio Talk
Rangers pick from a mixed bag of topics at 1pm daily at the visitor center.

Full Moon Hikes & Stargazing
Set off on a bright night hike (around full moon) or see the stars (around new moon).

Camping, White Rim Trail

uranium prospectors in the 1950s, the 100-mile primitive **White Rim Rd** encircling Island in the Sky is the top choice for 4WD and mountain biking trips. It generally takes two to three days in a vehicle or three to four days on a mountain bike. Because the route lacks any water sources, cyclists should team up with a 4WD support vehicle or travel with a Moab outfitter.

Day-use permits for one-day trips or overnight permits for trips on White Rim Rd are required. Overnight permits can be hard to come by in spring and fall. Permits become available four months before the start of the season (eg fall permits for September to December open in May). Walk-in permits are sometimes available. Check with rangers at the visitor center the day before or the day of your trip.

Potash Rd and the iconic switchbacks of the **Shafer Trail** do not require permits and make a thrilling dirt-road drive between the park and Moab, passing below Dead Horse Point State Park and the spot where the final scene of *Thelma & Louise* was filmed.

All-terrain vehicles (ATVs), utility terrain vehicles (UTVs) and off-highway vehicles (OHVs) are not allowed anywhere in the park. If you're bringing a rental car, make sure you've read the agreement closely. Most do not allow drivers to take their car off paved roads.

PERMITS FOR CANYONLANDS

In addition to the park entrance fee, permits are required for day use of White Rim Rd, overnight backpacking and river trips. Designated camp areas abut most trails and open-zone camping is permitted in some places.

One hundred day-use permits per day are issued for White Rim Rd (50 for motorized vehicles and 50 for mountain bikes). These permits cost $6 if reserved on recreation.gov, or they are free if picked up at the visitor center on the day of your trip.

Advance reservations are recommended for overnight backcountry permits, which often book out quickly in spring and fall. Some are kept open for first-come, first-served walk-ins. Permits cost $36, plus $5 per person per night.

GETTING AROUND

The easiest way to visit Canyonlands' Island in the Sky district is by car. Overlooks are easy enough to reach in standard cars, but to explore further, high-clearance 4WD vehicles are recommended.

MOAB

Moab

Doling out hot tubs and pub grub after a dusty day on the trail, Moab is southeast Utah's adventure base camp. Mobs arrive to play in Utah's recreation capital, from hikers to four-wheelers. While Moab doesn't have much going on between breakfast and dinner, it offers civilized comforts after a full day in the near-by nature. Operators in town can help you plan multisport and multiday adventures, from mountain biking and white-water rafting to backcountry ATV and Jeep tours.

It was nature of a different sort that brought most people to Moab in its 1950s boom years. Miners in search of 'radioactive gold' – uranium – forged the network of backroads that still runs through the surrounding canyons, now used by 4WD adventurers instead of truckers. Neither mining nor the hundreds of Hollywood films shot here have influenced the character of Moab as much as the influx of fat-tire mountain bike enthusiasts.

TOP TIP

Moab can feel overrun with national-park visitors from March through October. Main St (Hwy 191) is lined with shops, restaurants and hotels that book up quickly in season. Reserve as far in advance as possible. Prices drop by as much as 50% in winter.

Moab

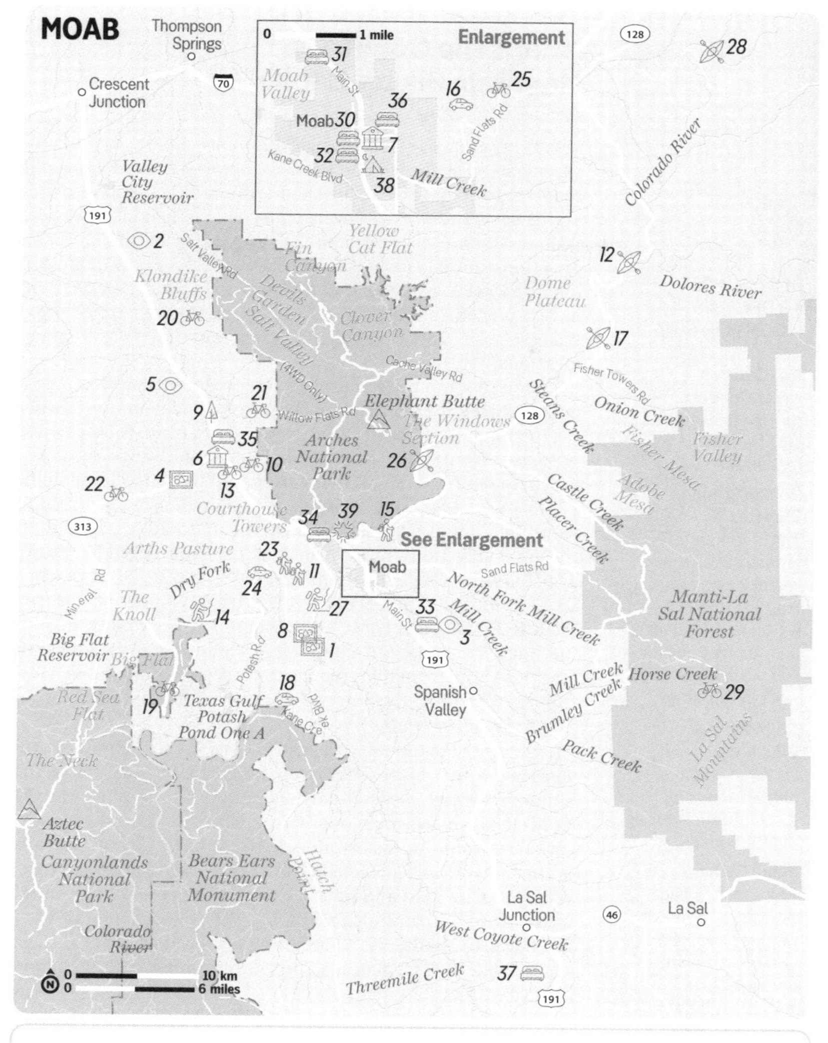

SIGHTS
1 Birthing Scene Petroglyph
2 Copper Ridge Dinosaur Tracksite
3 Golf Course Rock Art Site
4 Intestine Man
5 Mill Canyon Dinosaur Tracksite
6 Moab Giants
7 Moab Museum
8 Poison Spider Trailhead
9 Utahraptor State Park

ACTIVITIES & TOURS
10 Bar-M Trail
11 Corona Arch Trail
see 11 Bowtie Arch
12 Dewey Bridge
13 Gemini Bridges
14 Granary Canyon
15 Grandstaff Trail
16 Hell's Revenge
17 Hittle Bottom
18 Hurrah Pass
19 Intrepid Trail
20 Klondike Bluffs Trail
21 KlonZo
22 Navajo Rocks
23 Pinto Arch
24 Potash Rd
25 Slickrock Trail
26 Takeout Beach
27 Wall Street
28 Westwater Canyon
29 Whole Enchilada

SLEEPING
30 Best Western Plus Canyonlands Inn
31 Field Station
32 Gonzo Inn
33 Red Moon Lodge
34 Springhill Suites
35 Sun Outdoors Canyonlands Gateway
36 Sunflower Hill Inn
37 ULUM Moab
38 Up the Creek Campground

ENTERTAINMENT
39 Canyonlands by Night & Day

Moab: The Country's Mountain Biking Capital

SLICKROCK SESSIONS

Moab's mountain biking is world famous. Challenging trails ascend steep slickrock and wind through woods and up 4WD roads outside of town in every direction. Bike shop websites and Discover Moab (discovermoab.com/mountainbiking) are good trail resources and riders have an overwhelming number of options suitable for all skill levels. It's best for new mountain bikers to get a guide or join a tour. For rentals, reserve road or full-suspension bikes in advance. Day-use fees are charged in some areas and Moab bike shops arrange shuttles to many locations.

East of town in the Sand Flats Recreation Area, Moab's legendary **Slickrock Trail** will kick your butt. The physically and technically difficult 12-mile round-trip route is for experts only, as is the practice loop. Lots of elevation change and steep ascents mean riders will likely need half a day to complete it.

The lofty La Sal Mountains south of Moab provide a respite from the roasting weather and can be up to 20°F cooler than the lower elevations. Beat the heat on the **Moonlight Meadow Trail**, a 10.8-mile loop among aspens and pines that reaches 10,500ft altitude. Take it easy: you will get winded. The nearby **Whole Enchilada** trail system combines six routes, including Burro Pass, Hazard County and Porcupine Rim, which offer everything from high-mountain descents to slickrock. It's a full-day affair for advanced riders, with 7000ft of vertical drop and 34 miles of trails.

A few miles northwest of the entrance to Arches, **Moab Brand Trails** (named after brands of the cattle variety) skirt the boundary of the national park. Popular with families, **Bar M Trail** is an easy 8-mile loop with great views and short slickrock stretches. Connect from here to the more advanced trails in the network. The nearby **KlonZo Trails** are accessed from Willow Springs Rd and have a mix of flowing beginner, intermediate and advanced terrain. On the western side of Hwy 191, **Gemini Bridges** is a moderate full-day downhill ride past spectacular rock formations. This 13-mile one-way trail follows dirt, sand and slickrock.

On the 14-mile round-trip **Klondike Bluffs Trail**, further north on Hwy 191, intermediate bikers can learn to ride slickrock past dinosaur tracks to Arches National Park on mostly blue- and black-rated trails.

The highway to Dead Horse Point State Park and Canyonlands' Island in the Sky (p146) also has dozens of mountain

BEST PLACES TO RENT A MOUNTAIN BIKE

Rim Cyclery
Moab's longest-running family-owned bike shop offers rentals and repairs.

Poison Spider Bicycles
The friendly staff is always busy helping wheel jockeys map out their routes. Rents well-maintained road and suspension rigs and has a 'try before you buy' program.

Chile Pepper Bike Shop
Rents and repairs bikes, dishes out local trail info and has plenty of maps.

Moab Cyclery
High-performance bike shop offering rentals and sales. Offers biker shuttles and good half-, full-, multiday and multisport tours.

WHERE TO STAY IN MOAB

Field Station
If millennials renovated a Motel 6: sleek minimalist design; merch-filled lobby with a Phoebe Bridgers soundtrack. **$$**

Gonzo Inn
Cheerful spruced-up motel; great for cyclists, with secure storage and repair and wash station. **$$**

Best Western Plus Canyonlands Inn
A comfortable choice at the central crossroads of downtown with a lovely wraparound terrace. **$$**

Slickrock Trail

biking trails, including the epic multiday journey on White Rim Rd (p152). **Navajo Rocks** is an intermediate mountain biking area with good sandstone terrain that rides well even in the summer rainy season. Seven trails connect over 22 miles. The **Intrepid Trail** is an excellent single track on the rim of Dead Horse Point with great views. Rare for the Moab area, it's flat, so it's good for beginners and families, but its twists and turns keep riders on their toes.

White Waters of the Colorado & Canyons

RAFTING THE RIVERS

Whether you're interested in bashing through rapids or gentle floats for studying canyon geology, rafting might be the highlight of your visit to Moab. Choose from full-day floats, white-water trips, multiday excursions and jet-boating. Day trips are often available on short notice, but overnight trips should be booked well ahead.

Half- and full-day options stick to the Colorado River, northeast of Moab. **Hittle Bottom to Takeout Beach** with Class I to II rapids is the most popular stretch of river near town, perfect for first-timers. Families can safely bring small children without boring their teens. Like mellow water and just want to float along? **Dewey Bridge to Hittle Bottom** is a 7-mile section of flat water on the Colorado River with great scenery

THE BIG CLEAN-UP

Less than a mile from the entrance to Arches, unmissable on the drive south into Moab, is a government initiative that's the polar opposite of a national park: the Uranium Mill Tailings Remedial Action (UMTRA) project, a massive effort to remove 16 million tons of waste from mining uranium.

In the 1950s, the largest uranium deposit in the country was found near Moab and the radioactive element was processed next to the Colorado River. Waste slurry sat in an unlined pond and is thought to be leaching into the water. About 80% of the uranium tailings have now been moved 40 miles north and it's hoped the project will be complete by 2028.

Sunflower Hill Inn
Top-shelf adults-only B&B with a dozen rooms in a quaint cedar-sided, early-20th-century home. **$$$**

Red Moon Lodge
Sustainability-minded stay, with organic breakfasts, solar power and considerate xeriscaping on 6 acres. **$$**

SpringHill Suites
Closest hotel to Arches and Canyonlands; modern rooms with family amenities and huge pool area. **$$$**

and wildlife-watching.

Longer multiday expeditions head to Cataract Canyon, Westwater Canyon and Desolation Canyon. The legendary Class V rapids of **Cataract Canyon** are Utah's most intense stretch of white water. Outfitters run excursions lasting two to six days; shorter trips travel on motorboats instead of oar boats.

Find more serious white water at **Westwater Canyon**, which boasts Class III and IV rapids squeezed by 1200ft rock walls. Most people make the 17-mile trip in one long day (10 hours) from Moab, though some choose to camp and make it a two-day trip. If you don't go with an operator, you need to obtain the BLM permit yourself on recreation.gov.

On the Green River, **Desolation Canyon** is an epic adventure that starts with a scenic flight from Moab to the launch point. The remote location means that trips take between four and six days, covering 85 miles and more than 50 rapids. Ancient petroglyph panels and pioneer sites along the way shed light on the human history of the canyon.

Do-it-yourselfers can rent canoes, kayaks and rafts from outfitters in Moab. Many parts of the Colorado and Green Rivers require permits, but a section along Hwy 128 just beyond Moab

BEST RAFTING COMPANIES

Mild to Wild
Excellent rafting trips for any amount of time, including half-day sessions.

Adrift Adventures
Combine a trip on the river with a Jeep tour.

OARS
Has a permit for Canyonlands and runs epic weeklong expeditions that raft and hike to tough-to-reach parts of the national park.

Sheri Griffith River Expeditions
Operating since 1971, this rafting specialist offers a great selection of activities, from family floats to rapids.

Navtec Expeditions
Cool overland and on-water combo trips, plus DIY rentals.

Cataract Canyon

WHERE TO CAMP & GLAMP IN MOAB

Sun Outdoors Canyonlands Gateway
Tent and RV sites, plus wooden cabins and Old West–themed casitas; near the turnoff to Canyonlands. **$$**

Up the Creek Campground
Shaded tent-only urban campground within walking distance of downtown. **$**

ULUM Moab
Secluded luxe tents opened in 2023 on 200 acres with views of Looking Glass Arch. **$$$**

is the longest unpermitted stretch of the Colorado. Without permits, you'll be restricted to the more mellow stretches of the water, but depending on the season, you might still be in for some thrills and spills.

Rafting season runs from April to September; jet-boating season lasts longer. Water levels crest in May and June.

To get on the river without the adrenaline, **Canyonlands By Night & Day** runs an old-timey sound-and-light show projected on the canyon walls and accompanied by historical narration.

Moab's Top Spots for Rock Climbing & Canyoneering

GET A GRIP

Surrounded by high-quality sandstone cliffs, huge walls and tower formations, Moab is a great place to get up a wall. Climb up cliffsides, rappel into rivers and hike through slot canyons with local outfitters who have the inside scoop on the area's lesser-known gems. Moab's menu of routes will appeal to first-timers and families as well as those more chalked up. Operators offer a long list of options. DIY rock climbers gravitate toward **Wall Street** off Hwy 279. **Granary Canyon** is one of the best canyoneering routes near Moab, dropping into iconic rock formations over six rappels of up to 200ft and finding storage structures once used by Ancestral Puebloans that give the area its name.

Rock climbing and canyoneering are allowed in Arches and Canyonlands, but the National Park Service does not inspect or maintain any bolts or anchor systems. Some activities require permits, so check online or with rangers before you go.

Routes around Moab and in the national parks might be closed for several months of prime climbing and canyoneering season to protect nesting birds of prey and lambing bighorn sheep.

Hell's Revenge

Jeepers Creepers

SCENIC FOUR-WHEEL DRIVES FROM MOAB

Moab's hundreds of miles of primitive back roads are coveted by 4WD enthusiasts. **Hell's Revenge** is the best-known 4WD road around here, but the extreme terrain mandates solid driving experience. It's in the BLM

BEST CLIMBING & CANYONEERING COMPANIES

Windgate Adventures
Guided climbing, canyoneering, arch-rappelling and photo trips with a highly knowledgeable guide for all levels of adventurer.

Moab Cliffs & Canyons
Top-notch company with canyoneering, climbing and 'rockaneering' (combining elements of both, plus mountaineering) trips.

Moab Desert Adventures
Long-standing operator with climbing and canyoneering tours that scale area towers and walls.

Desert Highlights
Offers private canyoneering and packrafting trips that are big on personal attention.

Moab Adventure Center
This megacenter arranges activities of all descriptions, including beginner-level climbs and canyon descents.

WHERE TO EAT IN MOAB

Desert Bistro
Southeast Utah's top restaurant, serving perfectly plated game and seafood in an 1892 dance hall. $$$

Moab Food Truck Park
A dozen-plus trucks dishing up crowd-pleasing Chinese dishes, pizza, hot dogs, sushi and more. $

Sabaku Sushi
Hot dishes and fresh sushi with a Utah twist: elk tataki and rolls named after local rocks. $$

WHY I LOVE MOAB

Lauren Keith, writer

Is there any town in the world as geographically blessed as Moab?

Crowned by two jaw-dropping national parks, hugged by one of the country's most famous rivers and encircled by red-rock cliffs, Moab has everything an outdoor enthusiast could dream of, plus a shower and a soft place to rest your head after a big day.

Every time I come to Moab, I push the adventure a little further. More than a decade ago, my first visit – like most travelers' – took me only to Arches and Canyonlands, but Moab has so much more up its sleeve. On each subsequent trip, I've stayed longer, knowing this place has plenty more to show me.

administered area east of town and follows an 8.2-mile route up and down shockingly steep slickrock.

The 33-mile **Hurrah Pass** offers jaw-dropping vistas of the Colorado River, Dead Horse Point and Grand View Point in Canyonlands National Park. The route starts out west along paved Kane Creek Rd, off Hwy 191 in Moab, yielding to gravel and dirt as you enter Kane Springs Canyon. Standard cars can make part of the journey, past petroglyph sites and a rock climbing area. About 10 miles in you must ford the creek, which, depending on the weather, may be impassable. After 15 miles, you reach 4470ft Hurrah Pass; 4WD is mandatory beyond this point. South of the pass, the road descends toward the Colorado River, with views of the potash plant on the opposite bank (look for the blue ponds). Explore the desert before doubling back to Moab or continuing south on Lockhart Basin Rd toward Canyonlands' Needles district (p146). From Lockhart Basin Rd, the road is much more difficult and often confusing, eventually emerging about 50 miles south on Hwy 211, just east of the Needles.

On the other side of the Colorado River, the 15-mile scenic desert drive on **Potash Rd** passes mining remnants on the way into dry country with soaring rock walls and solitude. Just past the turnoff, you'll pass a radioactive tailings pond from Moab's uranium mining days (p157), while mid-route, stunning natural beauty abounds. Highlights include watching rock climbers clamber up Wall Street, Native American petroglyph panels (look for signs just beyond Wall Street), dinosaur tracks (bring binoculars for a better look) and a 3-mile hike to Corona Arch (p162). Past the potash plant, the road continues as a rough 4WD track into Canyonlands' Island in the Sky district, linking with the Shafer Trail (p152).

Outfitters such as **Cliffhanger Jeep Rental**, **Twisted Jeeps** and **Moab Adventure Center** rent Rubicons and Wranglers. Some also offer off-road utility vehicles such as Rhinos and Mules (seating two to four) or four-wheelers (straddled like a bicycle). Make sure you stay on established routes. It's illegal to go off-road. The desert might appear barren at first glance, but it's a fragile landscape of complex ecosystems. Biological soil crusts (p143) can take more than a century to regenerate after even one tire track (really).

If you'd rather someone else does the driving, join a group 4WD tour, dubbed 'land safaris,' in multipassenger-modified, six- to eight-person Humvee-like vehicles. Some rafting companies offer combination land/river trips that allow you to see Moab from many angles. **Coyote Land Tours** has daily drives in a bright-yellow Mercedes-Benz Unimog off-road ve-

WHERE TO EAT IN MOAB

Jailhouse Cafe
Where Moab gets breakfast: stacks of pancakes and eggs Benedict served in a former jail. **$**

Milt's Stop & Eat
Moab's oldest restaurant (established 1954). Classic diner grub: burgers, fresh-cut fries and milkshakes. **$**

Quesadilla Mobilla
Beloved food truck parked near Main St serving creative quesadillas on 10in tortillas. **$**

Hot-air balloon, Arches National Park

hicle that seats 12. **Dan Mick's Jeep Tours** is a highly regarded local operation that visits some 25 trails, including Hell's Revenge. With **High Point Hummer & ATV** you can take a thrill ride through Hell's Revenge in a Hummer. The company also offers guided self-drive UTV tours and rents UTVs and Utah-made Vanderhall Venices, sporty two-seater, three-wheeled 'autocycles.'

A Raven's-Eye View of Moab

THE SKY'S THE LIMIT

Moab's bounty of beauty is super scenic at ground level, but you can elevate your experience by seeing it from the sky. Set out at sunrise and soar over canyon country and the La Sal Mountains on a hot-air balloon flight with **Canyonlands Ballooning**, peacefully floating above it all. All flights take place in the morning when the winds are calmest.

Redtail Air Adventures is the only air-tour company allowed to fly above Arches and Canyonlands and offers combination tours that include both national parks, as well as longer trips to Monument Valley, Capitol Reef and Bryce Canyon.

Fall back to Earth with **Skydive Moab**. Choose from jumps at 8000ft (20 seconds of freefall) or 13,000ft (55 seconds of freefall) above ground level for a thrill like no other.

WHAT'S IN A NAME?

Readers of the Bible will recognize the name Moab, which refers to an ancient kingdom in the Levant, in modern-day Jordan.

However, the Moabites of the Bible were considered incestuous and enemies of the Israelites and later arrivals to the Utah town petitioned for Moab's name to be changed. One suggestion was 'Vina,' a nod to the town's location in a verdant valley where crops thrived despite the surrounding desert, but the petition lacked the required votes and the original name stuck.

WHERE TO GET SWEET TREATS IN MOAB

Moab Garage Co
Hip cafe with cupcakes, scones, brownies, excellent espresso drinks and more substantial savory dishes. $

Crystal's Cakes and Cones
Beat the Moab heat at this small shop with plenty of ice cream and cupcake flavors. $

Moab Diner
All the Americana classics: fruit pies, Blue Bunny ice cream, banana splits and sundaes. $

Two Arches for the Hike of One

CHECKING OUT CORONA AND BOWTIE

Corona Arch

Nearby Arches National Park might have the densest concentration of rock arches in the world, but that doesn't mean they are all found inside the park boundaries. At 335ft wide and 140ft tall, Corona Arch is big enough to fly an airplane through (and yes, that has happened).

The moderately easy 3-mile round-trip **Corona Arch Trail** is one of the best short hikes in the Moab area and is suitable for families with older children. Ascending a short ladder fixed to the rock is required to reach the arch. The trailhead is off Potash Rd (Hwy 279) and shortly after you set off you cross railroad tracks that are still in use by the potash plant further along the river. Some sections of slickrock have cables attached in case you need help getting up the steep surface. Shortly before you reach Corona Arch, look to your left to see **Bowtie Arch**, a pothole arch high up in the cliff. You start to get an understanding of the massive size of Corona Arch as you walk through it.

To tack on a third, take the spur trail to **Pinto Arch**, a large pothole arch that you can stand below. The elevated view over the Colorado River along this part of the trail is serene.

MUSEUMS IN MOAB

Moab Giants
This paleo-amusement park uses tech to transport you back to the land before time. A half-mile walking trail showcases more than 100 life-size replica dinos with Arches National Park and the La Sal Mountains in the background. A virtual-reality aquarium and 3D movie theater also help bring the creatures to life. The museum might be garish for some, but it's a must-stop for dino devotees.

Moab Museum
Regional exhibits feature everything from paleontology and archaeology to local crafts and Native American art.

Hiking the Grandstaff Trail

WATERSIDE CANYON WALK

Named for William Grandstaff, the first black rancher to settle in the Moab area in the 1870s, the moderately easy **Grandstaff Trail** is about 5 miles round-trip along a year-round stream closed in by high Navajo sandstone walls dripping with desert varnish. Beware of poison ivy growing along the trail – check the information board at the trailhead to make sure you know what it looks like. The elevation gain along the route is only 400ft, making this a good option for hikers of all abilities.

The conclusion of the hike is the 243ft-wide **Morning Glory Natural Bridge**, the sixth-longest natural rock span in the United States, in a box canyon. Plan on three to four hours. The trailhead is on BLM-administered land 3 miles north of Moab on Hwy 128.

WHERE TO DRINK IN MOAB

Proper Burger & Brewing Co
Southerly outpost of the Salt Lake City-based brewery; heaven for hopheads. Substantial food menu too.

Moab Brewery
The hometown brewery makes nearly a dozen beers in the vats just behind the bar area.

Moab Coffee Roasters
Low-key downtown spot to kick back with coffee, gelato and affogato; large outdoor patio.

Dinosaur tracks, Potash Rd (Hwy279)

Discovering Dinosaur Prints

FOLLOWING IN THEIR FOOTSTEPS

Incredible clues from Moab's past inhabitants hide in the rocks and cliffs around town. Dinosaurs crossed this land, stamping their prints into stone and the first fossils found in the western United States were discovered near Moab in 1859.

Just off Potash Rd (Hwy 279), the **Poison Spider Dinosaur Tracksite** has prints from at least 10 three-toed meat-eating theropods that are thought to have been walking at 3mph along the edge of a lake. The imprinted rock fell from the cliffside, revealing the tracks for the first time in 190 million years. Don't miss the panels of **petroglyphs** on the cliff face above, showing groups of people and hunting scenes with bows and arrows. The parking lot here is also the trailhead for **Longbow Arch**.

At the **Mill Canyon Dinosaur Tracksite** north of Moab, a raised boardwalk leads travelers along a short trail above prints discovered in 2009. At least 10 species of dinosaur, including sickle-clawed raptors, long-necked herbivores and crocodiles, walked here, creating the most diversity of any site in North America, with 200 individual tracks. Nearby **Utahraptor State Park**, created in 2021, is under development and slated to open in 2024. The site has seen a number of fossil finds, including its namesake dino – the velociraptors from *Jurassic Park* are based on the skeleton of a Utahraptor.

Copper Ridge Dinosaur Tracksite, is the first place in Utah where the prints of a Jurassic-period sauropod (a herbivore with a long neck) were discovered. About 150 million years ago, the large creature made a right turn and limped along from an injury. The site also has tracks from theropods and it's just 0.3 miles round-trip from the parking lot to see them.

BEST PLACES FOR PETROGLYPHS & PICTOGRAPHS

Potash Rd
Roadside site with several scenes, some carved as far back as 6000 BCE.

Poison Spider Trailhead
Panels of people hunting with bows and arrows; near the dino tracks.

Birthing Scene Petroglyph
Fallen boulder depicting the arrival of a baby feet-first, as well as bear paws, snakes and horses.

Intestine Man
Human with a curled-up snake in his stomach; on Hwy 313 toward Canyonlands.

Golf Course Rock Art Site
Spot *Moab Man*, a figure wearing earrings and a horned headdress.

GETTING AROUND

Downtown Moab is walkable and you can easily pedal around town by bike, but if you want to get to trailheads or the national parks, you need to have a car or join a tour.

Vehicle traffic can be heavy from April to October. In March 2023, Moab started a free-to-ride 'micro transit' system using 13-passenger vans. A fixed route runs along Main St from 9am to 9pm between mid-March and mid-October, while an on-demand service can take you door to door within the service area. Schedule a ride by downloading the Moab Area Transit app.

The small Canyonlands Field Airport, 18 miles north of town, has flights to Denver and Salt Lake City.

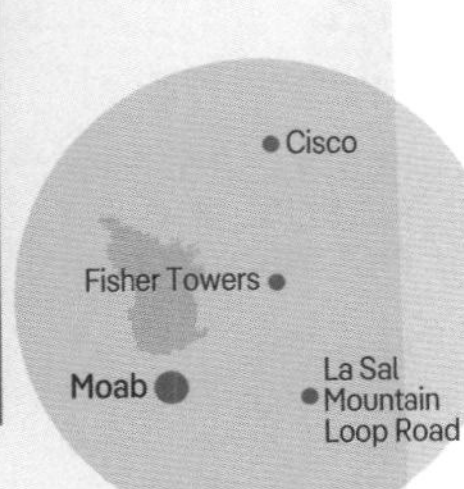

Beyond Moab

The landscape east of Moab is a dramatic shift from the red-rock desert found elsewhere in the southern part of the state.

Moab is the springboard for countless outdoor pursuits and activities not usually associated with the desert – charting the course of the mighty Colorado River and driving past patches of summertime snow in the lofty La Sal Mountains – are beautiful options for extending your adventure.

One of the most prominent rivers in the Southwest, the Colorado is the hardworking carver of the Grand Canyon in Arizona and part of Canyonlands National Park. It's also an incredibly important water source, providing water for 40 million people in seven states, as well as parts of Mexico. Looming over it all, the La Sal Mountains have their highest peak at 12,726 ft atop Mt Peale.

TOP TIP

From I-70, Hwy 191 is the usual way to reach Moab, but the Colorado River Scenic Byway is a gorgeous (though longer) alternative.

KRIS WIKTOR/SHUTTERSTOCK ©

La Sal Mountains

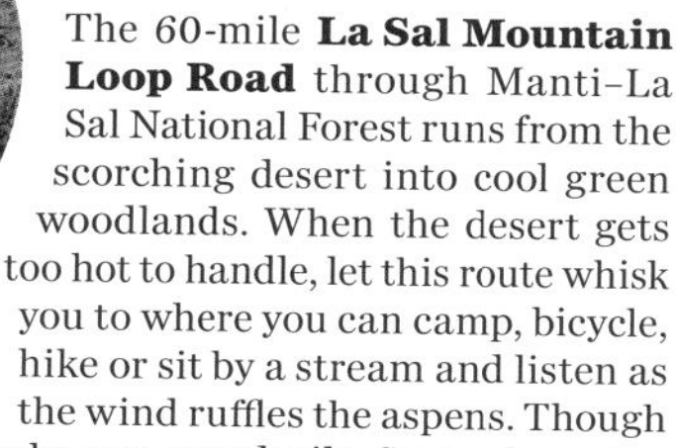

Castleton Tower

Driving the La Sal Mountain Loop Road

HIGH-RISE RESPITE FROM THE HEAT

The 60-mile **La Sal Mountain Loop Road** through Manti–La Sal National Forest runs from the scorching desert into cool green woodlands. When the desert gets too hot to handle, let this route whisk you to where you can camp, bicycle, hike or sit by a stream and listen as the wind ruffles the aspens. Though paved, it's narrow and lacks any guardrails. Snow closes the road between November and March.

About 15 miles northeast of Moab, off Hwy 128 (p167), the La Sal Mountain Loop Rd (aka Castle Valley Rd) climbs southeast up switchbacks into the national forest. Four miles from the turnoff, look to your left for the spires known as the **Priest & Nuns**, as well as **Castleton Tower**. The route winds past junipers and piñon pines, followed by scrub oaks and, finally, alpine slopes of majestic pines, firs and white-barked quaking aspens, the leaves of which turn a brilliant yellow-gold in fall. High above canyon country, you'll gain a fresh perspective on the vastness of the Colorado Plateau.

At the crest, you can turn left on a dirt spur road and climb 5 miles further to the picnic area and developed **campground** at Warner Lake. When it's 100°F in Moab, it might be a balmy 75°F by day and downright chilly at night at Warner Lake Campground, which sits at 9400ft. From the Warner Lake spur junction, the loop road descends to Hwy 191, 8 miles south of Moab.

Fisher Towers

On the Rocks at Fisher Towers

THE COUNTRY'S LARGEST FREE-STANDING SPIRE

Easily accessed from Moab but still far enough away to be forgotten by the national-park hordes, the 4.5-mile round-trip **Fisher Towers Trail** takes you past 300-million-year-old towering sandstone monoliths, the biggest of which (called the **Titan**) rises 900ft and is the tallest

GHOST TOWN RESURRECTED?

At the northern end of Hwy 128, **Cisco** might look like an abandoned ghost town, with half-collapsed and graffitied buildings, but there's life here yet. (The 2020 census noted a population of four.)

Established as a water stop for steam trains on the Denver and Rio Grande Railroad in the 1880s, Cisco once had 200 residents, a post office, a general store and a schoolhouse, but it was dealt a series of nearly fatal blows when diesel replaced steam engines and when the town was bypassed by I-70. But the tides of the town could be changing. In 2019, the general store was reopened (called Buzzard's Belly) and a residency for artists is in the works.

WHERE TO STAY ALONG HWY 128

Sorrel River Ranch
Southeast Utah's only full-service luxury resort was originally a 1903 homestead on 240 acres. **$$$**

Red Cliffs Lodge
Dude ranch meets deluxe motel, with horseback riding, an on-site movie museum and sunrise yoga. **$$$**

Lower Onion Creek Campground
Views of Fisher Towers and the canyons from these no-reservation BLM campsites. **$**

MOAB'S MOVIE HISTORY

Even if you haven't been to Moab before, you've almost certainly seen it. This stunning scenery has starred as the background of major films for nearly a century.

The free-to-visit **Moab Museum of Film & Western Heritage**, based at Red Cliffs Lodge on Hwy 128, has Hollywood memorabilia from locally shot movies and the ranch was the filming location for many of the first films set around Moab, such as *Wagon Master* and *Rio Grande*.

Movies as diverse as *Austin Powers*, *Thelma & Louise* and *Mission Impossible II* have been filmed here. Actor and director Kevin Costner has been particularly avid about filming in Utah and shoots for his passion project *Horizon: An American Saga* have begun.

ZOONAR GMBH/ALAMY STOCK PHOTO ©

Fisher Towers

freestanding rock tower in the US. The area is popular with rock climbers, who scale the otherworldly formations.

Much of the hike winds around the base of the sheer towers into short valleys that are occasionally shaded, depending on the time of day you visit. The west-facing monoliths can get hot in the afternoon, so wait for sunset, when rays bathe the rock in color and cast long shadows. After curving past the rock formations, the hiking trail climbs up to a ridge that provides views of the iron-red spires that you came through as well as over the other side to the majestic La Sal Mountains. The end of the trail is signposted near a rocky outcrop that's a good place for a snack and sitting to enjoy the scene.

The trailhead is 26 miles northeast of Moab, off Hwy 128. If you're visiting for sunset, don't forget to bring a flashlight to find your way back. There's a small five-site tent-only BLM **campground** near the trailhead with vault toilets but no water. Spaces cost $25 per night and are first come, first served.

GETTING AROUND

A car is necessary to travel the scenic drives and stay in the spread-out accommodation options.

CAR CRUISING ALONG THE COLORADO RIVER SCENIC BYWAY

The curvy 44-mile Colorado River Scenic Byway (Hwy 128) follows the winding waters through gorgeous red-rock country of high walls, mesas, alfalfa fields and sagebrush. Extend the trip by adding the La Sal Mountain Loop Rd (p165). The Colorado River forms the southern boundary of Arches National Park for the first 15 miles of this journey. Near the start of the 'river road' just east of Hwy 191, **1 Matrimony Spring** is said to have magical properties and couples who drink from it might soon hear wedding bells. Several BLM campgrounds are sandwiched between the river and the road. After the first major bend is the **2 Grandstaff Canyon Trailhead** (p162), which leads to a beautiful arch. At the head of the next bend (6 miles from Hwy 191), spot boulderers on the rocks at **3 Big Bend Recreation Site**, where you can picnic by the river. As you round the mesa near Red Cliff Lodge, look on the right for **4 Castleton Tower**, a narrow 400ft sandstone spire that rises above Castle Valley and is one of the area's most iconic rock climbs. In the 1960s and '70s, Chevrolet filmed TV commercials on top of it, helicoptering a car to the summit. Carry on to the turnoff for **5 Fisher Towers** (p165). The 900ft-high Titan, standing solemnly at the end of the formation, is the tallest freestanding natural tower in the country. The road finally crosses the river at **6 Dewey Bridge**, where you might spot rafters drifting by. The scenic byway soon ends at a three-way intersection. Return to Moab or double back to the La Sal Mountain Loop Rd. You're also less than 10 miles from I-70.

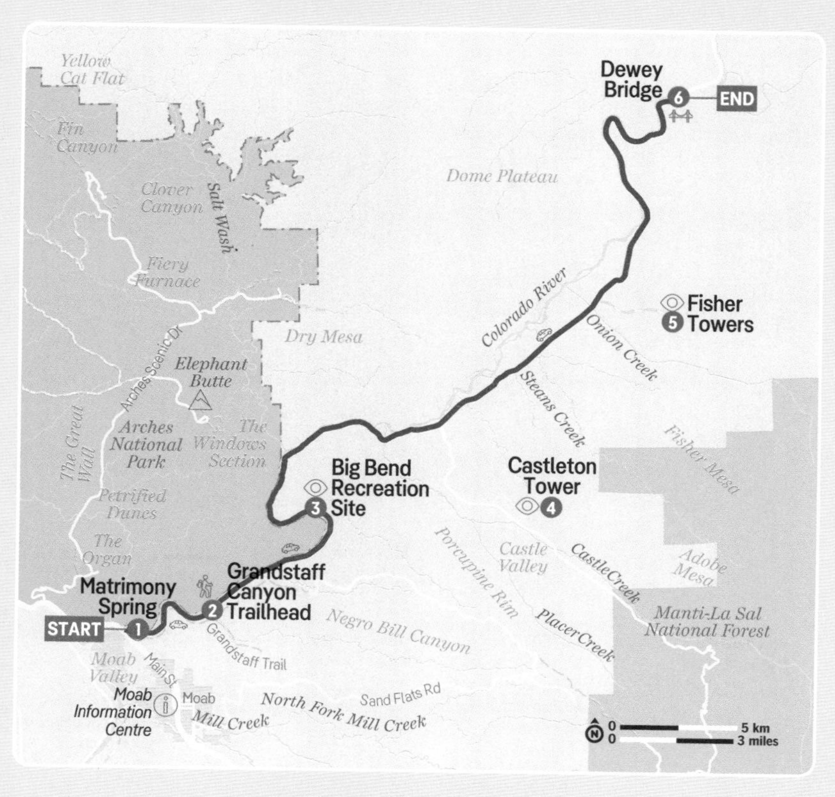

CANYONLANDS: NEEDLES DISTRICT

Canyonlands National Park
Needles District

Named for the spires of orange-and-white sandstone emerging from the desert floor, Canyonlands' Needles district is so different from Island in the Sky that it's hard to believe they're part of the same national park. The Needles receives only half as many visitors as Island in the Sky because it's more remote – but still only a 1½-hour drive from Moab – and there are fewer roadside attractions (but most are well worth the hike). The payoff is huge: peaceful solitude and the opportunity to participate in, not just observe, the vastness of canyon country.

The paved road in the Needles runs 6.5 miles from the visitor center to Big Spring Canyon Overlook. Parking areas along the way access several hiking trails to arches, Pothole Point, Ancestral Puebloan sites and petroglyphs, offering an overview of the region's human and geologic history. Many more miles of 4WD and mountain biking roads crisscross the district.

TOP TIP

The town of Monticello, pronounced mon-ti-*sell*-o, is the closest base to the Needles for non-campsite accommodations. You can take a shortcut to the Needles on County Rd 101 west to Harts Draw Rd (closed in winter). After 17 scenic miles, you join the main route on Hwy 211.

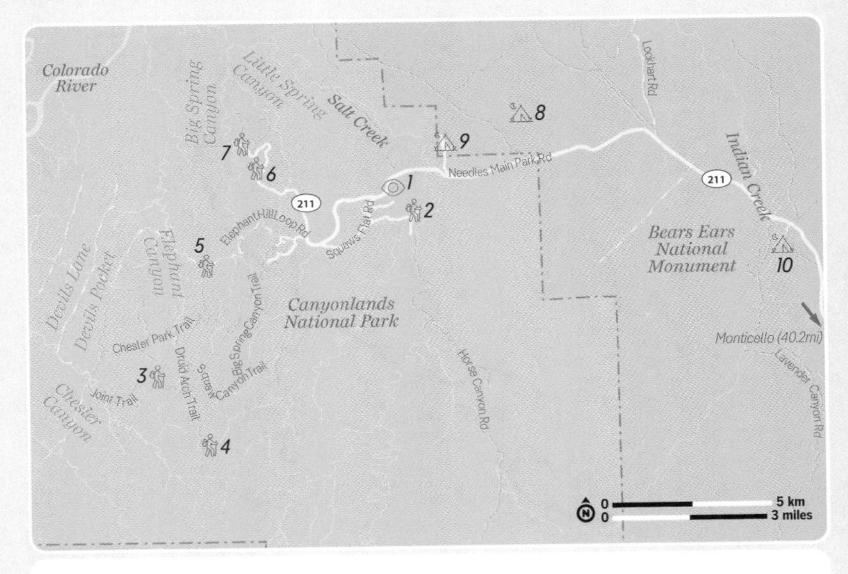

HIGHLIGHTS
1 'Roadside Ruin'

ACTIVITIES
2 Cave Spring Trail
3 Chesler Park Loop
4 Druid Arch
5 Elephant Hill Trailhead
6 Pothole Point Trail
7 Slickrock Trail

SLEEPING
8 Needles Campground
9 Needles Outpost
10 Superbowl Campground

Cave Springs Trail

PRISCILLA HAIGHT/SHUTTERSTOCK ©

Human History on Cave Spring Trail

DRAWN TO THE WATERING HOLE

Cowboy artifacts, historic pictographs, ladders and slickrock scampers: **Cave Spring Trail** is a fun-filled hike for history buffs and kids of all ages.

Pungent sagebrush marks this trailhead at the end of a well-maintained, mile-long dirt road. Hikers first reach an abandoned **cowboy camp** with miscellaneous remnants from the 19th and 20th centuries. The trail continues beneath a protruding rock lip to Cave Spring, one of the few perennial water sources in the Needles. Look for the rust-colored **pictographs** painted on the walls more than 1000 years ago.

From Cave Spring, you climb two ladders up slickrock for wraparound views of rock formations, steppes and mesas. The trail has awesome views of rock spires and the La Sal Mountains. After crossing the undulating sandstone, the trail drops into a wash and returns to the trailhead.

Pothole Point Trail

Pools of Life at Pothole Point

HERE TODAY, GONE TOMORROW

This short 0.6-mile **Pothole Point Trail** loop across slickrock explores the microcosmic ecosystems of potholes (naturally occurring dimples in the rock that collect water during rainstorms). The hike features views of distant cliffs, mountains and rock formations similar to those along the Slickrock Trail (p170).

To the naked eye, these potholes appear to be nothing more than mud puddles, but closer inspection reveals tiny organisms that must complete their life cycles before the water evaporates. Keep your hands and feet out of the potholes because these organisms are fragile. Though this is an excellent walk for contemplative souls and the scientifically inclined, it does lack drama, unless the potholes are teeming with life (which isn't always readily visible).

POWELL & THE WEST

In 1869, one-armed Civil War veteran and geologist John Wesley Powell became famous for being the first to descend the length of the Colorado River through the Grand Canyon. Thanks to his passion and rigor, Powell and his survey teams' geologic and ethnological work largely forms the basis of what we know about early southern Utah today.

Powell showed respect for the Southern Paiute, who gave him practical assistance and safe passage through the area.

You can track Powell's expeditions in Canyonlands and Zion National Parks and Grand Staircase-Escalante National Monument.

To learn about his famous boat trip, pick up a modern reprint of Powell's very readable *Exploration of the Colorado River and Its Canyons* (1875).

WHERE TO CAMP IN & AROUND CANYONLANDS' NEEDLES DISTRICT

Needles Campground
Some of the 26 in-park sites are reservable spring to fall; otherwise, it's first come, first served. $

Needles Outpost
Campsites, tipis and treehouse tents plus on-site store just outside the park entrance. $$

Superbowl Campground
BLM-administered spot with 37 sites, picnic tables, fire rings and vault toilets. No water. $

Scenery from the Slickrock Trail

NAVIGATING TO THE VIEWS

Slick Rock Trail

The ridgeline **Slickrock Trail** is high above the canyons with views below, almost entirely on its namesake type of stone. After ascending gentle switchbacks you'll follow cairns. This semiloop trail is tricky to trace in places. Brochures available at the trailhead describe four main viewpoints, each marked by a numbered signpost. Keep an eye out during your hike – bighorn sheep are occasionally seen here.

If you're short on time, at least visit **Viewpoint 1** for a panorama you simply can't get from the road. Giant red cliffs hang like curtains below high buttes and mesas, the district's eponymous needles touch the sky and the La Sal and Abajo Mountains lord over the whole scene.

Bear right at the 'Begin Loop' signpost to reach **Viewpoint 2**, where hearty vegetation clings to the desert crust and lines the watercourses. Scamper up the rocks for a primo view. At **Viewpoint 3**, giant boulders ring Lower Little Spring Canyon, where purple and gray rock layers offer telltale evidence of an ancient shallow sea.

Viewpoint 4 is a high promontory that overlooks Big Spring Canyon, a vast, rugged gorge. Watch overhead for birds soaring on thermals. To the north, you'll spot Grand View Point at Island in the Sky, perched high atop the red Wingate sandstone cliffs.

On the return path, you'll face the needles and spires to the south that define this district. The Abajo Mountains lie beyond.

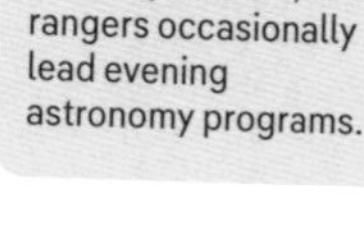

'HALF THE PARK IS AFTER DARK'

Canyonlands National Park is an incredible sight to behold by day and by night the landscape is blanketed by some of the darkest skies remaining in the US, perfect for stargazing.

On some nights, it's possible to see 15,000 stars twinkling overhead, compared to fewer than 500 stars visible in urban areas. The night sky at Canyonlands is so astounding that the International Dark Sky Association named Canyonlands a Gold-Tier International Dark Sky Park in 2015.

The park is open 24 hours a day 365 days a year, so stargazers can have a DIY dark-sky session, or rangers occasionally lead evening astronomy programs.

Connecting the Dots Around Chesler Park

LOOPING THROUGH CANYONLANDS' BACKCOUNTRY

Get among the namesake 'needles' formations on the **Chesler Park Loop**, an awesome 11-mile route across desert grasslands, past towering red-

Chesler Park Loop Trail

4WD & MOUNTAIN BIKE ROUTES IN THE NEEDLES

Colorado River Overlook
Jaw-dropping views of the canyon. Park and walk the final, steep 1.5-mile descent. No permit needed.

Elephant Hill
One of the most technically challenging routes in the state. Permits required for day and overnight use.

Salt Creek (Peekaboo) & Horse Canyon
aeology junkies love the rock art along this loop, but it's often impassable. Permits necessary for use.

IMAGEBROKER.COM GMBH & CO. KG/ALAMY STOCK PHOTO ©

Aerial view of Druid Arch

and-white-striped pinnacles and between deep, narrow slot canyons, some only 2ft across. Elevation changes are mild, but the distance makes it an advanced day hike. Make sure you plan your route and download maps in advance because this area has a number of intersecting circular trails.

Park at the **Elephant Hill trailhead**, 3 miles from Squaw Flat Campground on a gravel road that's suitable for sedans but in places is wide enough for just one car. From the parking area, the trail climbs to a bench and then undulates over slickrock toward rock spires. The next section is typically where people make a wrong turn. Cross the wash at the T-junction and follow signs to Chesler Park (not Druid Arch), descending 300ft along switchbacks into Elephant Canyon. Continue to follow signs along the canyon floor.

The final 0.2 miles to the **Chesler Park Viewpoint** climbs 100ft, topping out on the rocky pass amid spires. This marks the beginning of the 5-mile Chesler Park Loop. Five campsites lie southeast of the junction for backpackers.

If you're camping, leave your backpack at the campsite and explore the claustrophobia-inducing **Joint Trail**, where the fractured rock narrows to 2ft across in places. Pause just east of the Joint Trail for stellar views of the towering pinnacles that ring Chesler Park. On the southwest section of the loop, you'll follow a half-mile stretch of a 4WD road. If you're staying two nights, take the side trip to **Druid Arch**.

SHORT HIKE TO 'ROADSIDE RUIN'

The easiest hike in the Needles district is the 0.3-mile round-trip walk to the 'Roadside Ruin,' a remarkably well-preserved Ancestral Puebloan granary tucked into a hidden gap in the rocks. The trail takes only about 20 minutes to walk, starting out across uneven gravel and finishing over slickrock.

Ancestral Puebloan and Fremont people lived in this area, farming the locations that had enough water, such as nearby Salt Creek. Although the name 'Roadside Ruin' has appeared on the national park's maps since 1985, tribes today object to calling it a ruin, saying these places are still living and that their ancestors continue to use them.

GETTING AROUND

You need a car to get to and around Canyonlands. Make sure you have a 4WD and a permit if you're planning to venture into the backcountry.

Canyonlands: Needles District
Bears Ears National Monument
Monticello
Blanding
Bluff
Mexican Hat

Beyond Canyonlands: Needles District

A stronghold of Native history and heritage, the Four Corners region safeguards sacred spaces, ancient art and historic dwellings.

Utah's southeasternmost section offers the opportunity to connect with the original inhabitants of the land. Several Native American tribes still call this place home, including the Navajo, Southern Paiute and Ute Mountain Ute. Some trace their roots to the Ancestral Puebloans, whose fine artistic work and craftsmanship in construction can still be witnessed centuries after creation.

Their legacy lives on as today's tribes work together to preserve and showcase the rich culture and geology, including at Bears Ears, the country's first national monument established at the request of Native people. The pure night skies are some of the darkest anywhere in the US, providing starry scenes that the ancients also marveled at many moons ago.

TOP TIP

Many smaller restaurants, shops and even some motels close or have variable hours from November to April.

Moon House, Bears Ears National Monument (p175)

Petroglyphs, Newspaper Rock

Petroglyphs Aplenty at Newspaper Rock

STORIES IN STONE

On the way into Canyonlands' Needles district, don't miss the turnoff from Hwy 211 for **Newspaper Rock**. This single large sandstone rock panel, called Tse' Hane ('rock that tells a story') in Navajo, is packed with more than 650 petroglyphs, one of the largest known collections in the US. The carvings are attributed to Ute and Ancestral Puebloan groups and were etched over a 2000-year period. The many red-rock figures include humans, animals, tracks (many of which are polydactyl) and geometric symbols and are carved out of a black 'desert varnish' surface. Though protected by a fence, many of the petroglyphs are close to eye level, making for great photos and compelling viewing.

The town of Monticello is the closest to the site and has a few places to stay, eat and stock up on supplies.

Making History at Bears Ears National Monument

PRESERVING THE PUEBLOAN PAST

Valley of the Gods, Bears Ears National Monument

The first national monument created at the request of Native American tribes, **Bears Ears** protects more than 2100 sq miles of land and is named for a pair of reddish, nearly symmetrical buttes. The huge area protects important sites of cultural significance to Native people, with ancient rock art, cliff dwellings, ceremonial sites and granaries in a landscape of mesas, ponderosa forests and desert canyons.

Bears Ears has been the focus of political ping-pong for several years (p220). In one of his final acts as president, Barack Obama designated the land as a national monument in 2016, but when Donald Trump took over the White House, he cut the monument's size by 85%, down to just 201,876 acres. On President Joe Biden's first day in office in January 2021, he

NATIVE ARTIFACTS AT EDGE OF THE CEDARS

A museum with a small fenced-in outdoor area, **Edge of the Cedars State Park Museum** in Blanding protects ancient Native American artifacts and the biggest Ancestral Puebloan pottery collection in the Southwest.

It's built on top of a village lived in from 825 to 1225 CE and the encroaching subdivision makes you wonder what other sites remain hidden under neighboring houses. Informative displays provide a good overview of Native cultures in the Four Corners area and show off particular finds, such as a sash made of macaw feathers that dates from 1150. On the grounds outside, you can climb down a ladder into a preserved millennium-old ceremonial kiva.

WHERE TO STAY & EAT IN MONTICELLO

Grist Mill Inn
A 1933 flour mill-turned-B&B with comfy rooms, vintage furnishings, on-site restaurant and full bar. **$$**

Inn at the Canyons
Modernized motel rooms on Monticello's main drag with indoor hot tub and swimming pool. **$$**

Doug's Steak & BBQ
Utah might not be barbecue country, but the pulled-pork sandwiches and brisket are noteworthy exceptions. **$$**

sent out an executive order to review the rollbacks. That October, Biden issued a proclamation that restored Bears Ears to its original size.

Given its recent establishment and back-and-forth status, Bears Ears can be a little confusing when figuring out what to see and where to go. The monument doesn't have clear entrances and signage on the ground is minimal, so you might not even know when you're in it. Start your visit at the **Kane Gulch Ranger Station** (open in spring and fall only) on Hwy 261 or the **Bears Ears Education Center** in Bluff, a grassroots community-run information center with interpretative displays. At either spot, pick up maps and ask for advice on exploring the area. Bears Ears National Monument is divided into three sections: Indian Creek, Cedar Mesa and the San Juan River.

In the northern part of the monument, **Indian Creek** contains Newspaper Rock (p173) and world-renowned crack climbing routes, challenging rock climbers with vertical lines in a sea of sandstone. The **San Juan River** flows along the monument's southern edge, offering unforgettable scenes as you float by vertical red canyon walls and Ancestral Puebloan cliff dwellings and rock art. Outfitters around the town of Bluff host full-day rafting trips, as well as multiday adventures,

AROUND THE BEND AT GOOSENECKS

Head north of Mexican Hat on Hwy 261 and you'll come to a 4-mile paved road that turns west to **Goosenecks State Park**. The mesmerizing view of the serpentine San Juan River flowing 1000ft below is the work of 300 million years of erosion. See how the river snaked back on its course, leaving gooseneck-shaped spits of land untouched. The 'million-dollar views' promised by the park brochure cost $5 to see; bring cash.

Intrepid hikers can try the **Honaker Trail**, a steep 4-mile round-trip to the canyon floor with a 1400ft vertical drop, constructed in 1893 for gold miners to access the river. The road approach (from Johns Canyon Rd) normally requires a 4WD.

Rock climber, Indian Creek

WHERE TO CAMP AROUND BEARS EARS

Hamburger Rock Campground
Quiet BLM spot in the Indian Creek area, partially shaded by its namesake rock formation. $

Comb Wash Dispersed Camping Area
Enjoy million-dollar scenery for free; note there's no signage, water or cell service. $

Goosenecks State Park
Eight first-come, first-served sites along the canyon rim, with fire rings and picnic tables. $

from March to October. If you want to go on your own instead of with a commercial operator, you must get a permit for specific sections of the river from recreation.gov.

The **Cedar Mesa** section, which includes Natural Bridges National Monument (p176), is filled with remote hikes, archaeological sites and dinosaur tracks. Some spots, such as the 700-year-old **Mule Canyon Kiva**, are short and easy roadside stops, while others, such as the **Kane Gulch Trail** to the multilevel Junction Cliff Dwelling, are tough 8-mile hikes. Good in-betweens include the 1-mile round-trip **Butler Wash Trail**, which crosses slickrock to reach a viewpoint to a cliff dwelling across the chasm. An easy 2-mile hike along the South Fork creek of Mule Canyon leads to small Ancestral Puebloan granaries known as **House on Fire**, so named because one of the small dwellings appears to be engulfed in flames because of a rather unusual gold-orange sandstone overhang.

One of the largest and most evocative archaeological sites is **Moon House**, which has 49 rooms across three well-preserved dwellings. Its name comes from pictographs that show the lunar phases. Access to Moon House is limited to 20 people per day, doled out by permit on recreation.gov for $6 per person.

Hiking to Moon House, as well as other sites such as Kane Gulch and House on Fire, requires day-use permits ($5 per person per day, or $10 for seven days), which you can purchase on recreation.gov or by using the fee envelopes at trailheads. Backpackers also need permits to camp overnight.

Howenweep National Monument

Peering into Puebloan History at Hovenweep National Monument

STRUCTURES STILL STANDING

Meaning 'deserted valley' in Ute, **Hovenweep** is a remote area of Ancestral Puebloan settlements straddling the Colorado–Utah border. This area was once home to a large population before extended drought or conflict eventually drove people out of the region around the late 1200s. Today the site is best known for the remaining structures from this time period, but people have lived on this land since 8000 BCE.

The national monument contains six sets of unique tower

DRIVING THE TRAIL OF THE ANCIENTS SCENIC BYWAY

The **Trail of the Ancients Scenic Byway** loops around southeast Utah, linking the national monuments on Hwys 261, 95, 163 and 191 before crossing the state lines into Arizona and Colorado. The byway has tons of worthy roadside stops, plus longer hikes and larger parks, so leave room in the itinerary to do it justice.

Don't miss the sublime spires of Valley of the Gods (p177), the white-knuckle gravel switchbacks of Moki Dugway (p178) and the curving chasm of Goosenecks State Park (p174). At the border with Arizona, visit the Navajo village of Oljato for handcrafted art, including silver jewelry and intricately patterned wool rugs, all with cinematic Monument Valley (p178) for an unforgettable backdrop.

VISITING BEARS EARS WITH RESPECT

Keep Your Distance
Viewing sites from afar honors tribal beliefs and protects the space for future visitors.

Don't Touch
Oils from your hands can damage rock art; leave fossils, bones and historic artifacts in place.

Pay the Required Fee
The nominal amount supports efforts to preserve the area.

STARGAZING AT HOVENWEEP & NATURAL BRIDGES

Southeast Utah has some of the least light-polluted skies in the country and today's night sky is as clear as it was for the Ancestral Puebloans. In 2007, Natural Bridges was named the world's first International Dark Sky Park. Hovenweep was the second in Utah, earning the status in 2014.

Buildings and rock art tell of the Ancestral Puebloans' observation of solstices, equinoxes and other celestial celebrations. Structures were oriented to points on the horizon on the longest and shortest days of the year. Small wall openings focused the sun's light to fall in specific places to coincide with important dates in the agricultural year, creating a calendar showing when it was time to plant and harvest.

ruins, but only the impressive ruins in the **Square Tower** area are easily accessible. You need a high-clearance 4WD vehicle to explore further. Head to the visitor center to get advice about where to go.

The visitor center is the starting point for hiking trails that pass a number of buildings in the Square Tower area, which has the largest group of buildings, including towers, kivas, storage areas and living spaces, most of which were built between 1200 and 1300. The trails give both distant and close-up views of the ancient sites.

The national monument has a 31-site **campground** about a mile from the visitor center that's open year-round on a first-come, first-served basis. Toilets and picnic tables are available and some spots are suitable for RVs.

Hovenweep is a 45-minute drive from the town of Bluff, which has a few hotels and restaurants.

Hiking & Biking Natural Bridges National Monument

A BRIDGE TO THE PAST

Sipapu Bridge

Natural Bridges National Monument became Utah's first National Park Service land in 1908. The highlight is a dark-stained, white-sandstone canyon containing three easily accessible natural bridges. The flat 9-mile **Scenic Drive** loop winds past trailheads and viewpoints and is ideal for cycling.

The oldest natural bridge in the park, **Owachomo Bridge** spans 180ft but is only 9ft thick. **Kachina Bridge** is likely the youngest of the bunch and extends 204ft. The 268ft span of **Sipapu Bridge** makes it the second largest in the country after Rainbow Bridge, which is also in Utah. Sipapu is Hopi for 'place of emergence,' the opening through which Hopi ancestors came into this world.

Most visitors never venture below the canyon rim, but they should. Descents are a little steep, but distances to the bridges are short, between 0.5 miles and 1.5 miles. Enthusiastic hikers can take a longer 12-mile primitive trail that joins all three bridges. Don't skip the 0.3-mile path to the **Horse Collar Ruins Overlook** that takes in an Ancestral Puebloan cliff dwelling.

WHERE TO STAY & EAT IN BLANDING

Stone Lizard Lodge
Stylish Southwestern-themed rooms in a glow-up of Blanding's first motel, built in the 1940s. $$

Abajo Haven Guest Cabins
Solar-powered rustic cabins 7 miles northwest of Blanding; tack on a guided hike to ancient sites. $$

Patio Diner
Old-school diner eats since 1959; the massive milkshakes alone are worth the stop. $

The 13 first-come, first-served sites at the **campground**, about half a mile past the visitor center, are fairly sheltered among scraggly trees and red sand. The stars are a real attraction here: Natural Bridges National Monument was the world's first International Dark Sky Park and is one of the darkest places in the country. The campground has vault toilets and grills, but no electricity, running water or hookups.

The nearest services to the national monument are in the town of Blanding, about 40 miles east.

Classic Red-Rock Valley Vistas

DESERT DRIVES IN UTAH AND ARIZONA

Up and over, through and around: the 17-mile unpaved road (County Rd 242) that leads through **Valley of the Gods** is like a do-it-yourself roller coaster amid some mind-blowing scenery. In other states, this incredible butte-filled valley would be a national park, but such are the riches of Utah that here it is merely a BLM-administered area. The BLM Field Office in Monticello has a pamphlet (also available online) identifying a few of the sandstone monoliths and pinnacles, including

WEJ SCENICS/ALAMY STOCK PHOTO ©

Valley of the Gods

TRACKING DOWN PETROGLYPHS AT SAND ISLAND

On BLM land 3 miles west of Bluff, the freely accessible **Sand Island Petroglyph Panel** was created between 800 and 2500 years ago during the early Basketmaker through Pueblo III time periods. The rock wall is more than 300ft long and is covered with human figures, Kokopellis (a Native American fertility god who plays the flute and wears a feather headdress that's commonly seen around the US Southwest), animals and geometric patterns and shapes.

The petroglyph panel is scenically set near the San Juan River and you can stay nearby at the **Sand Island Campground**, which has 27 no-reservation sites. Boats launch from the nearby ramp for river trips.

WHERE TO STAY & EAT IN BLUFF

Recapture Lodge
Rustic motel with a hot tub, miles of trails and slide shows by local naturalists. **$$**

Comb Ridge Eat & Drink
Dinner-only restaurant serving burgers, barbecue poutine and even local wine – a Utah rarity. **$$**

Twin Rocks Cafe
Get fry bread as a breakfast sandwich, a Navajo taco at lunch or accompanying stew with dinner. **$**

DRIVING MOKI DUGWAY

Ready for a ride? Even though warning signs indicate the approaching curves, it still comes as something of a shock to leave the standard paved road for a roughly graded, hairpin-turn-filled route that's nonetheless considered part of the state highway.

The twists and turns of **Moki Dugway** ascend 1100ft in just 3 miles at an 11% grade. Miners dug out the extreme switchbacks in the 1950s to transport uranium ore from Cedar Mesa to a mill near Mexican Hat. This roller-coaster ride has a few wide pullouts that allow you to step out of the car and admire the view of the rock formations in the Valley of the Gods on the floor far below.

Monument Valley

Seven Sailors, Lady in a Tub and Rooster Butte, but there's no on-the-ground signage.

A high-clearance vehicle is advised for this drive. A car can make it on dry days, but don't go without a 4WD if it has rained recently. Allow an hour for the 17-mile loop connecting Hwys 261 and 163. Entrances to the road are near the corkscrew Moki Dugway and Hwy 163.

Free dispersed **camping** among the rock giants is a dramatic – if shadeless – prospect, or you can stay in a secluded refuge at **Valley of the Gods B&B**, a 1930s homestead with giant beam-and-post ceilings, stone showers and off-the-grid charm.

Across the state line in Arizona, **Monument Valley** is a larger and more accessible version of Valley of the Gods and as it rises into sight from the desert floor, you realize you've always known it. Its brick-red spindles, sheer-walled mesas and grand buttes, stars of countless films, TV commercials and magazine ads, are part of the modern consciousness. When you're driving here from Utah, stop at **Forrest Gump Point** on Hwy 163, the highway where Forrest finally stopped running.

This land is now part of the Navajo Reservation and at 27,000 sq miles it's the country's largest reservation, covering parts

WHERE TO STAY IN MEXICAN HAT & MONUMENT VALLEY

San Juan Inn
Motel rooms perched above the river; its restaurant is one of the few places to eat. **$$**

View Hotel
You'll never turn on the TV: the show from the balconies, especially at sunrise, is far more exciting. **$$$**

Goulding's Lodge
Historic hotel with a deep connection to Hollywood; the former trading post is now a museum. **$$$**

BELIKOVA OKSANA/SHUTTERSTOCK ©

of Arizona, Utah and New Mexico. Great views can be had from along Hwy 163, but to really get up close and personal you'll need to visit the **Monument Valley Navajo Tribal Park**. Travelers have two options for visiting: a rough and unpaved scenic loop that you drive yourself, or joining a Navajo-led tour on foot, on horseback or by vehicle. Tour operators have similar offerings and price points and you can find a full list online (navajonationparks.org/guided-tour-operators/monument-valley-tour-operators).

Guides shower you with details about life on the reservation, movie trivia and whatever else comes to mind. You'll see rock art, natural arches and coves such as the otherworldly **Ear of the Wind**, a bowl-shaped wall with a nearly circular opening at the top.

The only hiking trail you are allowed to take without a guide is the **Wildcat Trail**, a 4-mile loop trail around the West Mitten formation.

It costs $8 per person to visit the park and tours do not include this fee. Staying in the tiny town of Mexican Hat on the Utah side of the state line puts you between the two valleys; otherwise, a few accommodation options are scattered around the entrance to Monument Valley Navajo Tribal Park.

SHOT IN MONUMENT VALLEY

Stagecoach (1939)
Not the first movie filmed here, but the one that started the Valley on the path to silver-screen fame. A popular viewpoint is named after director John Ford.

Marlboro Man Ad Campaign (1950s)
Images of a macho man in the rugged landscape brought a spike in cigarette sales.

Back to the Future, Part III (1990)
Marty McFly and the DeLorean drive through the Wild West of 1885.

The Lone Ranger (2013)
Johnny Depp and Armie Hammer survey the scene on horseback.

GETTING AROUND

You'll want a car to get around sparsely populated southeast Utah.

CAPITOL REEF NATIONAL PARK

A GEM OF GEOLOGY

Called the Land of the Sleeping Rainbow by the Navajo, the colorful desertscape of Capitol Reef encompasses canyons replete with rock art, Mormon history and hiking trails.

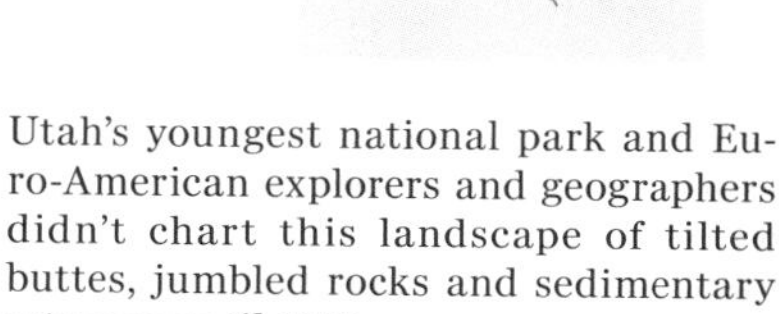

The showpiece of Capitol Reef National Park is the Waterpocket Fold, a 100-mile-long monocline (a buckle in the earth's crust) that blocked settlers' westward migration as a reef blocks a ship's passage. Also known for its enormous rock domes – one of which echoes the top of the US Capitol in Washington, DC – the national park harbors fantastic hiking trails, rugged 4WD roads and 1000-year-old petroglyph panels.

Capitol Reef wears its Mormon history on its sleeve more so than Utah's other national parks. Pioneer-planted orchards from the 1880s still grow heirloom varieties of fruits and nuts, watered by gravity-fed ditches – visitors can pick them straight from the trees to take home.

Established in 1971, Capitol Reef is Utah's youngest national park and Euro-American explorers and geographers didn't chart this landscape of tilted buttes, jumbled rocks and sedimentary canyons until 1872.

Often left off trip itineraries as travelers sail by on I-70, Capitol Reef is less famous than other Utah parks, but it's well worth visiting. The park's boundaries are only the beginning of the options for off-the-grid outdoor activities in the wider region. Two seriously remote areas of Canyonlands National Park – Horseshoe Canyon and the Maze – are more easily accessed from Hwy 24, which runs through Capitol Reef's front door, than they are from Moab. Grand Staircase–Escalante National Monument drips down from the park's southern border.

Opposite: Capitol Reef National Park; Inset: Mule deer, Fruita Orchards (p189)

THE MAIN AREA

CAPITOL REEF NATIONAL PARK
A wrinkle in time –
and the earth's crust.
p184

Find Your Way

Sitting in the south-central part of the state, remote Capitol Reef requires a car to visit. This part of Utah is all two-lane state highways and dirt backroads and the latter often require a high-clearance 4WD vehicle.

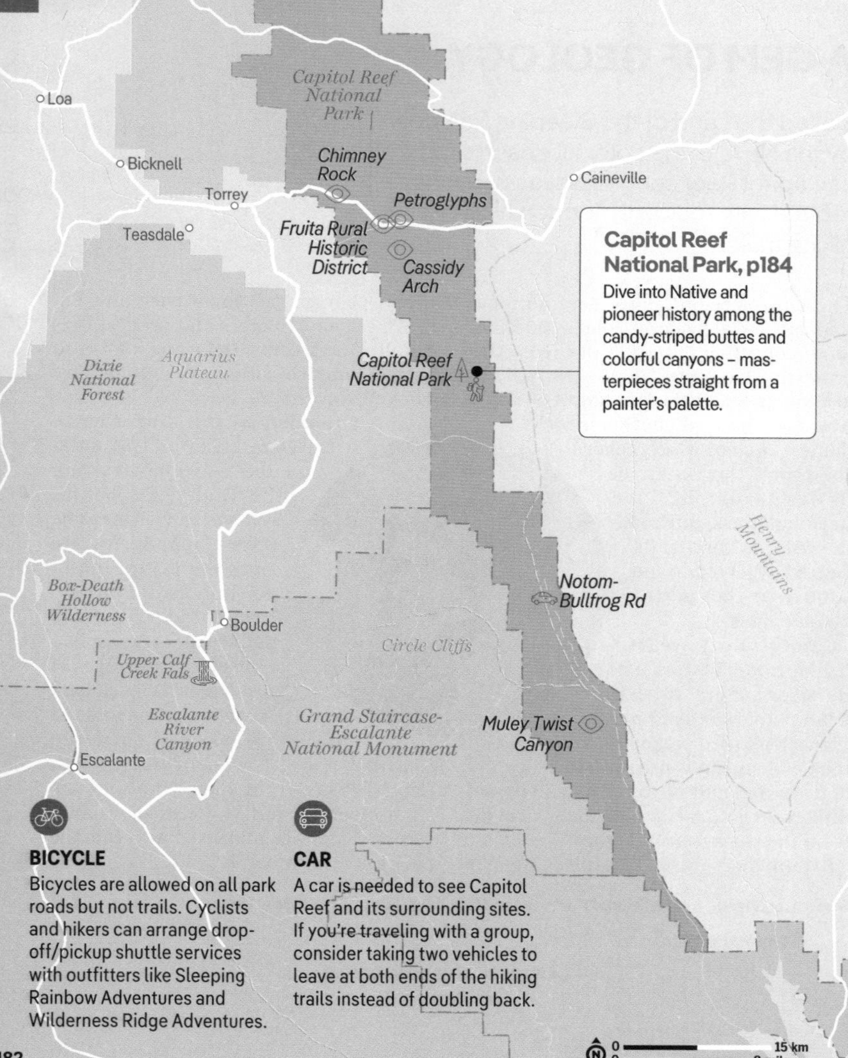

Capitol Reef National Park, p184
Dive into Native and pioneer history among the candy-striped buttes and colorful canyons – masterpieces straight from a painter's palette.

BICYCLE
Bicycles are allowed on all park roads but not trails. Cyclists and hikers can arrange drop-off/pickup shuttle services with outfitters like Sleeping Rainbow Adventures and Wilderness Ridge Adventures.

CAR
A car is needed to see Capitol Reef and its surrounding sites. If you're traveling with a group, consider taking two vehicles to leave at both ends of the hiking trails instead of doubling back.

MATTHEW CONNOLLY/SHUTTERSTOCK ©

Plan your time

Capitol Reef isn't a huge national park, but you can fill several days with hikes through slot canyons and up to grand viewpoints. Slow down to appreciate small-town life on the two-lane state highways.

Highlights of Capitol Reef

- If you have a day or less, take **Scenic Dr** (p194) through the heart of the park. At the end of the road, witness hundreds of years of history from petroglyphs to pioneer names in **Capitol Gorge** (p196).

- On your way back to Hwy 24, stop at the **Gifford Homestead** (p189) for its famous pie before choosing between hikes to **Cassidy Arch** (p186) or **Hickman Bridge** (p186).

Capitol Reef in Three Days

- Keep your hiking boots on after a few days in the park. Wander through the alien formations at **Goblin Valley State Park** (p199) and squeeze yourself through the slots of **Little Wild Horse Canyon** (p201).

- If you're not camping, base yourself in **Torrey** (p198) or **Green River** (p199) to get an early start to see the 'Louvre of the Southwest' at **Horseshoe Canyon** (p200).

SEASONAL HIGHLIGHTS

SPRING
Snow melts, wildflowers bloom and Capitol Reef starts to wake up. Gifford Homestead opens for the season on Pi Day (March 14).

SUMMER
Hike early or late – the sun is scorching before midday and monsoon rains often arrive by afternoon. The fruit harvest begins in the historic orchards.

FALL
Changing autumn leaves paint the vibrant landscape with even more colors. Apples are still in the orchards and ready for picking.

WINTER
Capitol Reef is mostly in hibernation mode, but solitude seekers are in their element. Reservations are not required at the Fruita Campground from November to February.

CAPITOL REEF NATIONAL PARK

In this forgotten fold of the Colorado Plateau, slot canyons appear as cathedrals cut from the earth and giant cream-colored domes arc into perfectly blue skies that hold fluffy clouds.

Capitol Reef doesn't always make it onto travelers' Utah national-park itineraries, lending it a carefree air that promises wide-open vistas, limited crowds (relatively speaking) and plenty of adventurous activities, from hiking through canyons and up to overlooks to dusty-bottoming your way out on rugged 4WD tracks. Or you can simply take in the history and geology that reveals itself in petroglyphs and early Mormon settlements, sandstone streaks and hidden arches and in a labyrinth of canyons that stretch back millions of years.

This narrow park runs north–south following the Waterpocket Fold. Unlike most national parks, there's no entrance station. Just follow Hwy 24, which cuts through the park, to the visitor center, where you can pay the entrance fee and pick up information.

TOP TIP

Capitol Reef's gateway town is tiny Torrey (p198), population 242, 11 miles west, where you'll find restaurants, gas stations and a multitude of accommodations options. Torrey doesn't have a full-sized grocery store, so if you need to buy specific items, head to Loa about 17 miles further west.

LISSANDRA MELO/SHUTTERSTOCK ©

Temple of the Sun, Cathedral Valley

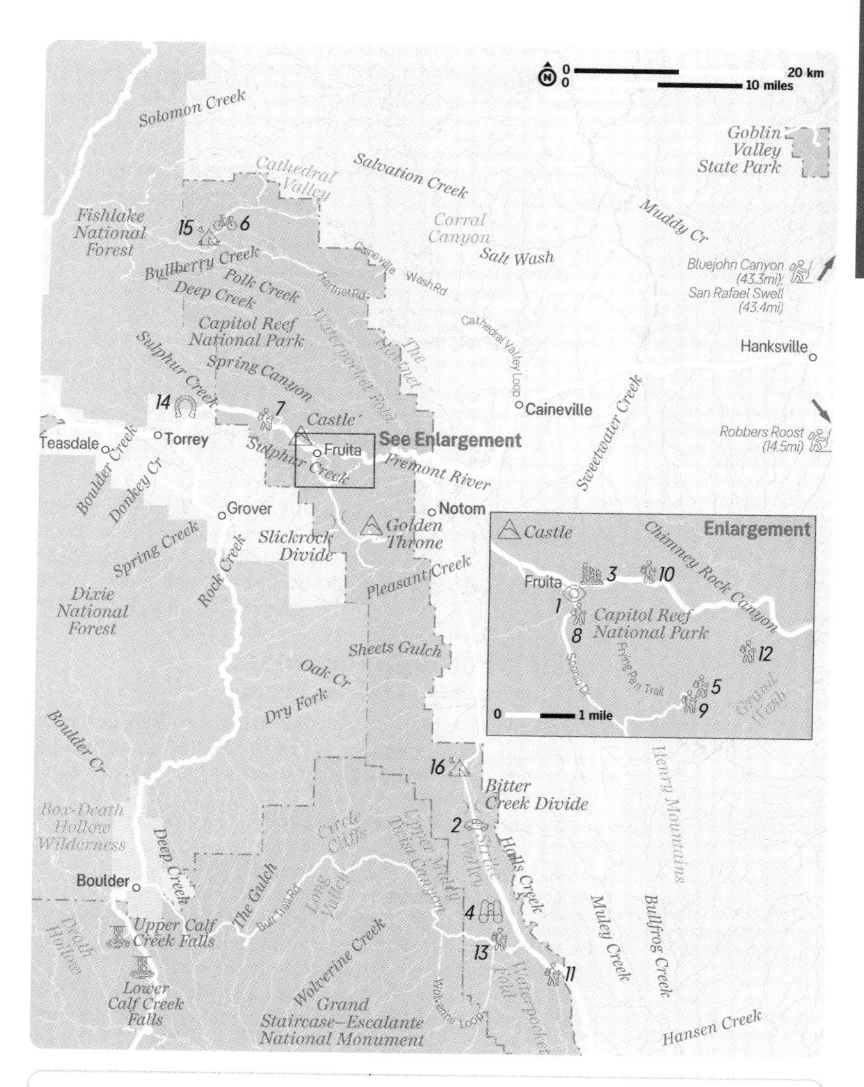

HIGHLIGHTS
1 Fruita
2 Notom-Bullfrog Rd
3 Petroglyphs
4 Strike Valley Overlook

ACTIVITIES
5 Cassidy Arch
6 Cathedral Valley Loop
7 Chimney Rock Trailhead
8 Cohab Canyon Trail
9 Grand Wash Trail
10 Hickman Bridge Trail
11 Lower Muley Twist Canyon
12 Narrows
see 10 Rim Overlook & Navajo Knobs
13 Upper Muley Twist Canyon
14 Wilderness Ridge Adventures

SLEEPING
15 Cathedral Valley Campground
16 Cedar Mesa Campground

The Drama of Capitol Reef

A WALK IN THE WASH

Grand Wash, Capitol Reef's most captivating canyon, is worth visiting just to walk between the sheer walls of the Narrows. This flat, easy hike with just 200ft of elevation change is sandwiched between the sides of a Navajo sandstone canyon that at one point tower 80 stories high but are only 15ft apart. Avoid this hike if rain threatens because the wash is prone to flash floods.

Along Scenic Dr, a good dirt road leads to the 2.2-mile one-way **Grand Wash Trail**. Start from the parking lot at the end of the Grand Wash spur road. It's an easy stroll up the packed-sand wash from the parking area. An offshoot path near the start of the Grand Wash Trail leads to Cassidy Arch and the Frying Pan Trail, but stay in the wash. The canyon's walls inch closer and closer together until, about 1.25 miles from the trailhead, you reach the **Narrows**, where the skyscraper-height canyon is barely more than two arm-lengths wide, a thrilling sight. The canyon walls shrink and spread out again as the flat trail approaches Hwy 24.

Return the way you came or arrange for someone to pick you up on Hwy 24, 4.5 miles east of the visitor center. Look for a trailhead marker on the south side of the highway, where there's a small gravel pull-off. It's also possible to start this hike from Hwy 24, but the parking area is significantly smaller.

SIDE TRIP: CASSIDY ARCH

A 3.3-mile round-trip side trail from Grand Wash leads to **Cassidy Arch**, a natural red-rock formation that you can walk on. With 670ft of elevation change, this hike is much more difficult than Grand Wash, switchbacking up the cliffside and traversing some sheer drops before flattening out on slickrock, but the views into the side canyons and from the arch are absolutely worth it.

The arch is named after Utah-born Butch Cassidy, one of the West's most notorious outlaws, who robbed banks and trains in the late 1800s. It's said that Cassidy hid out from the long arm of the law high up on these cliffs, which provided a good view of any action going on down below.

Hiking Through Hickman

NATIVE HISTORY AND A NATURAL BRIDGE

If you only have time for one hike, **Hickman Bridge Trail**, Capitol Reef's most popular, is diverse, offering a canyon and desert-wash walk to a natural bridge, plus long sky views and spring wildflowers.

This popular hike is easy enough for anyone from kids to grandparents to enjoy. Because the route is largely exposed, it's best to do it in the early morning. Cairns mark some of the route, which starts off the same way as the longer, more strenuous hike to the Rim Overlook and Navajo Knobs (p187). Pick up a nature trail brochure at the trailhead, which corresponds to numbered signposts along the way.

Starting from the Fremont River, the path ascends a red-rock cliff via a few easy switchbacks. As you cross an open area of desert vegetation strewn with volcanic black rocks, the highway vanishes behind giant white sandstone domes. A short spur leads to a tiny archaeological site where you can

WHERE TO CAMP IN & AROUND CAPITOL REEF

Fruita Campground
Terrific 71-site campground under cottonwood trees alongside the Fremont River, surrounded by orchards. Book well in advance. **$**

Singletree Campground
Closest non-park option to the visitor center, with lots of space and even wi-fi (for an extra fee). **$**

Sunglow Campground
Six first-come, first-served sites with good facilities (flushing toilets, sinks) on US Forest Service land. **$**

KIT LEONG/SHUTTERSTOCK ©

Hickman Bridge

AFTER MORE ARCHES?

Arches abound in Utah's national parks. **Arches National Park** (p136) is the most obvious example, home to Landscape Arch, the longest in North America, but **Zion National Park** (p52) and **Canyonlands** (p146) have a few too.

inspect the foundations of **Fremont pit houses**. A short distance further, look right to see the remains of a 700-year-old **granary** in a cliffside alcove.

The trail soon drops into a wash, where you can rest in a shady alcove before ascending over slickrock to **Hickman Bridge**, having gained 400ft in elevation from your start. While this chunky yellow arch can be tricky to spot from afar, the trail loops right beneath it for a marvelous appreciation of its mass. Hike counterclockwise and bear left beyond the arch to keep following the route. Pause to look over the rim and downriver to Fruita, an oasis of green.

Ascending to Rim Overlook & Navajo Knobs

SURVEY THE SCENE FROM 6000FT+

The **Rim Overlook and Navajo Knobs Trail** is a slickrock route to twin bumps of Navajo sandstone perched on the

QUIETER CORNERS OF CAPITOL REEF

Though Capitol Reef isn't Utah's least-visited national park – that designation belongs to the wild wonders of Canyonlands – this spot is decidedly less crowded than its neighbors to the southwest.

While in the busier spring and fall seasons you're not likely to have the trails to yourself, in some spots it's not uncommon to go for long stretches without seeing any other hikers. Once you get a mile or more away from the visitor center and Scenic Dr, you've left most travelers behind.

As with Utah's other national parks, winter is the season that sees the fewest visitors, but make sure you're prepared for snow, freezing temperatures and nearly closed-down gateway towns.

RANGER PROGRAMS

Geology Talk
Understand the many layers that make up Capitol Reef at this daily 30-minute talk, held year-round.

Archaeology Talk
Summertime half-hour chat about the people who have lived on this land.

Evening Program
Hour-long conversation about various topics, including the night sky. Meet at Fruita Campground.

precipitous western edge of the Waterpocket Fold that yields unsurpassed views. The 9.4-mile round trip is a steep, strenuous climb offering little shade.

Start hiking along the popular Hickman Bridge Trail (p186), but after 0.3 miles, fork right at the signed junction – you'll leave most of the crowds behind. Follow cairns along much of this dry-wash and slickrock route, which sidles around Capitol Reef's giant white domes. Pause at the well-marked **Hickman Bridge Viewpoint**. Blending in amid the surrounding rock, this natural bridge is visible across a small canyon at eye level with the overlook.

Onward, the trail zigzags along the edge of a south-facing side canyon. As you continue climbing, you'll wind past the mouths of three more side canyons before reaching the **Rim Overlook**, 2.3 miles from the start. Gorgeous views encompass a profile of the fold and its north end, along with mesas, domes, mountains and the town of Fruita more than 1000ft below.

After climbing up and down more sandstone pitches, you'll pass between cliffs and a radio repeater tower before reaching a broad ledge that faces the **Castle**, a large, eroded, freestanding

STARGAZING AT CAPITOL REEF

You're bound to be tired from all the hiking, but when it gets dark, it's not quite time for bed yet. Stay up late to watch the twinkling stars over Capitol Reef, which was awarded the status of a gold-tier International Dark Sky Park in 2015, an accolade acknowledging the highest quality of night sky.

Thanks to its remote location, Capitol Reef has pitch-black skies cut only by the Milky Way and the confetti of a million stars. Ranger programs occasionally include star talks and **Heritage StarFest** is an astro event held every September that celebrates the beauty of the area's night sky.

Navajo Knobs

WILDLIFE TO LOOK OUT FOR

Bighorn Sheep
These Utah natives have huge curved horns and are often depicted in petroglyphs.

Yellow-Bellied Marmots
Also called rock chucks, they are commonly spotted around the Fruita orchards and fields.

American Beaver
Rarely seen but look around the Fremont River for their dens along the banks.

chunk of the Waterpocket Fold. The trail rambles along this ledge to the northwest edge of a west-facing, W-shaped canyon. Following cairns, you'll climb the west rim and soon spot the **Navajo Knobs** (6980ft), which mark the high point on the next promontory. Watch your step as you clamber over loose rock to the double summit and then retrace your steps back to the trailhead.

EDMUND LOWE PHOTOGRAPHY/SHUTTERSTOCK ©

Cohab Canyon Trail

The Curious Story of Cohab Canyon

HIKING TO A HIDEAWAY

Often overlooked, the moderate 3.4-mile round-trip **Cohab Canyon Trail** deters crowds with a steep climb at the beginning, but exploring a hidden canyon and the views from atop Capitol Reef is worth every sweaty step.

Utah outlaw Butch Cassidy (p107) wasn't the only one who was said to hide out in the secret folds of Capitol Reef. Early Mormon settlers in the area were polygamists, also called cohabitants, shortened to 'cohab.' After Congress passed the Edmunds Act in 1882, which made plural marriages illegal, US marshalls were empowered to pursue them as felons.

Starting across the road from the **Gifford Homestead**, this trail makes a steep 0.25-mile initial ascent atop a rocky cliff. From here, it levels out through a desert wash, beside which small **slot canyons**, nicknamed 'the wives,' branch off from both sides.

About 1.1 miles from the trailhead, a short but steep spur trail veers off left to climb to two **overlooks** of Fruita and the orchards. After about 0.25 miles of switchbacks, this spur trail splits into separate branches heading toward the southern and northern overlooks. This is a good turnaround point if you'd rather do just a 3.2-mile out-and-back hike, instead of a one-way shuttle hike to Hwy 24. The trail to the right is the **Frying Pan Trail**, a moderately difficult route that leads to Cassidy Arch and Grand Wash (p195).

The path continues threading its way through Cohab Canyon, going down switchbacks to Hwy 24, ending almost opposite the Hickman Bridge trailhead, around 2 miles east of the visitor center.

FRUITA & THE ORCHARDS

Fruita (*froo*-tuh), a historic Mormon settlement established in 1879, is a cool, green haven, where shade-giving cottonwoods and fruit-bearing trees line the Fremont River's banks.

Fruita's final resident left in 1969 as the land became part of the national park. Most of the town's buildings were demolished, but the National Park Service maintains 19 **orchards** using historic agricultural practices. About 2000 trees planted by early settlers still grow cherries, apricots, peaches, pears, apples and more and you can pluck the ripe fruit between June and October.

You can also pick up one of the famous pies from **Gifford Homestead**, where Fruita's last inhabitants lived. Up to 13 dozen are sold daily (and they usually run out!).

UNIQUE SPECIES GROWN IN FRUITA ORCHARD

Capitol Reef Red Apple
Similar to Golden and Red Delicious apples; found as a unique variety in 1994.

Potawatomi Plums
From the Midwest but likely brought to Utah by pioneers and miners.

Native Pecans
These nuts are small and have thick shells, but also a rich flavor and a lot of oil.

CAPITOL REEF IN A DAY

Shauna Cotrell, Park Ranger at Capitol Reef, shares how to make the most of one day at the park.

Hike
One of the best ways to experience the park is hiking. Trails immerse you in the landscape while exploring at your own pace.

Visit an Orchard
Get a taste of Fruita and learn some of its history in the historic orchards. In season, you can pick and eat fruit fresh from the tree, including heirloom varieties you won't find at the store.

The Park after Dark
Enjoy the changing light on the cliffs near sunset and then stay until the stars come out. Marvel at the sky in one of the darkest places in the country.

DANITA DELIMONT/ALAMY STOCK PHOTO ©

Upper Muley Twist

Backpacking in Muley Twist Canyon

GOING OFF GRID

Two rugged backcountry trails, **Lower Muley Twist Canyon** and **Upper Muley Twist Canyon**, feature arches, sculpted sandstone slot canyons and long views of the Waterpocket Fold. Their name comes from the canyon's narrows, where the 800ft walls are less than 10ft apart at points, narrow enough to 'twist a mule.'

The National Park Service does not consider either of these trails 'official' and does not maintain them. Despite this, you must get a free backcountry permit from the visitor center for overnight trips. Make sure you have the necessary navigational skills and do not rely on markers like cairns. Check with rangers about current conditions and the weather forecast before heading out. The entire region must be relatively dry when you undertake these dangerously flood-prone hikes.

The Lower Muley Twist Canyon loop, once a wagon route for pioneers traveling south, follows the dramatic

FOCUS ON THE FREMONT

Fremont Indian State Park and Museum (p199), near the western end of I-70, preserves the largest Fremont site ever excavated in Utah including pit houses (one of which you can climb into), granaries and petroglyph panels.

TYPES OF WILDFLOWERS

Indian Paintbrush
Look for bunches of thin linear red petals in Cohab Canyon, Grand Wash and Capitol Gorge.

Prince's Plume
Vibrant yellow flowers that pop out from the whole stalk. Commonly seen along Scenic Dr and Hwy 24.

Sego Lily
Native people and Mormon pioneers used the Utah state flower as a food source.

lower area through narrow red walls and then returns through grasslands broken up by colorful hills. Starting from the Burr Trail trailhead makes a day hike possible.

Upper Muley Twist Canyon is less dramatic than the lower route, but it offers easier terrain and expansive views atop the fold. You'll pass arches and sculpted sandstone narrows along this hike too. Though you can approach Upper Muley as a long, difficult day hike, it's better to spend two days and enjoy the scenery. Most people camp near the Rim Trail junction and then hike the Rim Trail Loop without a pack.

Fremont petroglyphs

Park Petroglyphs

CARVINGS IN THE CLIFFS

Take a short drive east of the visitor center on Hwy 24, then pull into the parking lot and stroll along the wooden boardwalks to see dozens of **petroglyphs** pecked into the nearby rock wall. These rock-art carvings convinced archaeologists that the Fremont people were a group distinct from the Ancestral Puebloans. The shorter boardwalk leads to a panel of human-like figures who are wearing headdresses and are surrounded by bighorn sheep. The longer boardwalk runs closer to the cliffs, but the petroglyphs here can be more difficult to see. Bring your own binoculars for a better view. The longer you linger, the more you're bound to notice. The boardwalk is wheelchair accessible.

Chimney Rock

Getting a Close-Up of Chimney Rock

LAYERS ON LAYERS

The **Chimney Rock Trail**, a 3.6-mile loop, is a textbook on Capitol Reef's geology and is named after the magnificent red-rock formation that towers near the trailhead. Even though the trail skirts below Chimney Rock, you will get the best photos of it before you set off on the hike. The route climbs steeply to its namesake, stacks of banded Moenkopi

WHO WERE THE FREMONT PEOPLE?

The Fremont people, also called the Fremont culture by Euro-American archaeologists, inhabited much of what is modern-day Utah for more than 1000 years, from 300 to 1300 CE and the Hopi, Zuni and Paiute are thought to be their descendants.

'Fremont' comes from the Fremont River that flows just south of the petroglyph site, which was named after John C Frémont, who led expeditions into the West in the 1840s. However, Native tribes reject this name. Hopi call them Hisatsinom, 'people of long ago,' while Paiute use the term Wee Noonts, 'people who lived the old ways.'

They lived as hunter-gatherers and added to their diet with farmed corn, beans and other vegetables.

TREES OF CAPITOL REEF

Fremont Cottonwood
Found along the riverbanks; their seed 'fluff' looks like snow in spring and summer.

Two-Needle Piñon Pine
Twisted trunks growing in all directions dotted through the park's lower elevations.

Utah Juniper
Survives on little precipitation or cuts off water to a single limb to save the rest.

Formation rock layers crowned with a beige capstone, with 590ft of elevation change across the entire hike. Panoramic views of the Waterpocket Fold, the volcanic Boulder Mountain plateau, mesas and canyons unfold, their colors positively glowing in the waning light just before sunset.

The trailhead is off Hwy 24, between the Capitol Reef Visitor Center and the town of Torrey.

Tackling Capitol Reef's 4WD & Mountain Biking Trails

OFF THE BEATEN TRACK

Capitol Reef has just one paved road through the entrance-fee part of the park, meaning that adventurers on wheels will have a great time exploring beyond the concrete.

Long-distance mountain bikers and 4WDers love the 58-mile **Cathedral Valley Loop**, which starts 11.7 miles east of the visitor center. The bumpy, roughshod backcountry road explores the remote northern area of the park and its alien desert landscapes, pierced by giant sandstone monoliths eroded into fantastic shapes. Partway through, the **Cathedral Valley Campground** has six primitive no-reservation free campsites. Water is not available, but there are pit toilets, fire grates and picnic tables.

Leading to the Waterpocket District of Capitol Reef, **Notom-Bullfrog Rd** heads south from Hwy 24 (9 miles east of the visitor center), paralleling the Waterpocket Fold. It's paved for 15 miles at the start but switches to a maintained dirt road. Several backcountry routes have their trailheads along this road, such as Muley Twist Canyon (p190). Nearby **Cedar Mesa Campground** has five first-come, first-served free sites that lack water but have pit toilets, fire grates and picnic tables, as well as great views east along the fold. After 32 miles, you can turn west on Burr Trail Rd in Grand Staircase–Escalante National Monument (p117). Along the way, **Strike Valley Overlook** has one of the best comprehensive views of the Waterpocket Fold itself.

Thousand Lakes RV Park in Torrey rents Jeeps. If you'd rather someone else do the driving, get in touch with **Sleeping Rainbow Adventures** for private Jeep tours. All-terrain vehicles (ATVs) and utility terrain vehicles (UTVs) are prohibited in the national park.

BEST VIEWPOINTS

Panorama Point, Goosenecks Overlook & Sunset Point
Two miles west of the visitor center off Hwy 24, a short unpaved road heads to three overlooks. The dizzying 800ft-high viewpoints above serpentine Sulphur Creek are worth a stop. Afternoon light is best for photography.

Cassidy Arch
Walk atop the rock span and peer down at Grand Wash nearly 700ft below.

Golden Throne
A gold dome of Navajo sandstone cresting 600ft above its surroundings. Reached from the Capitol Gorge trailhead.

Scaling the Walls

ROCK CLIMBING AND CANYONEERING

In search of quieter climbs and canyons, more rock climbers, boulderers and canyoneers are going up and down Capitol Reef's sandstone walls. The hardness of the rock can vary – even the harder Wingate sandstone can flake off easily and unpredictably. Free day-use climbing and canyoneering permits are required and can be obtained at the visitor center or by email. The national park has a handful of different climbing zones and you must have a permit for each zone and each

AMYGDALA_IMAGERY/GETTY IMAGES ©

Robbers Roost

day you climb. A general permit (not for a specific zone) is granted for bouldering.

Commercial guides lead canyoneering adventures around Torrey and Hanksville, which have some of Utah's most famous routes. The **San Rafael Swell** and **Robbers Roost** are for experienced canyoneers and should otherwise only be attempted with a guide or group. **Bluejohn Canyon** gained infamy in 2003 when Aron Ralston spent more than five days pinned to a boulder before finally amputating his arm. His ordeal was captured in the 2010 James Franco movie *127 Hours*. Torrey-based **Capitol Reef Adventure Company** (capitolreef-adventurecompany.com) runs canyoneering trips, as well as guided hikes. **Get In The Wild** (getinthewild.com) in Hanksville offers trips throughout the wider region, including canyoneering in Goblin Valley State Park (p199).

On Your High Horse

IN THE SADDLE AROUND CAPITOL REEF

Horseback riding is permitted in some areas of Capitol Reef National Park, but most outfitters set off in the surrounding Bureau of Land Management and US Forest Service land, which have fewer restrictions. **Wilderness Ridge Adventures** (wildernessridgeadventures.com) runs one- and two-hour trail rides in the easternmost section of Fishlake National Forest, which borders the national park.

WHY I LOVE CAPITOL REEF NATIONAL PARK

Lauren Keith, writer

After visiting Utah's much busier national parks like Zion and Arches, Capitol Reef comes as a breath of fresh air. It feels more down-to-earth and less showy, even though it has just as much worth showing off.

As a history nerd, I love the hike through Capitol Gorge past panels of petroglyphs, rusted telephone wires and the foot-tall signatures and spelling errors of pioneers, prospectors and surveyors.

As then, this park still remains somewhat off the well-trodden trail, but the insistence of humankind to ensure our names are remembered even if our stories are forgotten – especially in the face of the flash floods that are Mother Nature's eraser in these narrow canyons – strikes a deep chord.

GETTING AROUND

There is no public transportation to or around Capitol Reef, so you'll need your own vehicle. Aside from Hwy 24 and Scenic Dr, park routes are dirt roads that are bladed only a few times a year. In summer, you might be able to drive Notom-Bullfrog Rd and the Burr Trail in a regular passenger car. Remote regions such as Cathedral Valley likely require a high-clearance 4WD vehicle. Check weather and road conditions with rangers.

ROAD TRIP

Scenic Drive Through Capitol Reef's Rainbow Rocks

This rolling drive along the Waterpocket Fold is a geology diorama come to life, with arches, hoodoos and canyon narrows easily within view, plus opportunities for hikes. The best of the route is its last 2 miles between the narrow sandstone walls of Capitol Gorge. You must pay the park's entrance fee ($20 per vehicle): there isn't a staffed entrance booth, so pay at the visitor center or the self-serve kiosk at the road's start.

1 Colorful Cliffs

For the first 2 miles after the self-serve pay kiosk, the road skirts the bottom of gorge walls that are striped in bands of colors, including layers of red-brown shale of the 225-million-year-old Moenkopi Formation and gray and purple volcanic ash. Stop at the pull-off to take a photo.

The Drive: After 2 miles, turn left on the dirt road to Grand Wash.

2 Grand Wash

Stretch your legs on the stunning Grand Wash Trail (p186), an easy hike that winds through a canyon that gets progressively narrower as you carry on. If you're up for a more active trek, hike up to Cassidy

Grand Wash Trail

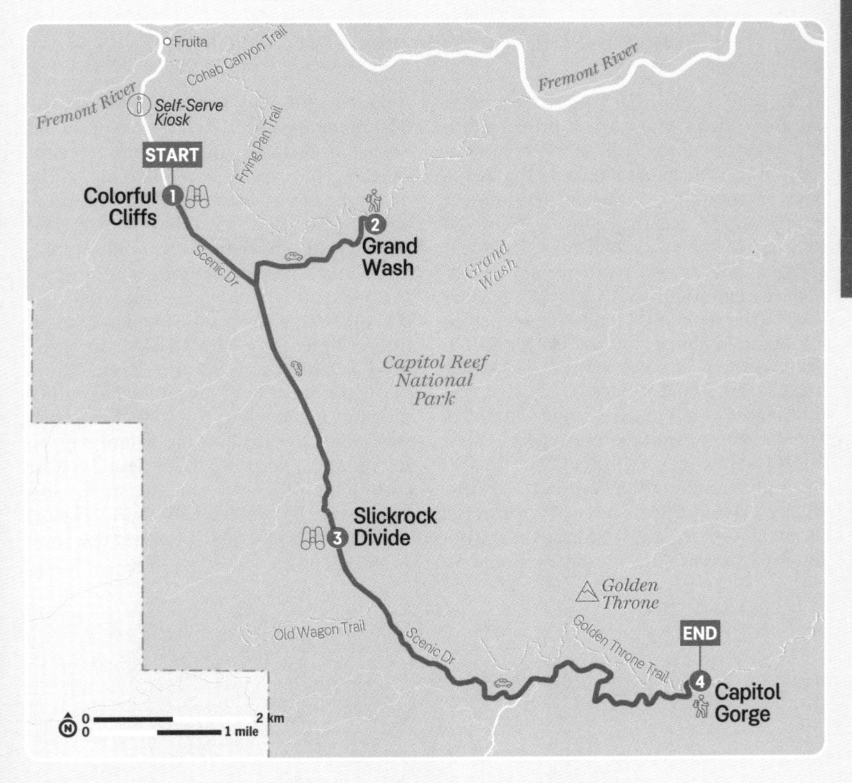

Arch (p186) for vertigo-inducing views of the canyon floor below.

The Drive: Head back the way you came to Scenic Dr. Stop at the information panels near the intersection to read about the abandoned Oyler Uranium Mine. It opened in 1901, long before the nuclear bomb and the Atomic Age. Uranium was used to 'cure' arthritis, rheumatism and similar ailments. The metal doors closing off the entrance to the mines are visible from the road.

3 Slickrock Divide

Scenic Dr winds on past soaring sandstone. About 2.5 miles after your last turn, a small pull-off marks the boundary between two major drainage systems in Capitol Reef: north to Grand Wash and south to Capitol Gorge.

The Drive: After 2 miles, the road curves to the northeast, leading to Capitol Gorge and switches to gravel after the sheltered picnic area.

4 Capitol Gorge

From 1884 to 1962, before Capitol Reef was a national park, you could drive – your car or wagon – through Capitol Gorge (p196), the primary route through the Waterpocket Fold until Hwy 24 was built in the 1960s. It took Mormon pioneers more than a week to clear the first road through the gorge, a process they had to repeat every time a flash flood blitzed through with more boulders and debris.

For a fascinating history lesson, hop out of the car and hike to the panels of Fremont petroglyphs and the names and dates of 19th-century pioneer passersby. Another trailhead from the parking lot heads to the Golden Throne viewpoint (p192).

The top layers of Capitol Gorge are part of the Navajo Formation. These white domes reminded early settlers of the US Capitol building, giving the park the first part of its name.

WRITING ON THE WALL IN CAPITOL GORGE

At the end of Scenic Dr (p194), leave your car behind for the easy 2-mile round-trip Capitol Gorge Trail, a historic wagon (and later automobile) route that leads past petroglyphs, 19th-century pioneer names carved into the rock and giant water pockets known as the Tanks. The sheer canyon walls are stained with desert varnish, which stands out in dramatic contrast to the red rock. Keep your eyes peeled for bighorn sheep and avoid this flood-prone route if rain threatens. The **1 trailhead** starts from the parking lot. Just 0.25 miles later, you'll reach a scoured panel of ancient **2 Fremont petroglyphs**. About 300ft further on, you'll spot signatures on the right-hand wall. These date to 1911, when a US Geological Survey team lowered its leader over the wall to incise the party's names – vandalism by today's standards.

A quarter-mile further, look up to see the **3 Pioneer Register**, a collection of carved names and dates. Despite more recent graffiti, you can clearly make out many of the historic carvings. Two gold prospectors, JA Call and Wal Bateman, etched the earliest names on this panel, in 1871. Look up to see the remnants of an early-20th-century telephone line. Just over 0.8 miles from the trailhead, bear left and follow signs to **4 The Tanks**, which lie atop a fairly steep 0.2-mile spur. These giant potholes hold significant volumes of water for much of the year. They were invaluable to early settlers and remain so for animals, so don't drink from or disturb them. When you're rested and ready, head back the way you came – the onward wash trail crosses park boundaries onto private land.

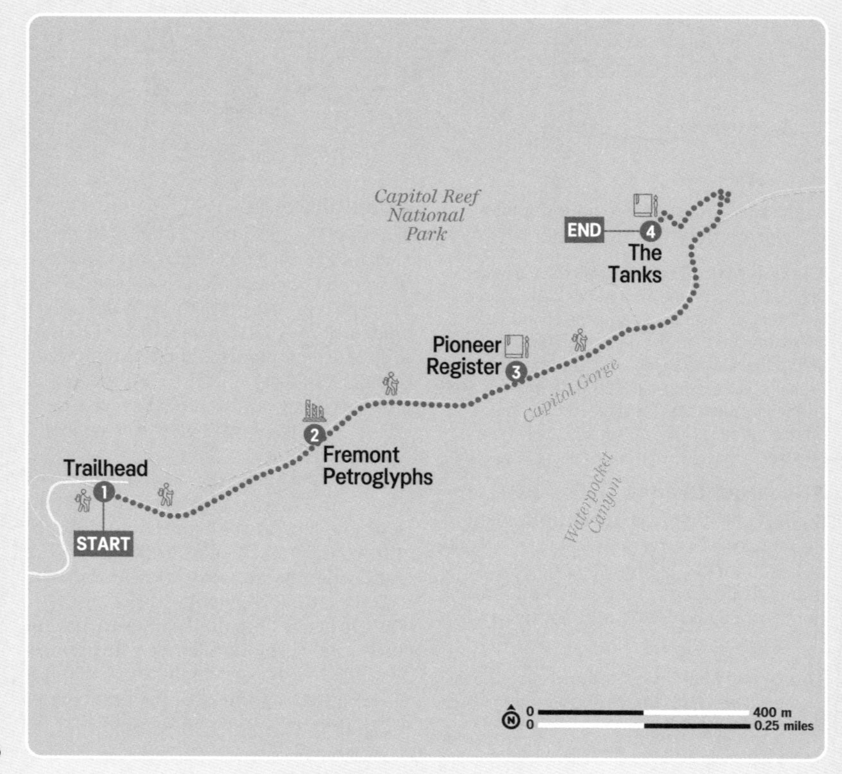

Beyond Capitol Reef National Park

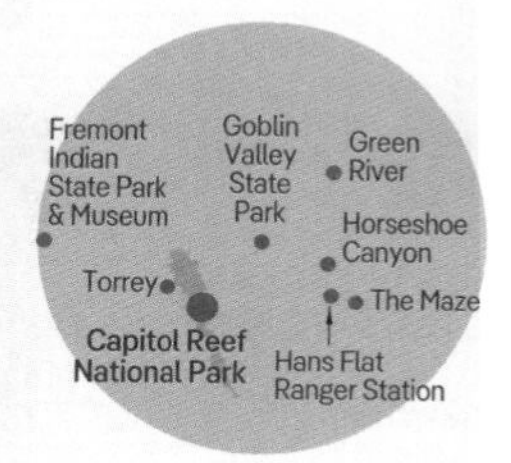

This quiet and remote section of Utah has stunning stop-the-car-now scenery that begs for road-trippers and backcountry exploration.

South-central Utah is so spectacular that the vast majority of the area has been preserved as national park or forest, state park or BLM wilderness. On the eastern edge of Capitol Reef, bizarre sandstone formations reminiscent of another planet poke from the ground in Goblin Valley State Park, while two nearby slot canyons pinch trails into crevices that aren't even wide enough for a single hiking boot. In a little-visited part of Canyonlands National Park, a meandering valley hides some of the most impressive Native American rock art on the continent.

The few small towns dotted along the highways are good places to stop and stock up – or even stay a while – before another jaunt into the wild.

TOP TIP

Cell-phone service is patchy in many areas, so make sure you have maps pre-downloaded and have let other people know your travel plans.

View from tent, The Maze Overlook

ANDREY DMITRIEV/ALAMY STOCK PHOTO ©

Ray's Tavern, Green River

Torrey: Gateway to Capitol Reef

SMALL-TOWN APPEAL

With pioneer charm and quiet streets backed by red-rock cliffs, **Torrey** lies just 11 miles from Capitol Reef and makes a relaxing stop. The town was a former logging and ranching center; its mainstay now is accommodations and outdoor tourism. Beyond the national park, Grand Staircase–Escalante National Monument is 40 miles south and national forests surround the town. A handful of outfitters are based here to help you get into the wild or to shuttle you to the national park. **Wilderness Ridge Trail Llamas** (wildernessridgetrailllamas.com) even offers day-long and overnight hikes with these adorable animals carrying your gear.

Torrey has pleasant and varied accommodations options, from basic motels and B&Bs to geodesic domes and Conestoga wagons. Most sleeping and eating options line the highway, which slows way down and becomes Main St through town. Outside of the spring-to-fall tourist season, the town shuts down. **Chuck Wagon General Store** sells camping supplies, groceries, beer and deli sandwiches to go. It's closed in winter, so you'll have to drive 16 miles on to the town of Loa for groceries from November to March.

The nonprofit **Entrada Institute** (entradainstitute.org) brings a whiff of countercultural sophistication. Its diverse events calendar includes music festivals and author talks. If you're here in late July, don't miss the **Bicknell International Film Festival**, a wacky B-movie spoof on Sundance that takes place just a couple miles up Hwy 24 in Bicknell.

BEST PLACES TO STAY IN TORREY

Skyview
Reach the guest rooms, some with private hot tubs, through a 'slot canyon' art installation, or spend a starry night in a geodesic dome. **$$$**

Torrey Schoolhouse B&B
A 1917 schoolhouse brought back to life as an elegant B&B. **$$**

Lodge at Red River Ranch
In the grand tradition of Western ranches, with rooms sporting open-beam vaulted ceilings, timber walls, Navajo rugs and fireplaces. **$$**

Capitol Reef Resort
Sleep in tipis, Conestoga wagons or standard resort rooms on this 58-acre complex. **$$$**

WHERE TO EAT IN TORREY

Torrey Grill & BBQ
A Culinary Institute of America graduate serves smoked meats on the back lot of Thousand Lakes RV Park. **$$**

Wild Rabbit Cafe
Cute family-run cafe with phenomenal all-day breakfasts, sandwiches and coffee roasted on-site. **$$**

Hunt & Gather
Surprising spot for fine dining, showcasing lovingly plated dishes of local ingredients. **$$$**

Green River Pit Stop

LAID-BACK INTERSTATE TOWN

Hugging I-70, the town of **Green River** offers more utility than charm, but its cheap motels and uncrowded restaurants can be a relief if you're coming from the swarms of Moab and Arches National Park, 53 miles southeast. It's also a useful base for boating the Green River or exploring parts of the San Rafael Swell, such as Goblin Valley State Park and Little Wild Horse Canyon.

The legendary one-armed Civil War veteran, geologist and ethnologist John Wesley Powell explored the Colorado and Green Rivers in 1869 and 1871. Learn about his amazing travels at the comprehensive **John Wesley Powell River History Museum**. It has good exhibits on dinosaurs, geology and local history.

White-water-rafting trips are popular, but the Green River is flat between the town and the confluence of the Colorado River, making it good for floats and do-it-yourself canoeing. The current, however, is deceptively strong, so swim with a life jacket. If you're passing through on the third weekend in September, be sure to attend the **Melon Days** festival – Green River is, after all, the 'world's watermelon capital.' Eat something more substantial at **Ray's Tavern**, a regionally famous local beer joint that opened in 1943. It draws residents and rafters alike for the best hamburgers and fresh-cut french fries around.

If you're headed west on the interstate, make sure you're fueled up. The 104 miles between Green River and Salina is the longest stretch of the Interstate Highway System with no services.

I-70 CONSTRUCTION & DESTRUCTION

As the bulldozers moved in to construct I-70 in the 1980s, they uncovered more than they bargained for. The largest known Fremont culture village was unearthed and the **Fremont Indian State Park and Museum**, near the intersection of I-70 and Hwy 89, was created to protect artifacts from the site.

While some parts of the village were still run over by the interstate after they were excavated, the state park contains one of the largest collections of Fremont rock art in Utah, with more than 500 panels on a dozen interpretive trails.

Get a better look with a pair of binoculars borrowed from the visitor center. You can also climb down into a reconstructed kiva.

WHO WANTS MORE HOODOOS?

Bryce Canyon National Park (p94) has the largest concentration of hoodoos anywhere on the planet and, similar to Goblin Valley, you can get up close and wander among them (though on designated trails, not anywhere that you please).

Far-Out Formations at Goblin Valley State Park

SPACE ODDITY

A Salvador Dalí-esque melted-rock fantasy, a valley of giant stone mushrooms, an otherworldly alien landscape or the results of a cosmological acid trip? No matter what you think the stadium-like valley

WHERE TO STAY IN GREEN RIVER

Skyfall Guestrooms
Three colorful riverfront rooms, each themed after a unique geological formation in the area. **$$**

River Terrace Inn
Well-kept waterside rooms; the swimming pool is a godsend on hot days. **$$**

River Rock Inn
Lovely Southwest-themed rooms, top-notch service and made-to-order breakfasts (get the famous pancakes). **$$**

WHAT IS BARRIER CANYON STYLE?

Formerly known as Barrier Canyon, Horseshoe Canyon is home to a handful of rock-art sites with a style so distinct that it has its own label. Barrier Canyon style shows front-facing human-like figures with broad, rounded shoulders but often no arms or legs. Many are painted in red, which was made from ground hematite (iron oxide).

The pictographs in Horseshoe Canyon are the oldest on the Colorado Plateau and their meaning isn't fully known. Some researchers think that the larger figures, such as the Holy Ghost, are shamans or spirits. The spirit figures have oversized eyes and are sometimes depicted with headdresses or horns. The torsos show life-giving symbols of water, such as waves, dots, zigzags or parallel vertical lines.

of stunted hoodoos resembles, one thing's for sure: **Goblin Valley State Park** is just plain fun.

At the end of the road, you'll reach the park's main attraction: the 3-sq-mile **Valley of Goblins**, punctuated with evocative hoodoos that rise up to 20ft tall. The three valleys are free to roam as you please, with no maintained trails, so you can temporarily forget the rules from the previous parks you've visited. Kids and photographers especially love it here. From the northeastern end of the parking lot, the **Caramel Canyon Loop** leads to the desert floor, connecting to the **Three Sisters** – the park's most famous goblins – and **Goblin's Lair**, which goes behind the valley and down into a cave (some scrambling is required).

The park's popularity is increasing, especially after Arches National Park instituted a timed entry system in 2022. Goblin Valley State Park tripled in size that year after the BLM transferred around 10 sq miles to the state. The park entry fee costs $5 extra if you arrive on Friday, Saturday or Sunday in April, May, September or October.

Goblin Valley State Park Campground has 24 sites that book up most weekends. If you'd rather glamp than camp, the grounds also have two canvas yurts with bunk beds, a porch and an indoor seating area.

"Holy Ghost" panel, Great Gallery

Hidden Art of Horseshoe Canyon

THE 'LOUVRE OF THE SOUTHWEST'

Part of Canyonlands National Park but detached by road from the park's other sections, **Horseshoe Canyon** shelters one of the most impressive collections of millennia-old rock art in North America. The centerpiece is the 200ft-long **Great Gallery**, where about 80 haunting human figures were painted in red, white and brown on the high rock wall between 2000 BCE and 500 CE, though they might be older. Similarly styled clay figures found in the vicinity date back more than 7000 years, meaning that this rock art could be twice as old as the Great Pyramid of Giza. The heroic life-size figures are magnificent, especially the 7ft-tall painting at the center of the scene, known as the Holy Ghost.

The Great Gallery is only one of four rock-art sites along this trail. Don't miss the other spots at **Horseshoe Shelter**,

MORE ACTIVITIES IN GOBLIN VALLEY STATE PARK

Canyoneering
Rappel 70ft down into Goblin's Lair, a sandstone cavern. Backcountry permit ($4) and technical gear required.

Mountain Biking
Five loops – each under 2 miles – make up the Wild Horse Mountain Biking Trail System.

Stargazing
Certified as a Dark Sky Park in 2016; ranger-led programs include full-moon hikes and telescope tours.

High Gallery and **Alcove Site**, which aren't well signposted on the ground.

This area was previously called Barrier Canyon, which hints at how difficult it is to get here. The Great Gallery lies at the end of a 7-mile round-trip hiking trail that descends 780ft from a dirt road, built by the Phillips Petroleum Company in 1929 to supply its oil wells. Plan on six hours. Rangers lead guided hikes most weekends in April, May, September and October; check Canyonlands' park calendar for specifics (nps.gov/cany/planyourvisit/calendar.htm). You can camp on BLM land at the trailhead, though it's really a parking lot. There is a vault toilet, but no water.

Aerial view, The Maze

TOM TILL/ALAMY STOCK PHOTO ©

Getting Lost in the Maze

LEAVE IT ALL BEHIND

Hardy backcountry veterans who truly want to get off the grid should head to the **Maze,** a 30-sq-mile jumble of high-walled canyons. This district of Canyonlands, Utah's least-visited national park, sees just a fraction of these bold travelers and is a rare preserve of true wilderness. The Maze's colorful canyons are rugged, deep and sometimes completely inaccessible. Many of them look alike and it's easy to get turned around, hence the district's name.

The rocky roads absolutely necessitate reliable, high-clearance 4WD vehicles. If you're at all inexperienced with four-wheel driving, stay away. Be prepared to repair your 4WD and, at times, the road. There may not be enough money on the planet to get you towed out of here. Most tow trucks won't even try.

Due to just how rough and remote this district is, plan on spending at least three days out here, though a week is ideal. Before you set off, contact the **Hans Flat Ranger Station** for conditions and advice. It has a few books and maps, but no other services. The closest towns are Hanksville (about 60 miles away, but 1¾ hours to drive) and Green River (83 miles, at least two hours' drive). These towns are your last chances to fill up on supplies and gas. The canyons are three to six hours' drive beyond the ranger station. The few roads into the Maze district are poor and often closed when there's rain or snow; bring tire chains from October to April.

SNAKING SLOTS OF LITTLE WILD HORSE & BELL CANYONS

West of the entrance to Goblin Valley State Park, a road heads to **Little Wild Horse Canyon** and **Bell Canyon**, a series of beautifully sculpted slot canyons. Sections of Little Wild Horse are too narrow to even fit your foot on the ground, so you have to shimmy sideways to carry on. If you're feeling the squeeze, Bell Canyon doesn't get nearly as narrow. At the end of Little Wild Horse, you have to climb about 6ft of rock to continue on the trail.

This hike is popular with families. You can walk as far as feels right before turning back, or make a loop along a 4WD road at the back of the canyons for an 8.2-mile circuit.

GETTING AROUND

You'll need a car to travel around this seriously remote part of Utah. Getting to some trailheads requires a high-clearance 4WD vehicle.

ROAD TRIP

Highway 24: Driving Capitol Reef Country

In just 48 miles, Hwy 24 packs in nonstop nature and history on a rural stretch of road between Torrey and Hanksville. Pass by tiny towns, curious rock formations and surprising spots to eat and fuel up. After Hanksville, the highway curves north to deliver you to otherworldly Goblin Valley State Park (p199), one of North America's most important rock-art sites, ending at I-70, just short of Green River (p199).

1 Torrey

Fuel up for the journey with a hearty breakfast at Wild Rabbit Cafe or grab a coffee and pastry to go from next-door Shooke Coffee Roasters. Walk one block west to see the one-room log school and church that opened in 1898.

The Drive: Hop in the car and sail downhill into Capitol Reef National Park.

2 Capitol Reef National Park

Capitol Reef is worth more than a passing glance, but save the hiking and cruising Scenic Dr (p194) for another day. It's free to stop at the roadside Fremont petroglyph panels (p191) just beyond the visitor center to see the impressive carvings of human figures, bighorn sheep and geometric designs.

PAUL BRADY PHOTOGRAPHY/SHUTTERSTOCK ©

Behunin Cabin

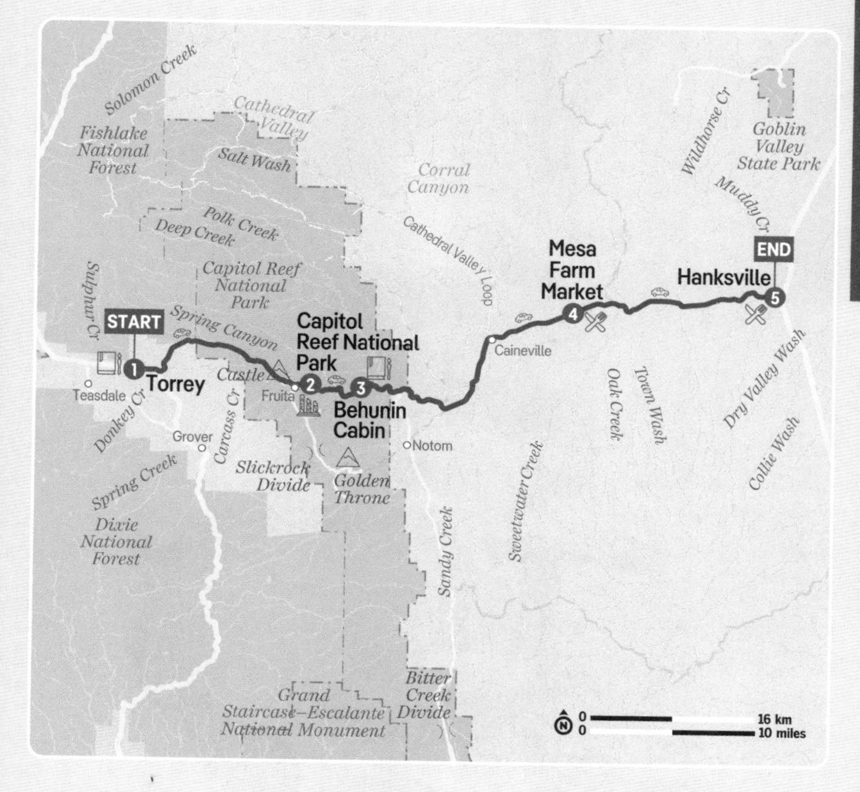

The Drive: Carry on east, as the road follows the curves of the Fremont River for about 5 miles. Pull off into the dirt parking lot at Behunin Cabin.

3 Behunin Cabin

Mormon settlers built this one-room sandstone cabin in 1883 for their family of 15 – all but the youngest kids had to sleep outside. After just a year, the Behunins packed up and moved east to Caineville.

The Drive: The mesmerizing rock layers continue outside of the national-park boundary, though they seem to have melted into softer, smaller hills of yellow sandstone and blue-gray shale. Drive on past blink-and-you'll-miss-it Caineville for 4 miles.

4 Mesa Farm Market

A foodie oasis in the desert, Mesa Farm Market offers straight-from-the-garden organic salads, juices, award-winning aged goat's cheese and freshly baked artisan bread from an outdoor stone-hearth oven. Have a seat and snack.

The Drive: The route starts to flatten out, though the Henry Mountains appear to the south. This range was the last to be named by Euro-American explorers in the lower 48. The drive ends after 14 more miles.

5 Hanksville

This small town at a highway crossroads is your chance to fill up on food and fuel – one of the gas stations has even been dug into a sandstone wall. Otherwise, there are no more services until you get to Green River (57 miles), Bullfrog Marina at Glen Canyon (67 miles) or Mexican Hat (130 miles).

TOOLKIT

The chapters in this section cover the most important topics you'll need to know about in Utah's National Parks. They're full of nuts-and-bolts information and valuable insights to help you understand and navigate Utah's National Parks and get the most out of your trip.

Rock climbing, Fisher Towers (p165)

Arriving

Most travelers to Utah arrive by air or car. Major airports include Las Vegas and Salt Lake City; Denver and Phoenix are manageable but further away. Smaller airports with flights to just a handful of locations are located in St George (near Zion National Park) and Moab (near Arches and Canyonlands).

Car & RV Rental

Traveling with your own vehicle is the easiest and most rewarding way to explore Utah's national parks. Car and RV rental is best in large cities such as Las Vegas or Salt Lake.

ESTA

Citizens of 40 countries do not need a visa for stays up to 90 days but do need to get an Electronic System for Travel Authorization (ESTA). Register online (esta.cbp.dhs.gov) at least 72 hours before your trip.

Cell Service

Cell-phone and data coverage are sketchy at best in Utah's national parks and wilderness areas. Don't count on having any. In most park gateway towns, reception is usually decent.

Groceries & Supplies

The small grocery stores in park gateway towns usually have a limited selection of items, sold at higher prices, so stock up when you arrive in larger cities, such as St George and Moab.

Distance & Driving Time from Airport

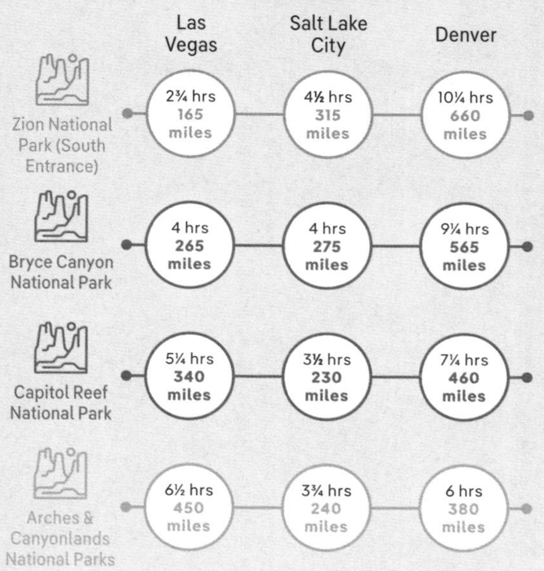

	Las Vegas	Salt Lake City	Denver
Zion National Park (South Entrance)	2¾ hrs 165 miles	4½ hrs 315 miles	10¼ hrs 660 miles
Bryce Canyon National Park	4 hrs 265 miles	4 hrs 275 miles	9¼ hrs 565 miles
Capitol Reef National Park	5¼ hrs 340 miles	3½ hrs 230 miles	7¼ hrs 460 miles
Arches & Canyonlands National Parks	6½ hrs 450 miles	3¾ hrs 240 miles	6 hrs 380 miles

TRAINS & UTAH'S NATIONAL PARKS

Riding the rails has always been intertwined with US national parks, and the potential of trains to bring huge volumes of tourists drove a flurry of development. The Utah Parks Company, a subsidiary of the Union Pacific Railroad, operated lodges, restaurants and bus tours to Zion, Bryce Canyon and beyond from the 1920s until the 1970s, by which time the automobile had truly taken over. Today, Amtrak runs only one train line, the California Zephyr, through Utah, which stops in just four places, including Salt Lake City and Green River. It's a super-scenic way to arrive but a completely impractical way to get around.

Getting Around

Public transportation does not run to any of Utah's national parks, so having your own set of wheels is essential for getting around.

TRAVEL COSTS

Car rental
From $35 per day

Gas
Approx $3.85 per gallon

RV rental
From $100 per day

EV charging
$10–30 for a full charge

Car Rental

Rental cars are readily available at airports and some city locations. To reach more remote trailheads and parts of the national parks, you'll need a high-clearance 4WD vehicle. If you have a choice, opt for a lighter-color car, which absorbs less of the blazing desert sun.

Renting an RV

RVs are a popular way to travel. Although larger models guzzle gas and can be difficult to navigate, they meet transportation, accommodation and cooking needs. If you're planning on driving an RV through the Zion–Mt Carmel Tunnel, you'll need to pay a fee and time your trip during specific hours.

TIP

The 104 miles between Green River and Salina on I-70 is the country's longest stretch of interstate without services.

ARE WE THERE YET?

Judging how long it will take to drive from point A to point B in southern Utah is an art form. Some highways drive like dirt roads, some dirt roads like highways, and slow-moving trucks and RVs can impede your progress for miles uphill.

If a dirt road is noted as 'good' and passable for passenger cars, you can usually drive an average of 30mph, but rough sections and washes could force you to slow to 20mph or less.

DRIVING ESSENTIALS

You must wear a seatbelt.

Yield to pedestrians at crossings and intersections.

.05

Blood alcohol limit is 0.05%, the strictest in the country.

Parking & Shuttles

Parking is usually easy to find in towns and at most trailheads. Zion and Bryce Canyon operate shuttles in the busy spring-to-fall season. When the shuttle is operating in Zion, you cannot drive your car along Zion Canyon Rd; Bryce does not have the same restriction.

Scenic Byways

Southern Utah is crossed by two interstates (I-70 and I-15), but avoid them whenever possible. Opt instead for the smaller scenic byways that show off the state's incredible topography and geology, sometimes even descending into switchbacks and unpaved surfaces that are part of the adventure.

On Your Bike

All of Utah's national parks have scenic drives that are open to recreational cyclists as well as cars, but the hiking trails are off-limits. Bicycles are allowed on Zion's Pa'rus Trail, and a paved multiuse path runs through Bryce Canyon to Red Canyon.

Money

CURRENCY: **US DOLLAR ($)**

Cash & ATMs

Have some cash on hand to pay fees at trailheads, state parks and campsites. ATMs are available in gateway towns and at some accommodations. Expect a surcharge of at least $2 per transaction on top of any fees applied by your bank.

LOCAL TIP

Single-use plastics will be banned in all national parks by 2032, and Utah's parks have already stopped selling disposable water bottles. Fill up your reusable bottle for free at visitor centers.

Tipping

Tipping in the US is not optional. Only withhold tips in cases of outrageously bad service.

Bartenders Per round 10% to 15%.

Guides Not required but recommended. A good start is $20 per day.

Restaurant servers Tip 15% to 20%, unless a gratuity is already added to the bill.

NATIONAL- & STATE-PARK PASSES

If you're headed to at least three national parks, buy an America the Beautiful Pass ($80; store.usgs.gov/pass). It's valid for a year and gives you access to all national parks across the country, as well as national monuments and other federal recreation sites. Seniors (62 and older) pay just $20 for the Senior Pass (or $80 for a lifetime pass), which has the same benefits.

The Utah State Parks pass likely isn't cost-effective. For nonresidents, an annual pass costs $175. State park passes expire yearly on December 31, regardless of when they were purchased.

Scan to buy the America the Beautiful Pass

HOW MUCH FOR...

a pass for all US national parks (America the Beautiful Pass) **$80**

an entry to individual national parks **$20–35**

an entry to state parks **$15–25**

an half-day tour or activity **$100**

HOW TO... Save Money

Prices skyrocket in the busy summer season (June, July and August), so plan a trip at other times for a cheaper – and quieter – experience. Camping costs significantly less than hotels, and many gateway towns have 'urban' campsites if you aren't prepared to fully rough it. Accommodation rates in towns a little further from the park entrances are lower, for example in Hurricane or Glendale (instead of Springdale) for Zion.

Accommodations

Camping

Utah is a camper's dream destination. Reserve months ahead, particularly for national parks and if you're in an RV. Use recreation.gov for federal lands and reserveamerica.com for Utah state parks. Show up early in the day at campgrounds that are first come, first served. Free dispersed camping is allowed in some areas managed by the US Forest Service and the Bureau of Land Management.

Hotels & Motels

Major hotel brands have outposts in Springdale (for Zion National Park), Bryce Canyon City (Bryce Canyon) and Moab (Arches and Canyonlands). Hotel choices are often limited in rural areas, but motels line the roadsides everywhere. The decor might be outdated and the buildings have seen better days, but most are still comfortable options for travelers on tighter budgets.

B&Bs

B&Bs in family-run homes generally offer good value and a heaping helping of personality. Hosts are eager to dispense helpful advice and assist with your onward travel plans. Rates often include a home-cooked breakfast, but some spots give vouchers for local restaurants instead to accommodate people who want an earlier start. Minimum stays are common in high season and on weekends.

HOW MUCH FOR A NIGHT IN...

Zion Lodge or Bryce Canyon Lodge

$160–340

an hotel outside the park

$200

a campsite

$20–40

Park Lodges

Zion and Bryce Canyon have in-park lodges with unbeatable locations steps from iconic landscapes and major trailheads. Both offer cabins and motel-style rooms – if you have a choice and the budget, opt for the pricier cabins, which have more personality. Rates are steep, and rooms are booked out far in advance. Check for cancellations to snag something last-minute.

Glamping

Utah has seen a huge increase in the number of glamping locations, including canvas tents, tiny homes and geodesic domes. Most lean high-end, with luxury linens and organic bath products, but a few are simply a small step up from camping. Under Canvas (undercanvas.com) has five locations in Utah, including the ULUM flagship that opened near Moab in 2023.

NO RESERVATIONS

Accommodations around Utah's national parks go fast, so it pays to reserve a place to stay as far ahead as possible for the widest selection and best price. If you're set on staying at in-park lodges and campgrounds, mark your calendar and book as soon as reservations open (13 months ahead for lodges and six months for campgrounds). The parks' gateway towns fill up in summer, but travelers on a budget and those making up their itinerary as they go will find rooms in towns a little further from the entrance gates.

Family Travel

Utah's national parks feature mind-blowing landscapes that seem like one ginormous playground, with wild rock formations to run around, slot canyons to squeeze into, gentle creeks to splash in and a variable level of adventure that can be tailored to every family's needs. A trip here promises priceless memories and might start a lifelong love of the outdoors.

Camping

No trip to Utah would be complete without at least one night in a tent – most kids love it. Look for a campground with fire rings so you can have the obligatory campfire and s'mores.

Plan Ahead

Most of Utah's park gateway towns do not have large grocery stores. Stock up on supplies for babies and toddlers at the start of your trip in urban areas such as St George, Las Vegas and Salt Lake City.

Safe Hiking

Many of the most famous hikes in Utah's national parks are physically demanding but not impossible for older children. Before you tackle a harder hike, start with a few easy warm-ups to get used to the desert environment and high altitude.

Children are particularly vulnerable to the heat: they dehydrate faster, and symptoms can turn severe more quickly. Make sure they drink plenty of water at regular intervals. To keep salts from being flushed out of the body when it is particularly hot, add a pinch of sea salt or electrolyte powder to drinking water. A wide-brimmed hat, sunglasses and sunscreen are absolutely essential.

Junior Ranger Programs

All of Utah's national parks offer junior ranger programs for ages four and up. Pick up an activity book at the park visitor centers, complete some of the pages during your visit and attend a ranger program. Upon completion, children are solemnly sworn in by a ranger as junior rangers, and they receive a certificate and a badge.

KID-FRIENDLY PICKS

The Narrows, Zion National Park (p54)
Splash through the canyon or pack a picnic to enjoy along the sandy riverside 'beach.'

Colorado River White-Water Rafting (p157)
Teens will love the thrills and (near) spills along this epic waterway outside of Moab.

Navajo Loop–Queen's Garden Combination Trail, Bryce Canyon (p103)
Bryce's most traveled trail has tunnels through rock walls and around otherworldly hoodoos.

The Windows, Arches National Park (p137)
Clamber below and around the park's iconic namesake formations.

TIMING YOUR TRIP

Traveling with children, especially during summer, means taking it easy. The hot sun, dry climate and occasionally high altitude can quickly turn into sunburn, dehydration and fatigue. Try not to squeeze too much in. Endless hours in the car can result in grumpy, tired kids and frustrated parents. After a while, canyon views start to look alike, and the trip can become a blur. Stop often and stay flexible.

Health & Safe Travel

DEHYDRATION

You don't need to do much to become dehydrated in the desert – just stand around. If you do engage in an activity, expect water and salts to leave your body at a vastly accelerated rate. Carry a large reusable water bottle or hydration bladder in your daypack and drink at least 1 gallon of water a day.

Blisters

Utah's national parks are all about the hiking, and blisters can easily derail your experience, no matter how beautiful the scenery. If you feel a blister coming on, find somewhere to sit and deal with it immediately. Apply moleskin, a Band-Aid or duct tape to the raw area. Wet and muddy socks can cause blisters, so pack spares.

Know Your Limits

One little-talked-about risk facing hikers is their own enthusiasm. Even in the middle of a national park, you're in a remote, wild place. Don't take on a trail that's above your skill level. Twisting an ankle or breaking a leg is surprisingly easy. It could take several hours or even days before a search and rescue team can get to you.

Altitude Adjustment

The rim at Bryce Canyon ranges in altitude from 8000ft to 9000ft above sea level, while Cedar Breaks rises above 10,000ft. A common complaint at high elevations is altitude sickness, characterized by shortness of breath, fatigue, headaches, dizziness and loss of appetite. Drink plenty of water and take a day or two to acclimatize before attempting anything strenuous.

SOLO HIKING

If you're hiking alone, tell someone in advance where you are going and when you expect to be back.

DANGEROUS PLANTS & ANIMALS

Southern Utah is awash in critters that, if bothered, can inflict a fair bit of pain. Among them are mountain lions, rattlesnakes, scorpions and tarantulas. Look before you put your hand on ledges or beneath boulders. Learn to identify poison ivy: serrated leaves that grow in clusters of three. This toxic plant grows in thickets, preferring moisture-laden canyons.

AVERAGE HIGH TEMPERATURES IN JULY

Zion National Park
93°F

Bryce Canyon National Park
80°F

Arches National Park
94°F

Canyonlands National Park
94°F

Capitol Reef National Park
89°F

Responsible Travel

Climate change & travel

It's impossible to ignore the impact we have when travelling, and the importance of making changes where we can. Lonely Planet urges all travellers to engage with their travel carbon footprint. There are many carbon calculators online that allow travellers to estimate the carbon emissions generated by their journey; try resurgence.org/resources/carbon-calculator.html. Many airlines and booking sites off er travellers the option of off setting the impact of greenhouse gas emissions by contributing to climate-friendly initiatives around the world. We continue to off set the carbon footprint of all Lonely Planet staff travel, while recognising this is a mitigation more than a solution.

Stay Local

Skip the hotel chains and stay in southern Utah's B&Bs, motels and other locally run accommodations. Hosts often dish out helpful advice alongside hearty breakfasts, and the buildings are characterful instead of cookie cutter.

Travel Slower

Water is precious in the desert. Hotels use nearly 400 gallons of water per day per room, so stay in one place longer to cut down on the amount of water used for changing sheets and towels.

Round Up

Nonprofit partners run the gift shops and bookstores at Utah's parks. When you make a purchase, staff will ask if you'd like to round up to the nearest dollar and donate your change to help preserve the parks.

The desert is an exceedingly fragile environment, easily damaged by feet, tires and fires, and slow to heal. Protect cryptobiotic soil crusts by staying on established trails and being mindful of where you're walking.

Know what to do when nature calls and restrooms aren't available. In the backcountry, come prepared with a disposable toilet system, such as a WAG bag that neutralizes pathogens and breaks down waste.

LEAVE NO TRACE

Practice the principles of Leave No Trace: plan ahead and prepare, travel and camp on durable surfaces, dispose of waste properly, leave what you find, minimize campfire impacts, respect wildlife, and be considerate of other visitors.

APPRECIATE NATIVE HERITAGE

Utah is home to eight federally recognized Native American tribes. Visit museums and parks that preserve their history, take a Navajo-led tour of Monument Valley, and don't touch the ancient rock art and buildings.

Wildfires burn millions of acres across the western US each summer. Always observe campfire restrictions.

Pack out your trash, including fruit peels, which can take years to biodegrade in the desert.

Get a Guide

You can visit many of Utah's incredible landscapes and natural features on your own, but going with a guide promises an in-depth and safe experience. Reserve part of your travel budget for guided activities.

Hiking Etiquette

Hikers heading uphill have the right of way, and it's polite to step aside to let faster hikes pass. Yield to horses and mules on the trail. Stay on the trail at all times.

Shuttles

Ride the seasonal shuttle to trailheads and viewpoints in Bryce Canyon National Park. The road is still open to private vehicles, but you can leave your car and let someone else do the driving.

Get Off the Interstate

To take the road less traveled, exit the interstate and drive Utah's scenic byways and backways. Support local economies by stocking up on supplies at mom-and-pop shops and stopping for a meal in small towns and lesser-visited areas.

5 million

By requiring visitors to use the shuttle bus, Zion National Park has eliminated 5 million pounds of carbon-dioxide emissions per year. A fleet of battery-electric buses is replacing the older propane-powered shuttles.

RESOURCES

zionpark.org
Nonprofit dedicated to conservation and education.

utahsown.org
Directory of farmers markets and local producers.

navajonationparks.org
Learn more about visiting the Navajo tribal parks.

FROM LEFT: JIM CUMMING/SHUTTERSTOCK ©, GEORGIAN BAY BOUDOIR/SHUTTERSTOCK ©, OLOS/SHUTTERSTOCK ©

Accessible Travel

The national parks exist for the enjoyment of all. Utah's parks have few accessible trails, but it's still possible for travelers with disabilities to experience the state's most epic landscapes.

Features for Wheelchair Users

All of Utah's national parks have wheelchair-accessible visitor centers, at least one accessible campsite in their main campgrounds, and a few viewpoints and trails that are open to wheelchair users.

Airport

All US airports must comply with the Americans with Disabilities Act (ADA) to provide accessible facilities and assistance to those who need it. Companies such as Thrifty, Wheelchair Getaways and Compassion Mobility offer wheelchair-accessible van rentals.

Accommodations

Accommodations must have at least one wheelchair-accessible room, though few are fully ADA-compliant. More often, these are ground-floor rooms with wider doorways, less furniture, and handles around the tub and toilet. Always ask exactly what 'accessible' means when making reservations.

ASL INTERPRETERS

If you're deaf or have hearing loss, you can request an American Sign Language interpreter for ranger programs. The National Park Service recommends submitting your request at least a week before your visit.

Visitor Centers

Visitor centers are wheelchair accessible, and some have tactile models and maps of the park for travelers who are blind or have low vision. Film screenings include subtitles, and museum exhibits sometimes have audio recordings.

Best Accessible Trails

The scenic Rim Trail at Bryce Canyon is paved between Sunrise Point and Sunset Point. A flat wooden boardwalk leads to Fremont petroglyphs at Capitol Reef. Part of the trail around Balanced Rock in Arches is paved.

SERVICE ANIMALS

Service animals (ie guide dogs) may accompany visitors on park shuttles, inside museums and visitor centers, and on trails. Ensure your service animal wears its official vest at all times to avoid misunderstandings with rangers or other visitors.

RESOURCES

nps.gov

The National Park Service has detailed accessibility information about each park online. Utah's state parks and the Bureau of Land Management also have webpages on their accessibility efforts.

alltrails.com

Popular hiking app AllTrails includes a filter for wheelchair-friendly trails in Utah's national parks and beyond.

travelability.net

Travelability offers state-specific information about accessible travel, including informative articles and a list of specialized travel companies.

Nuts & Bolts

Time Zones Utah, Nevada and the Navajo Nation observe daylight saving time from March to November, but Arizona does not. Keep the time difference in mind if you're going to or from the Grand Canyon.

Liquor Laws Utah has some of the oddest liquor laws in the country. All liquor stores are state run and close on Sunday. If you're drinking, there's a big difference between a restaurant and a bar. If the establishment is licensed as a restaurant, you must order food with your drink.

Marijuana Recreational marijuana is not legal in Utah, but it is in Colorado, Nevada and Arizona.

Tap Water

You can drink tap water in Utah. All the national parks have potable tap water.

Electricity

Electricity 120V/60Hz

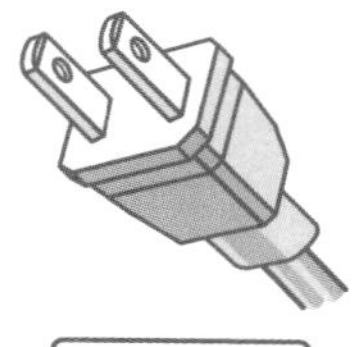

Type A
120V/60Hz

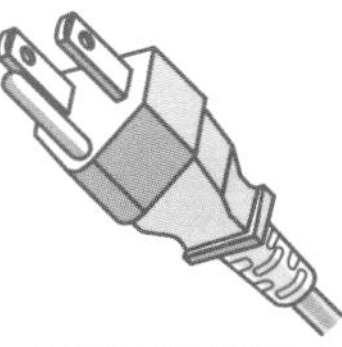

Type B
120V/60Hz

GOOD TO KNOW

Time zone
Mountain Time Zone (GMT-7)

Country calling code
+1

Emergency number
911

Utah population
3.3 million

PUBLIC HOLIDAYS

On summer holiday weekends, expect the parks to be ridiculously busy, with campgrounds full and all nearby accommodations booked out weeks, if not months, in advance.

All of Utah's national parks are open 365 days a year. Public holidays close visitor centers and can affect businesses in gateway towns.

New Year's Day
January 1

Martin Luther King Jr Day
Third Monday in January

Presidents' Day
Third Monday in February

Memorial Day
Last Monday in May

Independence Day
July 4

Labor Day
First Monday in September

Veterans' Day
November 11

Thanksgiving Day
Fourth Thursday in November

Christmas Day
December 25

THE UTAH'S NATIONAL PARKS

STORYBOOK

Lauren Keith delves deep into different aspects of Utah's National Park life.

Meet a Ranger

Ashley Dang is a ranger at Zion and shares her background and favorite parts of the park.

p218

This Land is Your Land: Public Land & Politics

More than 70% of Utah is owned by the federal or state government – but how should it be used?

p220

Uncovering Utah's Layers

Arches, hoodoos, fins and canyons reveal glimpses of the Earth's violent and fascinating geological history.

p223

Court of the Patriarchs, Zion National Park (p60)

MEET A RANGER

Having worked for the National Park Service for more than a decade, ASHLEY DANG is now a ranger at Zion. In this Q&A, she dishes on her background and favorite parts of the park.
By Lauren Keith

How long have you been a ranger at Zion National Park?

I've been a ranger at Zion National Park for a noncontinuous 2½ years. I started here as a seasonal Fire Effects Monitor some years ago and then came back as an Emergency Dispatcher for two years. I am relatively new in my current position as an Education Technician.

Have you been a ranger at other national parks?

I've worked for the National Park Service since 2011. In that time, I've had the privilege to work at more than a dozen different sites, and all of them have been unique experiences.

What is your favorite part of being a ranger at Zion?

As a ranger, I get to meet people from all over the world. It's fun and eye-opening to hear how Zion (and the national-park system as a whole) compares to natural and cultural landscapes around the world, as well as how Zion has changed as a park over time. Some of the most interesting stories come from people who have been visiting the park for decades or whose families have lived in the area for even longer.

Left: Mt Carmel scenic highway (p66), Zion National Park (p52)

What prompted you to become a national-park ranger?

The National Park Service offers opportunities to do almost anything, almost anywhere within the US and its territories. I became a park ranger because I believe in protecting the places that are naturally and culturally meaningful; I stayed because of the many ways it's possible to carry out that mission.

When did you visit Zion for the first time?

I first visited Zion in October 2011. It was rainy and overcast, and the most striking memory I have from that visit is an image of the Court of the Patriarchs surrounded by a beautiful moody mist.

> "NO MATTER WHO YOU ARE, YOU CAN COME HERE AND BE MOVED BY THE LAND."

EB ADVENTURE PHOTOGRAPHY/SHUTTERSTOCK © LEFT: CAT DANG PHOTOGRAPHY/SHUTTERSTOCK ©

What makes Zion such a special place?

Zion National Park is a place that means different things to different people, and I think that's what makes it special. Many people come here to find awe and wonder in the sweeping scenery, while others come to test their physical and mental limits on our challenging trails and technical canyoneering or climbing routes. Visitors with keen observation skills can witness firsthand the natural and physical sciences in motion or discover some truly compelling stories of human history. For some, Zion may be an unforgettable first outdoor experience: a first camping trip, wilderness hike, outdoor rock climb or canyoneering adventure. No matter who you are, you can come here and be moved by the land.

What are your favorite parts of Zion National Park?

I love the park's east side, the area from the historic Zion–Mt Carmel Tunnel eastward toward the park's East Entrance. The scenery feels simultaneously grand and intimate out there, and you can enjoy it in so many different ways. On low-energy days, I like to enjoy the sights directly from the comfort of my vehicle or find a quiet spot to hang out in the shade and look for wildlife. On days that I want an adventure, I bring a good map and explore some of the many routes the east side has to offer.

What do you wish more people knew before visiting Zion?

Many people think of Zion National Park as Angels Landing and the Narrows. While those are beautiful areas with amazing views and opportunities to challenge yourself physically (and mentally!), there is so much more to Zion. With some good planning, it's possible to have a unique, rewarding adventure. Remember to pack appropriately for your day (water, food, sun protection, extra clothing layers, appropriate technical gear etc), understand what current conditions are like in the park, and exercise situational awareness always

What are your favorite outdoor activities?

Good old-fashioned hiking.

THIS LAND IS YOUR LAND: PUBLIC LAND & POLITICS

More than 70% of Utah is owned by the federal or state government – but how should it be used?
By Lauren Keith

WHEN PRESIDENT BARACK Obama created Bears Ears National Monument in 2016, Utah found itself back at the center of a long-simmering controversy: how should the vast tracts of public land in the West be managed? Should they be set aside for recreation and environmental and cultural preservation, or sold off to private interests to promote economic growth in local communities?

With so much public land – Utah ranks second in the country for the most government-owned acres, after neighboring Nevada – it's no surprise that land use and stewardship is a continually contentious issue in the state. As administrations come and go, the political ping-pong carries on unresolved.

Buying – & Taking – the West

The federal government owns nearly half of the land in the West. As the 19th-century idea of 'manifest destiny' pushed Euro-American settlers to spread and stake their claims, the US government bought or took land, including from Native people, to fuel its expansion. Homesteading and

Pictured clockwise from top left: "Great Hunt" petroglyph (p199); Bears Ears National Monument (p175); Dixie National Forest (p107); Grand Staircase–Escalante National Monument (p220)

land grants brought land into the private hands of farmers, and ranchers were often permitted the free use of 'unclaimed' areas.

While this method worked in the Midwest, with flat landscapes and fertile soil, the mountain-filled and arid stretches of the West were not always well suited for agriculture. Over time, environmental conservation became a higher public priority, and some of the land became protected wilderness and parks.

National Park Versus National Monument

The difference between a national park and a national monument is simply to do with how the site is established. An act of Congress designates a national park, while a national monument can be created by presidential proclamation (as well as by Congress). National monuments established by a president can become national parks with congressional approval.

The 1906 Antiquities Act, brought into law by conservationist president Theodore Roosevelt, authorized presidents to create national monuments. The act was passed in response to concerns about the looting of Native archaeological sites in the West, and it permitted the president to preserve 'historic landmarks, historic and prehistoric structures, and other objects of historic or scientific interest' as national monuments, 'the limits of which in all cases shall be confined to the smallest area compatible with the proper care and management of the objects to be protected.'

A few months after the act passed, Roosevelt created the first national monument, Devils Tower in Wyoming, and the Petrified Forest and Grand Canyon in Arizona soon joined its ranks. Even then, the protection of the Grand Canyon was contentious – a mining claimant sued in federal court, arguing that Roosevelt had overstepped his power by setting aside the entire canyon. The Supreme Court ruled unanimously in Roosevelt's favor.Since then, seven Republican and nine Democratic presidents have used the Antiquities Act to create more than 140 national monuments across the country, including four of Utah's five national parks.

Grand Staircase–Escalante (p120)

The Controversy of Grand Staircase–Escalante & Bears Ears

Bill Clinton created Grand Staircase–Escalante (GSENM) in 1996. It was the country's second-largest national monument at the time, covering nearly 2 million acres. In 2017, just a year after Bears Ears was established, the Trump administration shrank the new monument by 85%, the biggest cutback of federal land protection in US history, further fanning the flames of national discord. And no wonder – Bears Ears has come to represent many hot-button topics in US political debates: federal versus state power, the influence of industry lobbyists among politicians, racism and Indigenous rights, and climate change versus natural-resource extraction. GSENM was downsized by almost half at the same time.

Within hours of Trump's proclamation, five Native American tribes, environmental groups such as the Natural Resources Defense Council and the Southern Utah Wilderness Alliance, and outdoor outfitter Patagonia filed lawsuits in federal court.

APINBEN4289/SHUTTERSTOCK ©

Angels Landing, Zion National Park (p58)

The cases remain in court, but one of President Joe Biden's first acts in office was ordering a review of these national monuments, and later in 2021, both were expanded back to their original boundaries.

This move launched a new wave of court cases. In 2022, the state of Utah, a mining company and recreationalists sued the Biden administration, and Native tribes have been granted motions to intervene. The federal government asked the court to dismiss Utah's lawsuit in 2023.

Are Tourists Loving Utah to Death?

Regardless of the political battle, one thing is clear: everyone loves Utah's parks. Visitation hit record highs in 2021, when 11.2 million people traveled to the state's five national parks. Zion leads the way, breaking records with more than five million visitors in 2021, becoming the fourth national park to ever reach that number.

While more visitation means more awareness of the need to protect Utah's wild lands and more funds for the National Park Service, the challenges are numerous and have put considerable strain on popular destinations. In Zion, for example, traffic jams to enter the park in summer can be up to an hour long. There are only 1200 parking spots, but some 10,000 daily visitors.

Finding a solution to increased visitation has not been easy: proposals have included increasing entrance fees by more than 100% during peak season, mandating a reservation system for park entry or installing a permit system for hiking certain trails. Some of these initiatives have been put into action: since 2022, hikers to Angels Landing are required to have a permit, and travelers to Arches National Park must have timed-entry tickets from 7am to 4pm from April through October. Both the National Park Service and many visitors say these restrictions are working.

In a region where life hangs by a slender thread, the heavy trampling of human feet leaves lasting impressions. Desert crusts, wet meadows, and riverside campsites are slow to recover from such use, and repeated visits can cause permanent damage. Other effects may accumulate so gradually that they almost go unnoticed: scientists at Bryce Canyon estimate that 3% of the vegetation disappears each year as people wander off-trail among the hoodoos.

The first paintings of Western landmarks such as Zion Canyon were instrumental in sparking the US conservation movement during the late 19th century, which in turn brought about the establishment of the National Park Service. But who owns Utah's land and how its beautiful spaces should be enjoyed are enduring questions with no easy answers.

UNCOVERING UTAH'S LAYERS

Arches, hoodoos, fins and canyons reveal glimpses of the Earth's violent and fascinating geological history like the chapters of a book.

By Lauren Keith

HOME TO ALL of Utah's national parks, the Colorado Plateau is a defining geologic feature of the West. The rise of the plateau, coupled with the effects of a million years of erosion by sand, wind and water, is fundamental to understanding the striated geologic history of these parks.

Building Blocks of the Colorado Plateau

Starting out as a shallow basin, the Colorado Plateau was uplifted some 60 million years ago. At that time, the plateau split along deep cracks called faults. Over hundreds of thousands of years, these faults have eroded to form stupendous cliffs.

From an aerial perspective, these lofty plateaus and cliffs form a remarkable 'staircase' that steps down from southern Utah into northern Arizona. Topping this so-called 'Grand Staircase' are the Pink Cliffs of the Claron Formation, extravagantly exposed in Bryce Canyon. Below them jut the Gray Cliffs of various Cretaceous formations. Next are the White Cliffs of Navajo sandstone that make Zion Canyon justly famous. These are followed by the Vermilion Cliffs and finally the Chocolate Cliffs abutting the Grand Canyon.

Devils Garden, Grand Staircase–Escalante National Monument (p142)

Another way of understanding the Grand Staircase is to visualize that the top layers of exposed rock at the Grand Canyon form Zion's basement, and Zion's top layers form the bottom layers of Bryce Canyon. You can imagine the parks as being stacked on top of each other, geologically speaking.

A Four-Act Play

Perhaps the simplest way to approach the geologic story of the Colorado Plateau is to think of it as a play in four acts. While this is an oversimplification and there's overlap between the scenes, it offers a framework for understanding the region's geologic history.

Sedimentation

More than 250 million years ago, the Colorado Plateau country was a shallow sea off the west coast of the young North American continent. The Paleozoic Era marked the beginning of life as we know it. Fossils and limestone from this era comprise nearly all exposed rocks in the Grand Canyon, and they form the foundation that underlies all of the Colorado Plateau.

At the close of the Paleozoic, the land rose, and the sea mostly drained away. During the Mesozoic Era (250 million to 65 million years ago), sedimentation continued as eroding mountains created deltas and floodplains. Meanwhile, the rise of a mountain chain blocked moisture-bearing storms, and a vast Sahara-like desert developed, piling thousands of feet of sand atop older sediments. Zion's Navajo sandstone cliffs and Arches' soaring spans of Entrada sandstone preserve evidence of these mighty sand dunes.

FROM AN AERIAL PERSPECTIVE, THESE LOFTY PLATEAUS AND CLIFFS FORM A REMARKABLE 'STAIRCASE' THAT STEPS DOWN FROM SOUTHERN UTAH INTO NORTHERN ARIZONA.

Canyonlands National Park (p151)

Lithification

Over millions of years, the weight of the accumulated layers (more than 2 miles thick) compacted loosely settled materials into rocks cemented together with mineral deposits, a process called lithification. Sandstone, siltstone and mudstone are cemented together with calcium carbonate.

Uplift

About 60 million years ago, North America began a dramatic separation from Europe, sliding west over another part of the Earth's crust and leaving an ever-widening gulf in the Atlantic Ocean. This movement caused the continent's leading edge to uplift, raising the Colorado Plateau more than a mile above sea level.

Erosion

As rock layers rose, gravity enabled watercourses to gain momentum and carve through stone, while sporadic rainfall and an arid climate ensured the soft layers would remain intact. These factors have remained consistent over millennia, enabling fragile hoodoos, fins and arches to develop.

Reading the Rocks

A complex geologic tableau characterizes the national parks of Utah, and each area reveals an astonishing geologic story.

Zion National Park

In Zion Canyon, massive cliffs expose more than 2000ft of Navajo sandstone, formed by ancient sand dunes. Nowhere else in the world do these rock formations reach such grand heights. In the park's Kolob Canyons area, sheer cliffs jut abruptly from the

Mesa Arch, Canyonlands National Park (p150)

Hurricane Fault as if they rose out of the ground yesterday. Bisecting the national park, the Virgin River continues its steady march, cutting downward about 1000ft every million years.

Bryce Canyon National Park

Bryce is not a canyon at all but a series of amphitheaters gouged from the gorgeous Pink Cliffs. Traces of manganese and iron account for the fetching pink and orange hues. The park features dramatic formations at all stages of development, from newly emerging fins to old weathered hoodoos beaten down into colorful mounds.

Grand Staircase–Escalante National Monument

This vast region reveals over 200 million years of geologic history. More than a dozen geologic layers document Mesozoic seas, sand dunes and slow-moving waters that once teemed with ancient life. Examples range from the lavender, rose, burgundy and peach colors of the volcanic ash and petrified forests of the Chinle Formation to the ancient sand dunes preserved in the bluffs of Wingate sandstone at Circle Cliffs.

Capitol Reef National Park

Along a 100-mile stretch, the Earth's surface is bent in a giant wrinkle, exposing multiple rock formations in tilted and upended strata. This unique step-up feature is known as a monocline, and the Waterpocket Fold is one of the longest exposed monoclines in the world.

Canyonlands National Park

Canyonlands is defined by the mighty Colorado and Green Rivers and is even more diverse than the Grand Canyon. Although the rivers have carved through 300 million years of Earth's history, only the oldest 125 million years' worth of rock layers remain – a staggering testament to the power of erosion. When you gaze into the canyon depths from Grand View Point, you're looking only at the middle slices of a giant geologic cake, with the top layers eaten away and the bottom layers still unseen.

To the south, the Needles district has colorful red and white bands showcasing a complicated 250-million-year-old history of retreating and advancing shallow seas. The red layers formed in river flooding after the sea's retreat, while the white layers represent ancient beaches and coastal dunes.

Arches National Park

Compared to the other parks, Arches' geologic makeup is relatively easy to understand. Ancient rock layers rose atop an expanding salt dome, which later collapsed, fracturing layers along the dome's flanks. These cracks then eroded along roughly parallel lines, leaving fins of freestanding Entrada sandstone. In the last 10 million years, erosion has removed roughly a vertical mile of rock, carrying away all older materials save for the freestanding fins. This process continues today: even as brittle arches occasionally collapse, new ones are always in the making.

INDEX

Map Pages **000**

Map Pages **000**

Map Pages **000**

"On previous trips to Arches, I had avoided the hike to Delicate Arch – the trail is completely exposed and too hot for me. This time, I set an alarm for 5am to reach it by sunrise, and now I understand why it's such a Utah icon."

LAUREN KEITH

"Angels Landing is certainly a quintessential Zion hike, but the trail to Observation Point was even more rewarding for me. Even loftier views and an almost flat path to get there? I'm sold."

LAUREN KEITH

Mapping data sources:
© Lonely Planet
© OpenStreetMap http://openstreetmap.org/copyright

THIS BOOK

Destination Editor
Sarah Stocking

Production Editor
Jennifer McCann

Book Designer
Aomi Ito

Cartographer
Christopher Lee-Ack

Cover Researcher
Norma Brewer

Assisting Editors
Sarah Bailey, Imogen Bannister, Melanie Dankel, Clifton Wilkinson

Thanks
Ronan Abayawickrema, Karen Henderson, Darren O'Connell, Katerina Pavkova

Paper in this book is certified against the Forest Stewardship Council™ standards. FSC™ promotes environmentally responsible, socially beneficial and economically viable management of the world's forests.

Published by Lonely Planet Global Limited
CRN 554153
6th edition – Feb 2024
ISBN 978 1838699857

10 9 8 7 6 5 4 3 2 1
Printed in China